R. B. Turton

Major Robert Bell Turton, second son of Captain E. H. and Lady Cecilia
Turton, was born at Upsall Castle, Thirsk, December 9th, 1859. He was
educated at Eton and Balliol College, Oxford, where, in 1882, he took his
B.A. (Hons. First-Class).   In 1883 he became a Barrister.   1884 he was
appointed to the Commission of the Peace. 1907 he was elected to the
County Council, 1922 appointed Alderman, and was Chairman from 1926
up to his death, March 15th, 1938. During the war he served as Major
with the Yorkshire Regiment.

THE ALUM FARM

TOGETHER WITH A HISTORY OF THE ORIGIN,
DEVELOPMENT AND EVENTUAL DECLINE OF
THE ALUM TRADE IN NORTH-EAST YORKSHIRE

by

R. B. TURTON

Printed and Published by
HORNE & SON, LIMITED, WHITBY
1938

INTRODUCTION

Only a very few words are needed to introduce this book. In the year 1884, Canon Atkinson, when editing the Quarter Sessional Records, Vol. 11, page 22, described the whole early history of the alum trade in England as " full of fable and error." He had previously in his then, and still, uncompleted History of Cleveland called attention to the many inconsistencies in the story as told in the various books of reference.

Since those days the task of tracing relevant documents has been made much easier, inasmuch as the work of indexing the public records has proceeded apace.

It must be nearly fifty years since my attention was first called to those Exchequer Depositions which suggested that the discoverer of alum was not Sir Thomas Chaloner but was another man of the same name.

Shortly afterwards the series of accounts known as A.O.1 were made accessible by an Index, and threw further light upon the subject. The series A.O.3 were divulged much later, and we have still to expect another book of the same nature as A.O. 3, 1243/3 carrying on the story with fuller details.

In the meantime, Mr. W. H. Price had published his English Patents of Monopoly, and devoted Chapter VII. thereof to the Royal Alum Works.

I had made a few notes from time to time, rather with the object of correcting errors in books already published than of adding to their number, and it was only gradually that the latter object took precedence.

Whilst the book has been in preparation many changes have taken place in the Public Record Office. Not only has the Index Department increased enormously, but the arrangement of Manuscripts has been much simplified. I have attempted to give the authority for each statement of fact, but in many cases I have given a reference that is now out of date. For instance, the Domestic State Papers are now classified by numbers, those for Charles II. being now known as S.P.29. I occasionally adopt the modern method, but I have found it impossible to alter all old references, and the two will be found side by side. I think, however, that anyone who desires to do so will have no difficulty in looking up the original.

In spelling I have almost entirely followed the modern fashion. I have no wish to justify my few deviations. Lord Sheffeild's name always appears as here spelt, and I have not altered it, though it would have been more logical, as I now see, to have written it as Sheffield.

On the other hand, I use the form Guisborough which occurs nowhere in any of the documents reproduced. Here the difficulty will be to decide which of the earlier forms to adopt. My own preference is for Giseburn, but I should probably have few followers.

I should like to thank Mr. H. N. Wilson, of the I.C.I. Ltd., of Billingham, for some very useful notes on the chemical reactions produced in the manufacture of alum.

I should also like to thank the Staff of the Record Office for the assistance which they afforded me, and I trust that the corrections which I have made in the dates of some of the letters which are to be found in the State Papers may be of use to them.

Finally, if I have robbed Sir Thomas Chaloner of the miraculous element attached to his reputation, I have at least preserved the memory of some of the much more valuable services which he and his father performed to the **State.**

R. B. TURTON.

Kildale Hall,
    December, 1937.

CHAPTER I.

THE EARLY HISTORY OF THE ALUM TRADE.

There are few events in history whose origin and development have been more distorted and misrepresented than the discovery and manufacture of alum in England. So far from being indebted to a fortuitous resemblance to some other locality for a potential source of wealth, those who were principally concerned in the adventure spent time and money without end, and he whose name is constantly associated with the discovery had less share in it than the majority of his associates; it may well be that some reaped where others had sown, but enormous sums had been spent upon its exploitation long before any profits were derived therefrom. The current legend is told in a variety of ways, each writer as he tells it produces out of his imagination an additional detail as improbable as it is untrue. The following are the general features of the legend.

The discovery of alum is attributed to Sir Thomas Chaloner, who was undoubtedly the Governor of Henry Prince of Wales, and who is usually described as a distinguished naturalist on the strength of a book called A Shorte Discourse of the most rare and excellent virtue of nitre. This book is attributed to him in the Index of the British Museum (no doubt on the authority of Anthony Wood in his Athenæ Oxonienses, Vol. ii., 157), but a very cursory examination of its contents should have convinced the compiler that Wood's information was unreliable. The story runs that during his travels in Italy Sir Thomas remarked the similarity between the delicate green tint of the vegetation near Guisborough and that of the alum-producing district of Puteoli [there is no evidence that he ever travelled South of Florence], and that he bribed some of the Pope's workmen to accompany him privately to England, whither he smuggled them in casks. This so exasperated the Pope, who had a lucrative monopoly of the alum trade, that he fulminated an anathema against both the seduced and the seducer.

The origin of the first part of the story will appear later. It rested upon a misreading of a Manuscript, and was followed with variations by Fuller (1) and John Aubrey (2).

The addition of the curse is much later. The earliest printed notice extant occurs in Pennant's Tour in Scotland in 1769, printed in 1771. A like account which may have

(1) Worthies, vol. ii., p. 490 (1662).
(2) Lives of Eminent Men, vol. ii., 281.

been the earliest in manuscript is to be found at p. 306 of the History of Whitby, published by Lionel Charlton in 1779. The story is also told in Vol. vi., p. 107, of the Antiquities of England, by Francis Grose (1785). No one can fail to notice the close correspondence in time between the first appearance of the curse in 1769 and the publication of Tristram Shandy in 1765. The latter admittedly borrowed the general form of excommunication used in the times of Bishop Ernulphus (who died in 1124), extracted from the Textus Roffensis and printed at page 490 of the Gentleman's Magazine for 1745, after the Jacobite rising. The form of the curse in Pennant and Charlton is almost identical. That there was a tradition of a curse by one of the Popes against those who competed with his alum works is probably correct. Those who imported alum from non-Christian lands in contempt of the prohibition of the Apostolic See were exposed to Ecclesiastical censures (1).

Dr. Edward Jordan, whose acquaintance we shall make later, in a letter written in December, 1615 (2) evidently had this in mind when he declared that the curse of the unpaid workman upon the works was more to be feared than that of the Pope.

But when we remember Sterne's frequent visits to Skelton Castle, and the high probability that either Pennant or Charlton (assuming that the former borrowed from a Manuscript of the latter) had interviewed the owner, John Hall Stevenson, whose knowledge of the Alum History was bound to be valuable, the origin of the particular curse embodied in the legend is not difficult to conjecture. Sterne had ridiculed the famous Antiquary, Dr. John Burton, under the name of Dr. Slop, in Tristram Shandy, and he was not likely to spare another of the same fraternity. A close neighbour and boon companion of Hall Stevenson was Zachary Harnage Moore, of Loftus Hall, who, through his father, Zachary Stewart Moore, and his great-grandfather, Zachary Stewart, had close relations with those engaged in the Alum Industry. It is true that Sterne left England in 1765, and only returned shortly before his death in 1768, the year previous to the publication of Pennant's Tour. If Lionel Charlton was the first to promulgate the story, there is nothing improbable in the suggestion that he was hoaxed by Sterne, but if he, in fact, got the story from Pennant, the credit of the hoax must be attributed to John Hall Stevenson or to Zachary Moore, either of whom was quite as capable as Sterne of inventing it.

(1) Rolls Series, vol. xxiv., pt. 2, pp. 167, 255.
(2) D.S.P. Jas. I. 84/2.

Lastly, it must not be forgotten that though workmen were said to have come from Italy to the Dorset works, in the sixteenth century, the foreign workmen who were imported in the seventeenth century came from Liége.

The true history of the early struggles of the alum trade is quite different from these empty legends. It is, in fact, very much more interesting, because there is hardly any aspect of the vicissitudes of modern industry upon which it does not throw some light.

The difficulty of providing capital, of estimating depreciation, the inconvenience of State trading, protection in the form of absolute prohibition of competing imports, sale at home at a high price and abroad at a less price, restriction on output, irregular payment of wages, forcing the wage earner to accept goods at a high price in lieu of his wages— all these find ample illustration in the pages that follow.

The importance of alum to the dyer, to the tanner and in medicine had been recognised from a very early period. At first, rock alum, probably from Roccha, near Edessa, in Syria, the natural and not the artificial substance, was employed. There is an early reference taken from the rolls of the Fair Court of St. Ives (A.D. 1317) (1), where Laurence the Dyer (le Teynturer) sued John of Grantham, the apothecary, and Bartholomew, his servant, for selling him a bale of alum (aluminis de plume) containing 216 lbs. for 26s. 9d., which was mixed with clay and not up to sample. The defence, which was successful, was that the alum was as well up to sample as such a mineral (mina hujusmodi alluminis) could be, so Laurence the Dyer took nothing by his plaint. The price, considering the relative purchasing power of money, seems enormous.

The author of the Libel of English Policy (2), written about 1436, speaks of the Genoese bringing into England

"Coton, roche-alum and gode golde of Jene,
And they be charged wyth wolle ageyne I wene,
And wollene clothe of owres of colours alle."

The earliest manufactury of alum was situated to the East of Commercina (Gumuljina), at a village called Cypsella or Chapsylar (probably the modern Ipsala (3)), on the high road leading from Durazzo to Constantinople, some miles due South of Adrianople. In the middle of the fifteenth century, alum works sprung up at Tolfa, about ten miles E.N.E. of

(1) Selden Society, vol. xxiii., p. 105.
(2) Rolls Series Political Poems, vol. ii., p. 172.
(3) Pierre Belon Les Observations de plusseurs singularitez, ch. lxi., p. 62, visited it in 1550.

Civita Vecchia, in the Papal States. Later, the manufacture was extended to Cartagena, in Spain. The fifteenth century also saw the establishment of the industry in Germany: the works at Schwemmsal, near Halle, claim priority in date. Not far off is Chemnitz, where Georg Bauer, known as Agricola, published De Re Metallica (1) and De Natura Fossilium in the early years of the sixteenth century, and described its manufacture and early history. These books soon came to England, and directed attention to the necessity for developing home resources. On New Year's Day, 1556-7, the famous bookseller, Reynold Wolf, presented a copy of the De Re Metallica to Queen Mary as a New Year's gift (2). The principal source of importation was still Civita Vecchia. The high seas in those days were not too safe for navigation. The State Papers are full of complaints from the Pope and others that ships which had been destined for a port of one state had been seized by subjects of another state and the cargoes confiscated. Our Ambassadors were kept sufficiently busy in all the Courts to which they were accredited, on the one hand in seeking to obtain restitution of cargoes of alum belonging to English subjects or destined for English ports, and on the other hand in excusing acts of violence perpetrated by English mariners on ships containing such cargoes and owned by foreigners. Henry VII. had not been many months on the throne when Pope Innocent VIII. complained of the seizure by certain English mariners of a Spanish ship laden with alum shipped from his possessions and on a voyage from Piombino to Flanders (3). A naval fight had ensued with many losses on either side, but the English, who were victorious, had taken the alum into an English port.

In reply the King declared that he desired to favour the Apostolic See, but he was new in the Kingdom, which was governed by its own ancient laws which he could neither oppose, infringe or abrogate. There was no prohibition against the importation of alum, but the capture of the ship without his consent should not remain unpunished. There is a constant stream of like instances running through the next century. In June, 1513, Margaret of Savoy, Regent of Flanders, complained of the action of William Compton, then of the King's household (4). His servants had seized and brought to Southampton the ship of a native of Biscay, carrying 1,685 bales of alum belonging to Andrew de la Coste, of Bruges,

(1) The late President of the U.S.A. has brought out a modern edition of this work.
(2) Nicholls Progress, p. 34.
(3) Rolls Series, vol. lx., p. 299, Memorials of Henry VII.
(4) S.P. Henry VIII. Dom and For, vol. i., Nos. 1,882, 1,957, 1,958, 3,141.

4

an officer in the service of her nephew, Charles V. A year later, Wolsey and Fox were promising justice to Andrew, but there is no evidence of the fulfilment of their promise.

That same year Pope Leo X. had suffered loss in that a ship of Rouen laden with alum of the Apostolic Chamber, and consigned to John Cavalcanti, had been seized and carried into Falmouth, on the ground that its destination was France (1). The ship with its cargo was worth twelve thousand ducats, and the cargo was confiscated for the benefit of Charles Brandon, Duke of Suffolk, the King's brother-in-law. Letters from the Pope, from Silvester, Bishop of Worcester, and from Ralph, Bishop of Ostia, Cardinal St. George, to Wolsey were only partially successful in obtaining restitution of a portion of the proceeds, and by November, 1518, there was still a large balance owing.

The difficulties incident to the trade are illustrated by an account of a voyage undertaken by Sir John Hawkins (then John Hawkins, armiger), for which there is only room here for a short summary (2). He had contracted with the well-known Genoese brothers, Horatio and Alexander Pallavicino, to carry 120 tons of alum from Civita Vecchia to the Port of London by way of Plymouth and Dartmouth. Disputes in the nature of a claim for demurrage arose between the parties. Hawkins affirmed that the loading of one of the ships engaged in the adventure had been purposely delayed for some nineteen days, in order that she might sail with an argosy whose departure was fixed for that period, and whose protection she thus hoped to obtain.

This escort would have been even more valuable the following year, when the Government of Spain gave instructions to stop the ships of Pallavicino wherever possible, on the ground that he had obtained the sole right for six years of introducing alum from Italy into the Netherlands, to the disadvantage of Spain (3). In 1579 one of his alum ships only escaped from Alicante, where it had put in from stress of weather, by weighing anchor at short notice and leaving behind a part of the crew. These and many other instances could be quoted to show the risks that importers of alum incurred, and there is no wonder that the Government was anxious to depend no longer on a foreign supply.

The desire to favour the Apostolic See had given place to an intention to do as much injury as possible to one who was considered an enemy to the Kingdom. So far as the

(1) Id. Nos. 3,092, 3,205, 3,241, 3,490.
(2) H.C.A. Libels 48/64, S.P. D. Eliz. 123/15.
(3) Cal. Spanish State Papers (1568-1579), pp. 609, 616.

alternative supply from Cartagena was concerned, our relations with Spain were tending from reciprocal suspicion to open rupture. There were, therefore, the strongest motives, political as well as pecuniary, to render this country self-supporting by the manufacture of this indispensable commodity within the four seas. Finally the discovery of the New World and of its mineral wealth aroused the spirit of rivalry amongst our countrymen. The rapid strides which Germany had made in the art of mining favoured the introduction of many of her workmen. As early as 1472 Hans Ducheman, whose name betrays his origin (1), was employed with others in examining the lead mines at Whelpington, in the Barony of Prudhoe.

Many of the same nation were imported into Ireland during the next century. Henry VIII. recognised the danger of England's position should war break out with a Continental Power whilst Ireland remained in a state of disorder. He took steps to strengthen his authority, and for that purpose despatched Deputy after Deputy with forces sufficient in his opinion to maintain a better standard of order. But the economical side was not neglected, and the Deputies in turn were instructed to develop the mining industry in order that the profits to be derived therefrom might liquidate the costs of administration. In that portion of Wexford that borders upon Waterford between the towns of New Ross and Clonmines, there were lead mines now unworked that then were thought to contain quite a fair proportion of silver. It was to these mines that attention was first paid. In March, 1545-6, through the exertions of Paget, Secretary of State (2), negotiations were entered into with a goldsmith of Antwerp, then residing in London, Garret Harman (probably more correctly Gerard Hermann), and with Joachim Gundelfinger, of Augsburg, for the supply of skilled workmen, amongst them a smelter and a mining surveyor. Garret Harman had lamented to Paget he would fain have had men of honest fashion, howbeit they were not easy to get. The scheme was not limited to silver and lead; by August following specimens of precious stones and of alum were produced before the Privy Council as having been found in Ireland (3), and preparations were being made for further progress when the death of Henry VIII. put a stop to the work.

In the reign of Edward VI. another attempt was made under the direction of Sir Anthony St. Leger, then Deputy,

(1) Surtees Society, vol. cxxxiv., p. 94.
(2) L. & P. For & Dom Henry VIII., Nos. 327, 402.
(3) Acts of P.C. 1st Aug., 1546.

and with the assistance of Gundelfinger (1). A staff consisting of some thirty-seven experts in the various departments (2) was to be engaged, and to include a man who understood the baking of rock alum, and two men to sow the seeds of deal and pine.

At the same time the services of a very well-known man had been secured, and he was entrusted with a band of English miners. This was Doctor Robert Record, sometime Fellow of All Souls College, Oxford, famous as the author of the first English Treaties on Algebra. The two ships conveying the respective parties arrived at Waterford about the same time, and by 17th July, 1551, the work was in full swing.

Like so many subsequent experiments in state mining, the enterprise was a failure. The two parties, German and English, kept themselves distinct. That the German miner should receive two shillings and a penny a day against the shilling paid to the Englishman was not conducive to harmony. Before the winter was over, each side was laying its complaints against the other. Record maintained that the English and Irish workmen were far more skilful than the Germans, and inveighed against the wasteful habits of the latter in the purchase of provisions and in smelting the ore.

Gundelfinger and Harman retaliated with charges against Record, of which the least was that he had neglected to survey the alum mines and to make use of the services of the men whom Gundelfinger had brought over for that purpose. The more serious charges against the Fellow of All Souls were that he had abused his power of provision; he had commandeered grain and fish at a low price beyond the needs of his men and sold the surplus, sometimes even the necessary provisions, for his own benefit at a higher price. The enterprise continued to swallow up money (3), and in July, 1552, it was thought advisable to send an independent mining surveyor of the name of William Williams, with full instructions to make an exhaustive report upon the chances of success. He was to be careful to distinguish between charges incident to establishment and to maintenance, respectively; he was to consider carefully a scheme of profit-sharing, taking every precaution lest the greediness of the workmen seeking to make much metal speedily should waste ore, out of which, with more labour

(1) S.P. Ireland Edw. VI., 4/70.
(2) S.P. Foreign Edw. VI., No. 244.
(3) S.P. Ireland Edw. VI., 4/52.

and less hasty expedition, they might obtain valuable metal. The alum mines were to be investigated with a view to their profitable exploitation, and if thought desirable the German alum workers were to be retained. The rest of the German miners were to be discharged by the following midsummer.

Williams landed at Dublin on the 12th July (1), and with the help of Sir Thomas Luttrell, then Chief Justice of the Common Pleas in Ireland, who had been appointed by Sir James Croft, the Lord Deputy, as his fellow Commissioner, at once entered upon his duties. The report of the Commissioners was not favourable to the continuance of the work. They considered that an Englishman produced ten hundredweight more lead in every three tons than a German; but the enterprise still showed a substantial loss. No attempt was made or possibly could be made to discriminate between capital and income expenditure, nor could the Germans, English or Irish be induced to adopt the suggested scheme of profit sharing; they utterly refused to " meddle after any such sort." The Commissioners suggested a reduction in the staff, but time had not served for a survey of the alum mines.

By February following, the expenses were on the increase (2), and it was finally decided to close down. Some months were spent in fruitless negotiations with Gundelfinger, who professed a desire to take the mines over. Then Edward VI. died, and Mary came to the throne in July, 1553. Nothing further was done during her short reign, but when Elizabeth succeeded her sister it was decided to secure, so far as possible, some benefit from the expenditure incurred in earlier years.

The results of state management had been too unfortunate to justify a repetition, but attempts were made to let the undertaking, and applicants were not difficult to find. The successful candidate was Walter Peppard. What his qualifications were as a mining expert do not appear, but the Irish State Papers give us ample information as to his career in the island. A kinsman of the Lord Chancellor, Thomas Cusack (3), and originally a retainer of Thomas Cromwell, we find him in Ireland towards the close of the reign of Henry VIII. (4), and he claimed to have letters of commendation both from King Harrie (as he called him) and King Edward for services performed on the borders of the English Pale. During the times of Sir Anthony St. Leger and Sir James Croft as Lord Deputies, he kept

(1) id. 4/59.
(2) id. 4/76.
(3) S.P. Ireland, Eliz. 10/37, 39.
(4) L. and P., Henry VIII., No. 212.

eighteen tall men fully furnished with horse and harness at his own expense, without receiving from the Crown the wages of a single man. He killed in one morning at Kyldingham thirty-two rebels of the Dempseys (1). For these and other services he received a lease of Slewmargy (Slieve Margy?), the town of Kilkea, and tithes and altar dues in Bally-Roan and Kilmahidé. These grants were of doubtful value. Their object was to interpose a safe barrier round the Irish who adhered to the English Crown against the contrariants. But Peppard was arrested as surety for Andrew Wise, the Irish Vice-Treasurer, and had to defend legal proceedings in England. On his return he found that the town of Kilkea (where he had resided), with fifty-three corn-ricks and eighteen hundred sheep, had been burnt, and that his kyne and stud of horses had been carried away. The rebels were in possession of the rest of the lands granted to him.

This was the selected candidate, and his enjoyment of the lease was neither very long nor very lucrative. The terms were of a similar nature to those contained in like leases (2). He was to have the use of all the tools, plants, stores and other necessaries formerly used in the mines, to restore them after the expiration of the term and pay for any deficiencies. He was granted a lease for twenty-one years of all mines of gold, silver, tin, copper and lead in Ireland; in return he was to pay one-twelfth part of all minerals actually gotten, and the Queen was to have the option of buying gold and silver, the former at five shillings an ounce and the latter at twopence the ounce below the market price. He was also to take over, at a valuation, the costs of which were to be shared equally between the Queen and himself, all the lead and ore then on the premises, and to pay for the same in five years. He had the usual powers of pressing into his service the various workmen required, and of commandeering provisions and necessaries, paying in each case such reasonable sums as were customary (3).

We are now about to make the acquaintance of John Chaloner, the father of Thomas Chaloner, who was the true discoverer of the alum mines, as well as the author of the Treatise of Nitre. The latter, at the time of his father's death (4), claimed that his father had served the Crown for thirty-four years and more, first under King Henry at Boulogne in the wars and the winning thereof, next at Calais as Auditor to the Forces, and afterwards for twenty-four

(1) S.P. Ireland, Eliz. 15/30.
(2) S.P. Ireland, Eliz. 15/31.
(3) Pat and Close Rolls, Ireland 2, Eliz. M.5 [May 28th, 1560.]
(4) S.P. Ireland, Eliz. 92/108.

years in Ireland. As he died in 1581, and Henry VIII. took Boulogne by siege in 1544, his service, if continuous, would have extended over thirty-seven years, but the point is immaterial. Probably the explanation is that there was a break in his service. Before the close of 1551 John Chaloner had obtained from George Browne, Archbishop of Dublin, with the consent of the Chapter of Holy Trinity Church, a grant in fee farm of the Island of Lambay at a rent of £6 13s. 4d., on condition that within six years he should erect a harbour and village for the shelter and refuge of fishermen. The island, which was about three miles from Dublin, was a common resort of pirates, and the object of the Archbishop in making the grant was the security of the City. John Chaloner's object in accepting it was to exploit its mineral wealth, of which he had already formed an exaggerated opinion.

The grant was duly confirmed by letters patent (1) of date September 21st, 1551, but the death of King Edward shortly afterwards introduced fresh hindrances. George Browne, who was an ardent Protestant Reformer, was deprived and replaced by Hugh Curwen, and an Act of Parliament was passed annulling all grants made by Browne while Archbishop. The title to Lambay was therefore in jeopardy, and John had also been a short time previously dispossessed (2) of the lease of a mill and fishery in Galway river, which appears to have devolved upon him on the death (10th June, 1550) of his father, Roger Chaloner (3). But notwithstanding the change in the established religion, John, like his brother Sir Thomas, kept on good terms with the ruling powers. His case was represented to the King and Queen, and the services which he had performed were called to mind, as well as the object for which the grant was made. His former possessions were restored, but in lieu of a grant in fee, a lease for three hundred years was granted to him. There is amongst the Admiralty Records in the Public Record Office a very interesting account of the experiences of a ship which he purchased in London, and christened Eugenius, on its voyage with a supply of materials for his mining operations in Lambay (4). No other description is given of these materials than that they were genera bombardorum bought from Sir Anthony Aucher and other goods brought from Calais. Sir Anthony Aucher was at Calais with John Chaloner, and later.

(1) Pat and Close Rolls, Ireland 5, Ed. VI., m.15, No. 109.
(2) S.P. Ireland, Mary 1/51-54.
(3) Inq. p.m. Ch. Ser. II., 34/6.
(4) H.C.A. 3 26/3 referred to as 27/3 in the Selden Society publications, vol. ii., p. 99. Possibly the number of the bundles have been changed.

The date appears to have disappeared from the extant records, but is given by an entry in Sir Thomas Chaloner's accounts (1) that he distributed five shillings amongst the mariners of his brother's ship when he supped there towards the end of 1554.

No sooner had the ship reached the open sea than a storm carried her past Jersey, past the Isle of Wight, and so westwards until eventually she gained harbour in the Scilly Isles, having had her mast cut down and having drifted before the wind. A weak make-shift was all that Scilly could supply, and the captain got a new mast in Waterford. The ship's stores now needed replenishing, and he had to retrace his steps to Youghal, where the ship was captured by a well-known pirate, Richard Cole, who carried her into Minehead. A writ was obtained from Thomas Luttrell (later of Dunster Castle), directed to his bailiff at Minehead, to arrest the ship, but before it could be executed Cole was off to Tenby, in Wales. Eventually he was captured at Beerhaven by Walter Tirrell, who had been commissioned from Portsmouth to pursue the pirates, but it was not until 1556 that John Chaloner obtained an order of restitution in his favour.

During the succeeding years he was fairly active in Dublin, supplying the forts with provisions, providing a ship to convey the Lord Deputy Henry Sidney to England (2). Then in 1558 he became Lord Mayor of Dublin, and was placed on the Commission of the Peace (3). He also acted as Clerk to the Signet. When the Earl of Sussex, in 1560, superseded Henry Sidney as Lord Deputy, John Chaloner was given the title of Secretary of State for Ireland; a new office of which he was the first holder. His duties as such soon brought him into touch with Walter Peppard. The Queen had derived no benefit from her lease, and in the autumn of 1560 John Chaloner was appointed, with the assistance of George Tresham, the uncle of Sir Thomas Tresham, to survey the mines in New Ross and Clonmines. They reported that Peppard had done nothing, had not observed the terms of the lease, and that the Queen was entitled to re-enter (4).

The next stage in the proceedings was one which in these days would have aroused a considerable amount of comment, but was then not at all unusual. Negotiations lasting four years ensued, under which John Chaloner,

(1) Lands 824/52.
(2) Sidney Papers Hist. MSS. Comm., vol. lxxvii., pp. 368, 370, 372.
(3) Pat Rolls 4 and 5. P. and M.m.4.
(4) State Papers Ireland Eliz. 2/49.

through the medium of George Tresham, though a commissioner, attempted to obtain a transfer of the leave from Walter Peppard. The latter was by no means loth to part with his bargain so long as he was released from liability in respect of the breach of covenants and got a substantial sum to boot (1). This sum was put at £100 a year, but in addition John Chaloner was to take over the ore and plant as they might be found, and yet be responsible for the original inventory as it appeared in the lease. This he declined to do, having, he said, no desire to buy " the pig in the poke as the proverb was " (2). He then, on the 10th May, 1564, applied to Cecil to cancel Peppard's lease, on the ground of failure to perform the covenants, and to grant a new lease to himself.

But by this time other rivals were in the field. The mining world was now divided into two principal groups; one, that which was eventually incorporated under the style of the Mines Royal, on 18th May, 1568, and the principal figures in which were at the time in question Thomas Thurland, Master of the Savoy, and two Germans, Hans Steinberg, a mining expert of reputation, whose terms were too onerous and who was dropped out, and Daniel Höckstätter, whose family remained in the northern counties for many generations.

The other group which, in like manner, was on the same day incorporated into the Mineral and Battery works, was represented by William Humphrey, Assay Master at the Mint, and a German named Christopher Shutz.

John Chaloner's application was supported by his brother, Sir Thomas Chaloner, then on the point of death, Benedict Spinola and Cornelius de Vos. At one time it looked as if the two last-mentioned groups would coalesce. Humphrey, who coveted the Isle of Lambay, declared that he was prepared to take in John Chaloner and Walter Peppard as partners, not for any science that he had heard to be in them, but because he had heard that Chaloner was well learned in Georgius Agricola as touching speculation. Georgius Agricola, he adds, is a present medicine to make a heavy purse light. The treatise to which he referred was evidently De Re Metallica. After endless negotiations, prolonged by the deaths of Walter Peppard and Sir Thomas

(1) S.P. Ireland Eliz. 10/54.
(2) id. 10/63.

Chaloner, the prize went to William Humphrey and his partner Christopher Shutz who, in September, 1565, obtained the right to mine for calamine stone (carbonate of zinc) (1) in certain named counties, and in addition was granted very wide powers of getting all manner of minerals in that part of Ireland called the English Pale.

John Chaloner had now to content himself with the Isle of Lambay. He first attempted to resign his Secretaryship of State, the fees of which amounted to £50 a year only, in favour of his brother Francis, but Francis was too well known, and the resignation was not accepted. Then, when it pleased God, as he put it, to take out of this life John Parker, Master of the Rolls, he applied for the vacant post, not as one that was more remunerative, but one that would afford him more leisure for his mining speculations.

Lambay was not a safe abode (2). About All-Hallow Tide, 1563, two French ships of war came unawares to Lambay and spoiled brother John of all that he had that might be taken away. So wrote Francis to Sir Thomas. John himself lamented to Cecil on 23rd April, 1564, that he had lost £300 by spoil of Frenchmen and no more substance left him than his corn and plough-horses (3). His debts then amounted to £200. Nevertheless, he is still sanguine. He had there discovered by May, 1563, a dozen large veins of copper (4), mines containing silver enough to bear the charge and clear the copper. Lawyers had told him that he might dig up and enjoy whatever metal it contained in stone or ore, yet so that it might not be an example to those of the Irish Pale who haply had the like, he begged for the Queen's licence with such a licence and commission dormant for taking up necessaries as was granted to Walter Peppard for Clonmines. On 14th August, 1563, he wrote from Dublin to his brother (5), Sir Thomas, then in Spain, that he had found four rich veins of ore near the surface on the slope of hills, and asking leave to transport his metal from time to time to St. Bees, in Cumberland, where there was water and coaling wood (charcoal) suitable for smelting. On 5th March, 1569-70, a correspondent sent to the Earl of Leicester specimens both molten and unmolten of the Lambay mine (6). What gold, silver or copper it contained he could not say. Certain French Finers said that it was

(1) P.R. 7 Eliz. Pt. 8 and see Selden Society Publications, vol. xxviii., p. 16.
(2) State Papers (Foreign) 1563, No. 1,500.
(3) S.P. Ireland Eliz. 10/54.
(4) id. 8/51.
(5) S.P. Foreign (1563), No. 1,139.
(6) S.P. Ireland Eliz. 16/45.

very rich. Notwithstanding this, it had made Mr. Chaloner poor, and for lack he did scrape the ground though he had four mines going.

The letter ends with a panegyric on Chaloner. He knew where the most of the mines in Ireland were both of lead, gold, silver and alum, and was himself skilful in finding, melting, fining and boiling of alum. For some time John Chaloner had been engaged in experiments in making alum, following the instructions contained in Georgius Agricola— that present medicine to make a heavy purse light. Meantime he was being out-stripped in England. In 1564, as we shall see, a patent had been granted to Cornelius de Vos to mine and dig for alum and copperas and an Act (8 Eliz. c. 21) which tranferred this right to James Lord Mountjoy, the husband of Sir Thomas Chaloner's step-daughter, granted an exclusive licence for twenty-one years. Lord Mountjoy was anxious to obtain an Irish Act of Parliament confirming this licence (1), and the Privy Council on the 8th March, 1567-8, sent a recommendation to that effect to the Lords Justices in Ireland. Whether or no John Chaloner, as Secretary of State, could put a spoke in the wheel does not appear (2), but the request of the Privy Council met with no very ready response. Just a year later, on the 10th March, 1568-9, a correspondent wrote to William Cecil that the Irish Parliament was inclined to grant Lord Mountjoy a privilege for ten years, but not without Mr. Chaloner's great exclamation, who was making importunate suit to have his little kingdom of Lambay excepted, alleging that he had travailed there five years past about the discovery of alum and copperas (3). The writer of the letter added that surely whatever show he made, Lord Mountjoy might be more afraid than hurt of him for any ability he had to follow these enterprises to good effect. Eventually the Act of the Irish Parliament was duly passed in December, 1569 (4). During the next ten years the progress of the works at Lambay can only be a matter of conjecture. It would appear as if the grant of exclusive privileges to Lord Mountjoy for ten years was an insuperable obstacle to the further development at Lambay. But that some form of activity was proceeding continuously we cannot doubt. At length the ten years having come to an end, on the 11th August, 1579, John Chaloner obtained his licence (5) to search for minerals in Ireland. The patent recited that since 1558 he had bestowed great travail and expenses in the discovery of mines of alum, copperas or vitriol, otherwise called atrament or calcanthum

(1) S.P. Ireland Eliz. 23/68.
(2) id. 25/24.
(3) id. 27/44.
(4) Journals of H.C. 8 Eliz. C. 21.
(5) Pat Rolls. 21 Eliz. Pt. 8.

mysi, melantery, sorios and of sulphur and nitre, as also of other metals and minerals within the Isle of Lambay. The Queen desired the mines to be worked for the benefit of her kingdom, and the remuneration of his expenses, especially as both the Isle of Lambay and the Isle called Ireland's Eye were separated from the English Pale by the sea, and therefore not included in the grant to Humphrey and Shutz.

He was therefore fully licensed to search the Isle of Lambay for mines and minerals, paying the royalties therein mentioned, amongst others one-twentieth part of the value in money of all alum, vitriol and copperas tried out from time to time.

As he had invented the making of nitre within the realm, which had previously been imported from Egypt or Turkey, and was of great utility in medicine, linen and cloth working and dyeing, there were to be no customs for nitre unless imported. Finally, there was a prohibition upon pain of six months imprisonment against others mining in Lambay, or making nitre anywhere in England or Ireland.

John Chaloner had now attained the summit of his ambition, but he was far from realising a fortune, though his experiments increased his high reputation with his contemporaries for scientific knowledge. When Walter, Earl of Essex, died after a short illness in Ireland in 1576 (1), there were many who attributed his death to poison. Sir Henry Sidney was convinced that there was no truth in these rumours. Besides the opinion of Irish Physicians, he relied upon that of Mr. Chaloner, the Secretary of State, who, as he told Walsingham on 20th October, was not unlearned in physic, and often for goodwill gave counsel to his friends in case of sickness.

But now Chaloner was getting past work (2). Unkind critics said that in the past ten years he had not written ten letters on matters of state. He was grown old, he coveted rest, he had neither body nor purse to bear the attendance at Court, though he was honest and a good counsellor. His years made him unfit to travel. It was meet that some well qualified person (3)—Geoffrey Fenton, his successor, in fact— was sent from England to act as Secretary of State, and that he should enjoy his pension.

But this he was not fated to do. On the 13th May, 1581 (4), he died and left his affairs in the deepest confusion.

(1) Collins (A) Sidney Papers 1.140.
(2) id. I. 280. S.P. Ireland Eliz. 71/40.
(3) Carew MSS., Nos. 317, 377, 421.
(4) S.P. Ireland Eliz. 73/15.

Had not his son, Thomas Chaloner, in response to his petition to the Lord Deputy and Council (1) received £15 from the Treasurer of Ireland for his interment, he could not have had a funeral meet for the degree of a Privy Councillor. On the 15th July following, Thomas, the son, obtained protection for a whole year against his father's creditors for debts exceeding two thousand marks, while he collected the property (2). When that period expired we have a succession of petitions from Thomas, describing himself as only son and landless heir of John Chaloner, who, during his thirty-four years' service, had not been in any way mindful or provident by suit or otherwise for "himself and hizzen," and begging for a lease for forty years of certain lands lately owned by rebels who had been recently executed.

After some three years he seems to have attained the object of his petitions, but the enjoyment was short, for on 25th October, 1589, we learn that rebels preyed on his lands in Connaught (3). We get one last notice of him in the Irish State Papers of 1592, a complaint against William Usher, son-in-law of Archbishop Loftus, who was alleged to have wrested the Isle of Lambay from him, notwithstanding the lease to his father for three hundred years. Shortly after his father's death he published the treatise on nitre which in most books of reference is incorrectly attributed to his cousin, Sir Thomas. It was printed for Gerald Dewes at the Sign of the Swan, St. Paul's Churchyard, in 1584, and professes to be a copy of a discourse written from the Isle of Lambay, on the East Coast of Ireland, by Thomas Chaloner, gent., unto his cousin, John Napper, apothecary, dwelling at the sign of the Ewe and Golden Lamb in Cheapside, opposite Soper Lane (4).

He claimed, following almost precisely the words of the letters patent, that his father's industry introduced the manufacture of nitre into the realm, and he professed to impart what he had heard from his father's discourse, partly gathered of good authors, partly of his own experience. One of the good authors, possibly the only one, was no doubt George Bauer, surnamed Agricola, the present medicine to make a heavy purse light, as William Humphrey called him.

Here for a time we must leave Thomas Chaloner. Some ten years later we find him in Yorkshire; it is not a very wild

(1) id. 92/107, 108.
(2) id. 15/47, 48, 121/66, 67.
(3) id. 147/41.
(4) John Napper apparently dwelt at the junction of the present King Street and Cheapside.

16

conjecture to suggest that when the rebels re-took the lands which had been granted to him, and when William Usher deprived him of the Isle of Lambay, he applied to his cousin, Sir Thomas. He was mentioned in his uncle's will, and there had been no cause of difference between his father and his uncle. It is therefore most probable that his cousin, the younger Sir Thomas, offered him an asylum at Guisborough, and called his attention in language which he later reproduced in the Cottonian Manuscript (1) to the geological treasures to be found in the adjoining hills.

(1) Julius F. VI.

CHAPTER II.

THE CHALONER FAMILY.

In order to follow with greater clearness the connection between those to whom the establishment of the alum industry is due, it is proposed to insert here a short history of the Chaloner family which sticklers for relevancy are advised to skip. The most reliable pedigree of that family is to be found in the Visitation of Cheshire, made by Richard St. George, Norroy King of Arms, in 1613 (1). The Manuscript (2) containing the Visitation was the work of Jacob Chaloner, an arms-painter, son of Thomas Chaloner, Ulster King of Arms, who was second cousin of his better known namesake. There is therefore peculiar authority to be attributed to this pedigree, more especially as it is confirmed from other sources. The family sprung originally from Ruddlan, in Flint, represented phonetically in the manuscript by Rithland, whence members of the family spread to Denbigh and Chester. One member of that family, Roger Chaloner, found his way to London at an early age, entered the King's Household, where he must have met Richard Cecil, the father of William Cecil, and the intimacy between the two families was exceedingly close. On the 13th October, 1538, he received a grant of the lease for forty years of the Mill and Fishery in Galway, to which reference has already been made (3). He was then one of the Ushers (4) of the King's Chamber. In addition, he held, jointly with his son Thomas, the lucrative post of a Teller of the Exchequer, and he was also engaged in trade.

He married Margaret, daughter of Richard Middleton, of London, one of the same Welsh family as Hugh Myddleton of New River fame, and as the owner of Chirk Castle, Margaret would appear to have been a widow at the date of her marriage, and the mother of Jasper Alleyn (5).

By her, Roger Chaloner had three sons—Thomas, John and Francis—and a daughter, Ellen, who married firstly Thomas Farnham, of Stoughton, Leicester, also one of the Tellers of the Exchequer, a member of the same family as the Farnhams of Quorn, and secondly, Richard Saunders, of Welford, Northamptonshire, Barrister-at-law. Roger died on the 10th June, 1550 (6), and owned considerable property in the City of London and elsewhere. At the date of the

(1) Harl. Soc. Publn., vol. lix.
(2) Harl. Ms., 1535.
(3) Ante p. 10.
(4) Dapiferi.
(5) Calendar of Wills Court of Hustings, 7, Edward VI., 2nd part, p. 655. Jasper Allen is mentioned in Cal. State Papers, Ireland (Henry VIII.), 2/10.
(6) Inq. p.m. (Ch. Series II.), 94/6.

Inquisition in February following, his son Thomas was described as his heir, and of the age of thirty years and more; therefore presumably born in 1520 or thereabouts. He is generally assumed to have been educated at St. John's College, Cambridge, and his connection with the Royal Household, and intimacy with William Cecil, renders the assumption probable.

Before he had taken his Degree, Thomas, accompanied, as his Secretary, Sir Henry Knyvett, when the latter was sent to Ratisbon as Ambassador to the Court of Charles V. He was thus employed from 1538 to 1541, and took part in the Naval attack on Algiers. The ship in which he was sailing was wrecked, and he told a story which perhaps should not be taken too seriously, that, as he was being hauled to safety, his arms grew too tired to hold the cable (1), and he seized it with his teeth, thus saving his life. Shortly after his return he was promoted Clerk of the Council, an office which he nominally held for life, although his yearly salary of £50, paid during the reign of Edward VI., ceased when Mary came to the throne, and was not renewed by her sister.

In 1547 he was Knighted by the Protector Somerset after the battle of Pinkie, and the same year he married Joan, widow of Sir Thomas Leigh, LL.D., who had died in 1544. Leigh had been the most active of the Commissioners employed by the King in visiting the Monasteries prior to their dissolution, and the very careful surveys that he made of their possessions enabled him to gauge with accuracy their value. He acquired an interest either by lease or purchase in the monastic lands of Guisborough, St. Oswald's (Nostell) and St. Bees in Cumberland.

Lady Leigh was the daughter of Sir Wm. Cotton, of Oxon Heath (now the residence of Sir W. N. M. Geary, Bart.), near Hadlow, in Kent, which he acquired through marriage with Margaret, only daughter of Richard Culpepper, who married for her second husband Richard Welbeck (2).

Joan Cotton was one of a moderate-sized family; her sister Anne married a Yorkshireman, Sir Thomas Gargreave, and their son eventually became Sir Cotton Gargreave. On the Welbeck side she had a first cousin (3), whose son was named George Carlton, of Wollaston, in Northamptonshire, and whose daughter Catherine married Francis Blount, brother to James Lord Mountjoy.

(1) Hakluyt Voyages, vol. ii., p. 210.
(2) C. 3, 104/100.
(3) Or possibly half-uncle.

Sir Thomas Leigh left an only child, Katherine, not quite five years old at his death. By various transactions St. Oswald's devolved upon Katherine, whose wardship and marriage Chaloner obtained; he also in July, 1547, procured a transfer of the cell of St. Bees to himself and Dame Joan Leigh, widow, in advancement of a marriage to be made between them, and a lease in reversion expectant upon the determination of the twenty-one years' lease to Sir Thomas Leigh for a period of thirty years of the site of Guisborough Priory and lands adjacent, and finally, in 1550, consolidated his title to Guisborough by purchasing the freehold estate for the sum of £998 13s. 4d. (1), to be held as the fortieth part of a Knight's fee, Dame Joan enjoying a joint life estate.

Besides these lands he had a house in Clerkenwell (still or lately known by his name) and a small estate at Steeple Claydon, in Buckinghamshire, which, until its sale to Sir John Verney in the eighteenth century, was the principal seat of the family; their visits to Guisborough being few and far between.

The experience which Sir Thomas had gained as Secretary to Sir Henry Knyvett, aided no doubt by his close intimacy with William Cecil, brought him ample employment as a diplomat. At the close of the reign of Edward VI. he had been sent as joint Ambassador to France with Dr. Wootten and Sir William Pickering, in a fruitless attempt to reconcile Henry II. of France with the Emperor Charles V. Queen Mary continued him at the French Court for a few months, and then recalled him merely because it was no longer necessary for her to retain there more than one Ambassador. Soon afterwards he was sent upon an important mission to Scotland to protest against an unprovoked attack upon Ireland. Next he was employed as a Commissary for the ill-fated expedition to succour Calais, and was entrusted with the task of providing carriage for troops at Dunkirk.

His wife died on the 5th January, 1555-6; the Inquisition (2) taken on the 5th May following described Katherine as her heir and aged 15 years and thirty-five weeks at her mother's death, therefore born about 6th May, 1540.

There was no issue of her second marriage. Katherine Leigh was an heiress, even if St. Oswald's possessions were all that she secured of what her father had once owned. Sir

(1) P.R. 4 Ed. VI., Pt. 3. This works out at twenty years purchase of the then rent, £49 18s. 8d.
(2) Inq. p.m. (Ch. Series, II.), 109/24.

Thomas's account book (1) notes on the 11th February, 1556-7, a payment of two shillings to Lord Mountjoy's man that brought " Venison pastes " (2), a propitiatory gift, to her stepfather. Shortly afterwards Lord Mountjoy married Katherine with the full consent of her guardian (3), yet " because Maister Chaloner's haste " was very great for the payment of the purchase money of the marriage, he had to raise it by borrowing upon heavy bonds.

When Queen Elizabeth succeeded her sister, Chaloner at once found employment, no doubt again through the influence of his friend William Cecil. The Emperor, Charles V., had now abdicated in favour of his son, Philip II. of Spain, and it was to the Netherlands that Chaloner was sent. The Count of Feria, who married the daughter of a Buckinghamshire neighbour (Jane, daughter of Sir Robert Dormer, of Eythorpe, by his first wife Mary, daughter of Sir Wm. Sidney), and who was afterwards to be on most intimate terms with him, described him in a letter written to King Philip as a man of a little over forty, who spoke Latin, Italian and French well. In a later letter he thought him a great talker, and a person of no authority.

But in July, 1559, the Queen had already made up her mind to transfer him from the Low Countries to Spain. For some reason the transfer hung fire. On 5th February, 1559-60, he and Sir Thomas Gresham, his successor, had an audience with the Regent and presented the letters of recall and substitution. He then returned to England, where he remained for a year-and-a-half, notwithstanding the piteous appeals to be released of Sir Thomas Chamberlain who was then accredited to Madrid and only too anxious to get home.

At last, in the early part of November, 1561, he started: his heavy baggage went by sea to Bilboa, while he crossed the channel, spent a little time at Paris on State affairs, and then posted slowly to his destination. The journey had been most painful both on account of the ill, stoney ways of the mountains, and the mirey ways of the plain country. The fare and lodgings were worse; in eight weeks he had not dared to undress three times before going to bed. He could get no bread (4).

He crossed the frontier near Vittoria towards the end of December, and reached Madrid early the following

(1) Lands 824. Those who are interested in accounts should peruse this account book, where every pecuniary transaction is recorded in detail.
(2) Pasties.
(3) D.S.P. Eliz., Add 13/49.
(4) S.P. Foreign. Eliz. 1561, No. 740.

January, only to find that his heavy baggage had been detained on arrival at Bilboa by the Officers of the Inquisition, the trunks broken open and searched and his books examined and condemned as forbidden. The King of Spain himself could do no more than negotiate where the functions of the Inquisition were concerned, but eventually, through his good offices, the property was restored and reached him on the 13th March. No sooner had he reached his destination than he longed to get home. His services in Spain must have been highly valued by the Queen, and the strongest proof of this was her reluctance to recall him. His friendship with the Count and Countess of Feria brought him into close contact with the King, who held the Count in the highest esteem, and not long afterwards promoted him to a Dukedom. Notwithstanding that the Duchess (to give her her later style) as a former Lady in Waiting of Queen Mary, and a Dormer adhered to Roman Catholicism, she still retained the affection of Queen Elizabeth, who had spent a day in her company at her home at Eythorpe (1) in the troublous times that succeeded Wyatt's rebellion (2), and as late as August 22nd, 1568, in disregard of the modern conventions of International law, described herself as her Sovereign and friend (3). The Duke and Duchess resided at Zafra, and here Chaloner was always sure of a welcome and of a refuge from the heat in Summer and cold in Winter, from which he suffered in Madrid.

From his arrival in Spain in January, 1561-2, until his departure on 30th April, 1565, Chaloner poured forth an unceasing stream of complaints and requests to be recalled. His health suffered, and his purse was insufficient. His " diets would not bear " at the prices in Madrid, which were double, treble or quadruple those in England. If he kept but a dozen servants their wages, liveries and clothing would cost 600 ducats a year. Lodging and bedding alone came to 38 ducats a month.

During his first month there had not been so much rain for twenty years. " Spain, nay, rather, pain," was his comment to his friend Sir John Mason. Seven years in Flanders were a less penalty than seven months in Madrid. " Hispania vallis miseriæ, fons superbiæ, beati qui non viderunt et crediderunt," he writes six weeks later to the same friend.

(1) S. E. of Waddesdon, not Heythrop, as in D.N.B.
(2) Holinshed's Chronicle, iv., p. 129.
(3) S.P. For. Eliz. 1568, No. 2445.

He suffers from ague tertian and has tasted a piece of Spanish " reumatizos." In Lent he feeds on poison, no fresh milk, fish or butter is to be had. The salt fish is worse than what would satisfy the meanest boy in his kitchen at home. In October, 1563, he suffers from calculus renium, and reminds the Queen that his father died of the same ailment. Rest at Madrid and the drinking of Spanish wines had increased it, more especially as the wines were adulterated with lime and other filthiness to make them look whiter. He became a total abstainer, and was reduced to drinking a decoction of liquorice and barley—all to no purpose, his health grew steadily worse. At the end of 1563 a ray of hope dawned. His brother Francis wrote to him that he had at last obtained his letters of recall, and the draft in Cecil's handwriting of a letter to be written by the Queen (to be found amongst the Foreign Papers) shows that it was not an idle boast (1). But serious matters arose, and the difficulty of finding a successor caused the postponement of the recall for another fifteen months.

He had had to follow the Court from Saragossa to Montzon and thence to Barcelona, and was not back in Madrid until April, 1564.

He had now been a widower for some years with no direct heir. In a letter dated 20th August, 1562 (2), to one of his most intimate friends, the Marchioness of Northampton, sister of George and Henry, successive Lords Cobham, he laments that he has no child to inherit what God has sent him, his next brother's children not being what their father and he think much of, an apparently unfounded aspersion upon his nephew Thomas Chaloner, the discoverer of alum, and his niece Bessie. He thinks it time to wed. He confides to the same correspondent that one of his reasons for wishing to go home was to find a wife and raise a family. The rumour that Sir Maurice Berkeley was about to marry Elizabeth, daughter of Sir Anthony Sondes, of Throwley, Kent, a gentlewoman of the Chamber to Queens Mary and Elizabeth (3), was communicated to him by Sir Nicholas Throckmorton, on the 14th June, 1562, with the comment : " You are too cold in your suits." This may have been the lady to whom he alluded in another letter to Lady Northampton (4).

He regretted that in this treeless country (i.e., Spain) he could get no green willow to make a garland. These fair

(1) S.P. For. (1563). No. 1563.
(2) S.P. For (1562). No. 509.
(3) Nicholls Progress.
(4) S.P. For. (1562). No. 257.

women that are young will bid have away the old man.   Later
we find his brother Francis reminding him that there were
two Countesses to be had: but at that very time, or certainly
very shortly afterwards, a young lady whose surname does
not appear in the Foreign State Papers, but whose Christian
name, Audrey, sufficiently identifies her with Miss Ethelred
Frodsham, must have been paying him a visit.

There appears to be no record of her arrival; but a
letter which Chaloner received (1) at Balbastro from Madrid
containing commendations to Mistress Audrey, implies that
certainly she was in his company in January, 1563-4, and
most probably had accompanied him thither from Madrid.
She left Spain on 6th July, 1564, sailing from Portu Galete
(2); with certain persons whom Chaloner described as his
folk.

There is no mention of any child, and it is probable that
Thomas the younger was not born until about 16th November,
1564.   The Christmas of that year found Chaloner distinctly
worse (3), and now he was a confirmed invalid.   He had had
to forgo his visit to the Ferias at Zafra, the one bright spot
in his banishment; in declining the invitation on 27th June
he wished that the Countess could, for three or four months,
visit the green fields of Buckinghamshire (4), where he hoped
to make his nest.   Letters received from England are not
cheering, his affairs there are in a state of disorder.   Needless to say, he redoubles his attempts to get home.   He begs
the Queen to provide a new broom to sweep the cleaner, for
he was worn to the stump.   He appeals to the Privy Council
on the ground of his long service in Spain; he sends to his
friend, Sir John Mason, fifteen pages of Latin verse to be
presented to the Queen; all to no purpose; finally he solicits
the help of the Earl of Leicester, who is at last succcessful
in obtaining his recall.

He packed his belongings preparatory to a sea voyage,
for he felt too weak to travel by land, and on Friday, 24th
April, 1565, he embarked at St. Sebastian in a ship of Lyme.
Four days later he arrived at Exeter, where he rested at the
house of his old Steward and friend Roger Hooker (otherwise
Vowels), the father or uncle of Richard, the well-known
divine, and brother of John Hooker, not unknown in the
literary world (5).   By slow stages he reached his house at

(1) S.P. For., 1564, No. 15.
(2) id., Nos. 539, 652.
(3) id., No. 725.
(4) id., No. 444.
(5) The Ency. Brit., 11th Edn., gives the father's name as
    Richard.   D.N.B. gives Roger.

St. John's, Clerkenwell. The home-coming was not conducive to peace of mind.

On the one hand his friends, amongst them Sir Ambrose Cave and John Jewel, Bishop of Salisbury, urged him to marry Etheldred Frodsham (1); on the other hand his brother, Francis, was wild at the thought that the possessions to which, or at least to part of which, he expected to succeed, should slip from his grasp. The admonitions of the Bishop had their desired effect. The long delayed marriage took place; when and where we cannot learn. As Sir Thomas was then on his death-bed it was most probably solemnised under licence from the Archbishop of Canterbury, but there is an unfortunate hiatus in the records of the allegations for marriage licences issued from the Faculty Office of the Archbishop in London, and those for the years 1549 to 1566 are missing (2).

But approximately we know the date—Richard Clough wrote on 20th November, 1565, to their mutual friend William Phayre, who had been left in Spain as Chargé-d'affaires—Sir Thomas Chaloner has changed his life, being but one month married (3).

In a scurrilous letter actuated by his disappointment at the frustration of his hopes (4) Francis described the hasty summoning of a scrivener on the morning of Saturday, 25th July, and the execution of a will devising all his lands to the " bastard " only, and bequeathing all his goods to the " danderly," by which opprobious terms he referred to the younger Sir Thomas and Lady Chaloner, respectively.

Marriage at that period did not necessarily revoke a will, but obviously if the will of 25th July had ever been executed, prudence dictated a revision of its provisions, as well as a modification of its language. In effect, the ultimate dispositions were similar to those that Francis had feared. They were three in number. An Indenture, dated 11th October, 1565 (recognised by Sir Thomas on the 12th October), by which he conveyed to Sir William Cecil and other trustees his possessions at Saint Bees, Steeple Claydon and Guisborough (5): a declaration of trust contained in another Indenture made on the same day and between the same parties as the enrolled deed, whose import can only be conjectured: the will, dated 13th October, 1563, which does not differ materially from that sketched by Francis (6).

(1) D.S.P., Eliz., 37/1.
(2) Harl Soc. Publns., vol xxiv., p. 14.
(3) For. S.P., Eliz.
(4) D.S.P., Eliz., 37/1.
(5) Close Rolls 7, Eliz. pt. 17 m.1.
(6) Bacon 47, Surtees Society, vol. cxxi., p. 44.

The infant is described as the *said* Thomas, son of
Audrey, the draughtsman evidently having drawn the will
after the declaration of trust, and with its phraseology in
his mind. Lady Chaloner (described as Audrey, my wife)
was to have the care and custody of Thomas for six years
after her husband's decease, with an allowance of £20 a
year for his finding. After the expiration of the six years
the testator most humbly desired the " Right Honourable
Sir William Cecil Knight, the Secretary to the Queen," to
take the order and rule of his body. Cecil, Lady Chaloner,
and young Thomas were appointed executors. There were
several legacies, amongst others ten marks to Thomas, son
of John Chaloner, our alum discoverer. Francis, needless to
say, gets nothing. Then the following day he died, and was
buried at St. Paul's with great pomp, Cecil attending as
Chief Mourner.

What steps Francis could have successfully taken to
upset the dispositions in favour of his nephew are not very
obvious. But that Cecil anticipated some such steps is
evident from the very careful manner in which he calculated
how the income of the estate was to provide for payment of
the legacies and incidental charges, not forgetting ample
provision for the costs of litigation. He was not in too
great a hurry to prove the will; indeed it was not proved
until 20th November, 1579, and then by the oath of Lady
Chaloner only. He had no intention to exhibit too much
altruism in his administration. A letter from Sir Henry
Percy, written from Tynemouth Castle on 27th October,
1566, desiring to know his pleasure whether certain stones
from Guisborough Abbey were to be sent to Burghley or
London, tells its own tale (1). But that he took his duties
very seriously is shown by the careful calculations to which
reference has been made (2). Then his anxiety ceased. The
litigious Francis died. He had married Agnes, the illegitimate daughter of Sir William Bowyer, a former Lord Mayor
of London, and at the time of his death was engaged in
disputing the claim of a nephew (whose father, John, was
living but had been passed over) to succeed another of the
brothers of Agnes, who had died without issue, on the ground
that the remainder was to the " heir of John " and that John
could have no heir until he died (3). As the remainder
to Agnes was conditional upon failure of John's issue, which
obviously had not happened, his chances of success were small,
but before the cause was heard he died and the proceedings

(1) D.S.P. Eliz., 13/35.
(2) Lands 8/60, 9/50.
(3) C3 7/47.

dropped. The material point is that he was dead before 23rd January 1565-6, and, therefore, he could not have survived his brother more than three months.

John Chaloner was too much engrossed with his alum experiments to make any unpleasantness, although we read of an action in Chancery (1), Thomas Chaloner v. John Chaloner, respited on 16th July, 1580, the subject matter of which is not to be found. This much appears to be clear, that the will of Sir Thomas Chaloner was carried into effect.

Lady Chaloner did not long remain a widow. She had been left the house in St. John's, Clerkenwell, but she soon gave it up to reside at Steeple Claydon, where she lived with her second husband, Edward Brockett, of Wheathamstead (2), the second son of Sir John Brockett, of Hertfordshire, by whom she had a son and two daughters. He also pre-deceased her, and then on the 25th August, 1601, when she could not have been far short of sixty years old, she married Robert Charnock, a college contemporary of her son (3). She died on the 25th December, 1603 (4). Under his father's will the younger Thomas passed the first six years under his mother's care. At an early age he was sent to St. Paul's School for the headmastership of which William Malim had recently deserted Eton. Then, at a correspondingly tender age, he was entered at Magdalen College, Oxford. On the 6th November, 1578, he wrote from this College a Latin letter addressed to Lord Burghley (5), soliciting his influence with Dr. Laurence Humphreys, the then President, to secure for him rooms in the College. There is an allusion in the letter to some insult which he had suffered at " Gysborowe," and which would do him much harm if it were not put right. There is no hint as to the nature of the insult.

Burghley's intervention proved successful (6). On the 4th April, 1579, Thomas Chaloner was admitted as of Magdalen College and Buckinghamshire, fourteen years old, and the son of a Knight, and on the same day his serviens (not improbably his tutor), Thomas Ward, twenty-seven years old, was likewise admitted (7).

On the 17th November, 1581, he was one of that College who subscribed to the Thirty-nine Articles, and in May, 1582, he was admitted B.A. (8). His half-brother, John Brockett,

(1) S.P. Ireland, Eliz., 72/48.
(2) Harl Soc. Publns., vol. xxii., p. 32.
(3) Lipscomb Bucks ii. 517, citing Register of Adstock.
(4) Lipscomb Bucks iii., 83, citing Register of Steeple Claydon.
(5) B.M. Lands, 27/22.
(6) Clarke's Register of Oxford, vol. ii., part 1, p. 391; part 2, p. 138; vol. iii., p. 101.
(7) id., vol. ii., part 2, p. 101.
(8) Clark's Register, by a printer's error, describes him as of Magdalen Hall; College is correct.

followed him to Magdalen on the 30th October, 1584. Mention has already been made of the probate of his father's will on the 20th November, 1579, and another event of almost equal importance was the publication in the same year of his father's great Latin poem, upon which he spent so much time in Spain, and which was to rival the Aeneid of Virgil, in length if not in reputation, De Republica Anglorum instauranda. William Malim, the son's headmaster, acted as Editor. Burghley and young Thomas both contributed verses, while Malim in his introduction sketched the life of the author.

Though never called to the Bar, on the 13th November, 1583, young Thomas was admitted to Gray's Inn (1), and shortly after taking his degree he married Elizabeth, daughter of Sir William Fleetwood, Sergeant-at-law, and recorder of the City of London, who was a neighbour at Great Missenden, in the same County as Steeple Claydon ; the date of the marriage can be fixed approximately by the baptism of his eldest son Thomas (who died young) at St. Olaves, Silver Street, on the 24th February, 1586-7. Meantime, on 16th November, 1585, on the Recoveries Roll of Mich. Term 27 and 28 Eliz. (2), three separate deeds were enrolled dealing in turn with the Manors of St. Bees in Cumberland, Steeple Claydon and Guis-borough. The exact object of the transaction is uncertain, it most probably marked the attainment of his majority and was a method of conferring the legal estate upon him, or it may have formed part of the settlement executed upon his marriage.

A few days afterwards, in December, 1585 (3), with two horses and two servants he formed part of the train of the Earl of Leicester in his expedition to the Netherlands.

As an interlude it may be in his military duties he sat in the short Parliament that lasted from the 15th October, 1586, to the following 23rd March as Member for St. Mawes in Cornwall, a county which then returned forty-four members against twenty-three for the combined three Ridings of Yorkshire. There again we expect to find the influence of Burghley. St. Mawes was one of the recently-created boroughs. When a new Parliament was summoned

(1) Foster's Admissions to Gray's Inn, p. 63.
(2) Recovery Roll, C.P., 43/1.
(3) Cal. Spanish State Papers, p. 554, citing Paris Archives, K. 1564, 19.

28

in 1588 two new members, John Potts and Walter Cope (afterwards Sir Walter Cope), sat for St. Mawes. It is probable that Chaloner was then serving either in Flanders or Brittany, though his name has not been discovered in the very voluminous accounts preserved in the Record Office, possibly because he was then not yet a Company Commander. His step-grandfather, Sir John Brockett, levied some hundred-and-fifty men and supplied them with coats. Chaloner might have gone out with them. Charles Blount, later Lord Mountjoy, and still later Earl of Devonshire, his father's step-grandson, also commanded another company, but there is no evidence that there was any great intimacy between him and the sons of Katherine Leigh.

It is generally admitted that he was knighted by Henry IV., King of France, in company with Sir Anthony Shirley, at the seige of Rouen. When we call to mind his father's friendship with the Earl of Leicester, we could have felt no surprise to learn that he was included in the latter's retinue in the Netherlands, and it is equally natural to find him serving his step-son, the Earl of Essex, for whom he acted as special correspondent in Florence during the years 1596 to 1597. The letter books of Anthony Bacon, of which the originals are in Lambeth Library, and abstracts in the British Museum, contain enough of his correspondence to date his movements (1). On 25th October, 1595, he thanked Anthony Bacon for recommending him to Lord Essex, and promised to testify something worthy of his notice. He sailed from Gravesend two days later, and for the next few months he reported everything of importance that occurred in Italy, and a mass of second-hand information from France.

His intimate acquaintance with Anthony Bacon appears from a suit commenced in the Court of Requests (2) shortly after Bacon's death, who was said to have borrowed £100 from Richard Synhouse (? Senhouse), one of the household of his father, Sir Nicholas Bacon, Lord Keeper. In addition to other security, Chaloner and Bacon gave Synhouse a joint bond for £200. Chaloner sued to restrain Synhouse from enforcing the bond, on the grounds that in lieu of interest Synhouse was to have a very competent gentlemanlike diet and other valuable benefits and gratuities, and that Synhouse had realised the other security which was ample to cover the debt. Synhouse denied that there was any such arrangement, and alleged that there were two bonds given for £100

(1) B.M. Add., 4121, and following.
(2) Court of Requests, Eliz., 189/21, 192/16.

29

and £66, respectively, to be paid in the Chapel at Essex House, otherwise called Leicester House without Temple Bar.

The details of the case which was not finally settled when Synhouse died about Michaelmas, 1602, are not relevant, but the connection between Chaloner, Bacon and Essex can thus be traced as existing shortly before the execution of the last mentioned. But it is quite clear that he took no part in the rebellion, the cause of the execution. Some of his letters, signed Thomas Bentivolus (1), to Anthony Bacon and to Essex are to be found amongst the manuscripts at Hatfield, written respectively from Pisa and Florence in January and March, 1596-7, from Lyons in June, 1598, and from Paris in March, 1598-9. The probability is that when Essex quarrelled with the Cecils he sided with the latter. It may be that, like his father's step-grandson, Charles Lord Mountjoy, he realised to what lengths Essex was prepared to go, and left his service. Or it may be that he was one of those sent in the interests of Essex to the King of Scotland, and so was out of the country when the crisis came. He was certainly there at the time of the death of Queen Elizabeth (2). Thomas Lord Burghley wrote on the 2nd April to his brother, Sir Robert Cecil, that young Sir Thomas Chaloner was in great favour with the King.

He accompanied him on his journey South to take possession of the English throne, and stayed with him at York, where in the same month of April he received the thanks of the Lord Chancellor (Lord Ellesmere) for having recommended the King to continue him in Office. In reply, Chaloner referred to the alliance in blood between them as a sufficient explanation of his action (3).

In August following, Prince Henry was placed in a separate establishment, and Sir Thomas was put in charge of his person and household with the title of Governor (4). Here he was brought into close connection with his brother-in law, Sir David Foulis, who held the Office of Cofferer to the two Princes Henry and Charles, and who was afterwards one of his fellow-patentees in the grant of alum rights under circumstances to be detailed later.

It was mainly through information conveyed to him that the Gunpowder Plot was discovered. His first wife died

(1) Cecil MSS., vols. vii., viii. and ix.
(2) id., vol. xv., p. 28.
(3) Egerton Papers Camden Society, vol. xii., pp. 359, 363.
(4) S.P. Dom. Jac. I., 3/15.

22nd November, 1603, and on 10th July following he married Judith, the daughter of Sir William Blount, of the City of London, and widow of John Gregory, of Hull. She died on the 30th June, 1615, and he on the 17th November in the same year; the dates of his birth and death corresponding very closely to those of William Shakespeare.

By his will dated two days before his death he confirmed an assignment made on 28th February, 1607-8 to his brother-in-law, Sir William Fleetwood, of two-thirds of the profits arising from the alum mines for the benefit of his children by his first wife, and bequeathed the remaining third amongst the children of his second marriage, and in addition provided that his daughter, Dame Mary Fisher (1), who had had no portion from him, was to have £1,200 out of the alum mines by instalments of £300 a year. His children were destined to receive very little, if any, benefit from these gifts.

Under the arrangement with the Crown, the terms of which will appear in due course, no payments were due to his estate until the 1st of May following his death, but when that date occurred the beneficiaries were not much better off than before. The actual payments were set out in a Privy Seal Warrant dated 16th March, 1636-7 (2). All that Sir William Fleetwood received was the sum of £500, due on 1st May, 1617, and £750 for three-quarters-of-a-year ended on 1st February, 1617-8, as appeared from a certificate given by Sir Robert Pye, Auditor.

Before the payments fell due, on 25th November, 1616, Sir Edmund Fisher, the husband of Mary, filed his bill in Chancery (3) against the executors of Sir Thomas for specific performance of an agreement to settle £3,000. He alleged that in November, 1603, his father, Edward Fisher, settled upon him the Manor of Odeston or Orleston in Berkshire, and also Mickelton in Gloucestershire. At once he received many offers of marriage, among them one which he accepted from Sir Thomas Chaloner, who offered his daughter Mary with a portion of £3,000.

The answer to the bill was sworn by William Smeeth, the only one of three executors who proved the Will. Sir Thomas's estate was much encumbered, and unable to satisfy the liabilities which could be enforced upon it. But apart from this he tells quite a different story. The generous

(1) Fisar, in MSS.
(2) P.S.O.2, No. 108.
(3) C2, Jas. I., F. 11/44.

gift of the elder Edward Fisher was merely made to avoid the possible consequences of a number of lawsuits in which he was involved. The younger Edward had heard that Sir Thomas had a fair, comely young gentlewoman to his daughter, and was then greatly in favour with the late Prince Henry. He demanded no money, but was quite satisfied with his countenance in his lawsuits.

The marriage, in fact, was arranged by Judith Lady Chaloner, who perhaps was not sorry to get her eldest step-daughter off her hands. In any case, through Chaloner's good offices, Fisher was knighted, and his wife was left a legacy of £1,200.

Like so many other Chancery suits, we must wait until someone has patience and leisure to transcribe the weighty volumes of Chancery Decrees and Orders before we can speak with certainty, but it is a not improbable conjecture that the executor's answer was accepted by the Court. On one point only do we feel confident, and that is that Lady Fisher received no part of her legacy other than possibly a small portion of the two payments made to Sir William Fleetwood. A petition from Mary's next sister Elizabeth and her husband, Robert Barnfield (1), shows that she was not much more fortunate. The petition is undated, but from internal evidence must have been presented shortly after her marriage, the licence for which was granted 15th June, 1627 (2).

It recites a pension due to the petitioners of £166 13s. 4d. for ten years then to come, payable out of the alum works. The prayer is that the arrears might be paid and the petitioners express their willingness to accept £100 a year in future, and so make a sacrifice in ten years of 1,000 marks. Again, though it is impossible to speak with certainty, there seems little doubt that the sacrifice was not accepted, and that Mrs. Barnfield received nothing.

So far as the sons were concerned, the eldest, William, was created a Baronet in 1620 (3), and died in Turkey in 1641, without issue. We hear of him later protecting his interests by an appeal to the Treasury when rumours were going about that Thomas Russell intended to sell some of the fittings of the works. But there is no intimation that he received any portion of the annuities. Edward, the second son, was a Doctor of Divinity; he seems to have taken no part in the alum negoti-ations. It is from him that the present line is derived. The two youngest sons of the first marriage were the two

(1) D.S.P., Chas. I., 102/63.
(2) Clay, vol. ii., 231.
(3) id.

so-called regicides, Thomas and James, but of these only Thomas actually took part in the sentence on King Charles I. While the story is obviously untrue that their adherence to the Parliamentary party was caused by the action of the Crown depriving them of their alum mines, it is not improbable that they were irritated beyond measure by the non-performance of the promise to pay them their share of the annuities. James died in 1660, possibly as the result of his imprisonment in Peel Castle in the Isle of Man. For thirty years, or thereabouts, he had been struggling to get his share of the alum monies. His first step was to induce his uncle, Sir Wm. Fleetwood, by an indenture dated 2nd February, 1627-8, to convey to him his sixth share of the annuity of £1,000, and all arrears accrued up to date. He then, on the 13th March, 1637-8, succeeded in getting the warrant for a Privy Seal (1), to which reference has already been made, entitling him to receive from the Treasury the sum of £3,291 13s. 4d. The state of the Kingdom at this date was hardly favourable for the payment of so large a sum. Nearly twenty years were to elapse before we find the sequel (2). On the 12th August, 1657, he was again presenting a petition. He alleged that before the Civil War he had been secured in the Tower, and his papers seized by order of the Privy Council. He had been extremely oppressed by the late King in his alum rights, so that £6,000 was owing to him, while the King got £100,000 from the alum (a sum which can only be correct, if at all, by taking no account of the outgoings incidental thereto). He then begged payment of the sum of £3,291 13s. 4d., for which he had obtained the Privy Seal, but found that his Parliamentary friends were quite as bad payers as the Royalists had been.

Thomas took advantage of the first proclamation after the Restoration to surrender himself, but found himself excepted, both as to his life and estate, from the Act of Oblivion. Opinions were divided whether the exception was justifiable, and it may be that eyes were wilfully closed when he escaped to the Low Countries. He lodged in the house of Constancia Lee at the Sign of the Red Cross, in High Street, Middleburg (3), and was buried under the name of George Saunders on 26th August, 1660. He was recognised by Mr. Spang, Minister of the English Corporation, who was unkind enough to say that he should have been buried under

(1) P.S.O. 2, No. 108.
(2) S.P., 1657, vol. clvi., 1, 93, No. 43.
(3) E. 134, 20, Chas. II., Mich., No. 58.

a gallows as a traitor to the King. An almanack found amongst his possessions was sent to England in 1668, and clinched the identification.

From this short sketch of the family it will be seen that while undoubtedly its members had claims under the letters patent, none of them, other than Thomas Chaloner of Lambay, had any actual share in the discovery of alum.

CHAPTER III.

THE DORSET MINES.

James Blount Lord Mountjoy, who married Katherine Leigh, the step-daughter of Sir Thomas Chaloner the elder, was descended from Walter Blount, a retainer of John O'Gaunt and Constable of Tutbury, drawing a competent salary from the revenues of the High Peak (1). During the next two centuries the family rose to greater importance, usually, but not always, on the Lancastrian side. Indeed, the peerage was in the first instance conferred upon Sir Walter Blount, in 1465, by Edward IV., for services rendered.

William Blount, 4th Lord Mountjoy, was a pupil of Erasmus, and famous as a scholar and patron of learning. He was Chamberlain to Queen Catherine of Aragon from 1512 onward, and was married four times. His first wife, Agnes Vanegas, who died early without issue, was one of the Queen's gentlewomen when she was Princess of Wales, and accompanied her from Spain. By his second wife, the daughter and co-heir of Sir Wm. Say, he had a daughter, Gertrude, who married in 1519 Henry Courtenay, Earl of Devon (2), afterwards created Marquis of Exeter, but later committed to the Tower for High Treason, condemned, beheaded, and attainted. By his third wife, Alice, the widow of William Browne, a former Lord Mayor of London, he was the father of Charles Lord Mountjoy, and grandfather of James Lord Mountjoy. His fourth wife, who survived him, was the widow of Robert Lord Willoughby de Broke. The only issue of the Exeter marriage was one son Edward, who died without issue at Padua, on the 8th September, 1556, never having enjoyed the title of Marquis of Exeter. He owned the Manor of Canford, in Dorset, and devised it to his mother, who survived him for two years only; she in turn devised two-thirds of the manor to her nephew of the half-blood James Lord Mountjoy (3). This manor, which stretched as far south as the English Channel, including much of what now is Bournemouth and Poole, was the site of the earliest attempts to manufacture alum on a commercial scale.

Charles, 5th Lord Mountjoy, who married Anne, daughter of Robert, 2nd Lord Willoughby de Broke, and of his step-mother, died on 10th October, 1544 (4). His son James was described as eighteen years old on 1st October, 1552, and his difficulties began at a very early age. He had

(1) Camden Society, N.S., vols. xx., xxi. Passim.
(2) Inq. p.m. 3/23.
(3) Rot. Parl., 5, 311.
(4) Inq. p.m. Ch. Series, ii., 93/34, and see. 238/75.

not yet come to his lands, and sued out his livery when the Coronation of Queen Mary took place (1), and as a token of misplaced gratitude for the services of his grandfather to her mother, he was commanded to be one of her Knights of the Bath. He had to borrow money from his tenants to enable him to bear the expense. A succession of law-suits with his step-father, Sir John Bonham, and with Lord Windsor, who claimed through his grandfather, increased his debts. Even his marriage with the heiress of Thomas Leigh brought no immediate relief. He had, as we have seen, to buy his wife's marriage and to satisfy " Maister Chaloner's haste " for the purchase money by borrowing upon heavy bonds.

He married Katherine Leigh in 1557 or 1558, a few days before he received an order to report himself at Calais, and though under the circumstances he was granted leave of absence, he was put to considerable expense in raising and equipping troops for the service. His wife was only eighteen years old at this date, and therefore could not assist him by charging her lands. When she came of age her services were soon required. On the 31st Deecmber, 1562, Sir Thomas Chaloner directed his brother Francis to ascertain whether Lord Mountjoy would sell Hoxton House (2), where Sir Thomas Leigh died. Apparently the answer, which is not preserved, was in the negative, but a year later Francis reported the intention of Lord Mountjoy to go to Terra Florida (3), and added that St. Oswald's was mortgaged to Robert Saville for £3,000. In fact, the fine completing the mortgage had been enrolled in favour of this Robert Saville in Hilary Term 1561-2, a few months after Lady Mountjoy attained her majority. Several other fines relating to the same or adjoining lands and evidencing further mortgages or transfers of mortgages followed in quick succession. Most of these mortgages eventually became vested in John Browne, a retired barrister of the Inner Temple, then living at Horton, in Kent. He was a son of the former Lord Mayor, William Browne, and therefore a half-uncle to his mortgagor. James Lord Mountjoy, besides Canford, had also the Manor of Puddleton, in Dorset, but it was mortgaged for £1,200 to Sir Matthew Arundel. In order to carry out necessary financial arrangements, John Browne was induced to release the St. Oswald's Priory lands and to accept in their stead a mortgage of two-thirds of Canford, reserving to Lord Mountjoy power to dig for ore within (4) Canford Waste and to make alum and copperas.

(1) D.S.P., Elizabeth, Add. 13/49.
(2) S.P., Foreign, 1562, No. 1,320.
(3) S.P., For., 1563, No. 1,500.
(4) Godbolt's Reports, p. 17.

Then the property so discharged was, in Michaelmas, 1568, sold outright to Lady Mountjoy's uncle by marriage, Sir Thomas Gargrave and her first cousin, Cotton Gargrave. Thus the last of the possessions which Sir Thomas Leigh secured on the dissolution of the monasteries passed out of the hands of his daughter. When we remember that these lands comprised a good slice of the West Riding coalfield, it is one of the ironies of life that they should have been exchanged for a small quantity of alum, the cost of production of which far exceeded its profit. The proceeds of sale of St. Oswald's enabled Lord Mountjoy to satisfy some prior charges on his Dorset property, and also to build and furnish houses for his alum works. One whose estates were so encumbered was hardly in a position to enter upon extensive mining operations, but Lord Mountjoy was of a sanguine temperament and not easily discouraged.

So far as the Southern Counties were concerned, the earliest experiments in alum making were made in the Isle of Wight, and their memory is preserved by the name of Alum Bay, on its West Coast. They were connected with one William Kendall, of Launceston, who is probably the same as a person miscalled Bendall in a transcript of an order dated 7th March, 1562, and printed by Richard Worsley in his History of the Isle of Wight (1). The order stated that the Queen had been informed of the existence of alum, and had sent Bendall (sic) to try and prove it. In any case William Kendall, on 31st December, 1562, received letters patent entitling him to the exclusive rights for twenty years of making alum within the Counties of Cornwall, Devon, Somerset, Dorset, Hampshire, Sussex, and Surrey (2). He could only enter upon lands after agreement with the owners thereof. He had the rights to requisition provisions, necessaries, workmen and transport at reasonable prices.

There is no trace in the Calendar of the State Papers of any acts performed under these letters patent. Kendall seems to have been connected with tin works at Lostwithiel, in Cornwall, and to have soon abandoned his interests in alum for presumably more remunerative pursuits. His rights were nominally reserved when a little more than a twelvemonth later another grant was made. On the 3rd July, 1564, Cornelius de Vos (3), described as a merchant, of London, and a " liege-made subject," was rewarded for having found alum, copperas and other minerals within the

(1) Appendix II., p. xvi.
(2) P.R., 5 Eliz., pt. 5, m. 8.
(3) P.R. 6 Eliz., pt. 8, m. 38.

Isle of Wight and elsewhere by the grant of a licence to dig for the same for twenty-one years from the 1st August, 1564. There were very similar clauses to those contained in the grant to William Kendall. For his part, Cornelius de Vos entered into two Indentures with the Queen by which he covenanted not to take more than three strangers as partners with him, and to observe the restrictive covenants in his licence. The Queen was to have one-tenth of the produce as compensation for any duty or custom, and also a right of pre-emption of the residue of the alum. De Vos, whose connection with mining operations in Ireland (1) we have already noticed, seems at a very early stage to have found a difficulty in raising the necessary capital, and very soon moved from the Isle of Wight to Canford Cliffs.

Negotiations associating Mountjoy with the work soon followed. An incomplete draft, attributed to the year 1565, of a transfer of one-twentieth part of the profits to some right honourable unnamed may have been a stage in these negotiations (2), but the final agreement was embodied in an Act of Parliament (8 Eliz., C. 21) passed in the following year.

The Queen (so the preamble says), being desirous that the hidden riches of the earth should by search and work of skilful men be found and brought to the use and commodity of the realm, had granted the letters patent to Cornelius de Vos inasmuch as she had been informed that there was some hope of his discovering alum and copperas which had been often previously attempted but never heretofore brought to effect. The ores and other necessary requirements for the work had been found most abundantly within Lord Mountjoy's lands, and he had himself grown to such knowledge and perfection as had never been attained before. He had made good copperas, and hoped to get alum which was very necessary for the use of drapery. He had also compounded with Cornelius de Vos, who was not of sufficient wealth, to carry out the work.

It was therefore enacted that, subject to the rights of William Kendall, no one for twenty-one years from 1st April, 1567, other than Lord Mountjoy and those duly licensed by him, should dig for alum or copperas upon pain of forfeiture of the proceeds and a penalty of £100, of which one-half was to go to the Queen, and the other half to Lord

(1) p. 14, ante.
(2) D.S.P., Eliz., 36/77

Mountjoy. Finally the latter undertook all the obligations of de Vos.

From the start difficulties hampered the progress of the work (1). To remedy the inexperience of the men of Dorset, de Vos brought certain men out of Italy at an expense to Mountjoy of £300, upon the pretext that they would make the mines yield nine parts in ten more than before, but when they arrived they could not make so much by nine parts in ten as the natives, and could only make that by copying their example. So said Lord Mountjoy later, but his complaint reads like that of a disappointed man. Though the legend of the importation of workmen from Italy to Guisborough is false, it is noteworthy that there was some connection at an earlier date. When things went the wrong way, de Vos returned to his native land, Liège. He had married on 11th December, 1558, Helen, widow of John Gylmym, alias Gilimene, Vintner, who had died on the preceding 5th June at Little Saint Bartelmews. In 1573 Helen complained that de Vos had left the realm some eight years previously (i.e., in 1565) (2) about some great and weighty affairs, and that she, being a very simple old woman, had been dispossessed of her land by strangers. Attached to the petition was a certificate dated at Wood St., 31st May, 1573, and signed by Lionel Ducket, then Lord Mayor, to the effect that Cornelius de Vos was then alive and residing with a cousin named Arnould, at Luick, the name by which Liège was then known. Some thirty-five years later the connection between Liège and England was to be renewed, with more profit to the alum trade.

Mountjoy had now to bear the whole burden of the work upon his own shoulders. He abandoned his residence at Brook House, in Wiltshire, and moved his establishment to Canford (3) Manor, which his mother then occupied. According to his statement, the change entailed a much greater expense for him. That his debts increased at an enormous rate is proved by the countless recognisances enrolled in his name on the Close Rolls of the relevant years.

Attention has previously (4) been called to his struggles to secure an Act of the Irish Parliament securing his rights in that kingdom. Part of the year then was passed at Canford and the remainder in London. His town house was known as Mountjoy House, just off Knightrider Street, of which he held the residue of a term of fifty years created by

---

(1) D.S.P., Elizabeth, Add. 13/49.
(2) Court of Requests, Eliz., 28/60, 134/4.
(3) Misread as Tunford in Cal. D.S.P., Eliz., Add. 13/49.
(4) Ante p. 14.

the Dean and Chapter of St. Paul's Cathedral. This was the building subsequently (1) leased to Dr. Henry Harvie, Master of Trinity Hall, Cambridge, and for the Fellows and Scholars thereof in trust for the Society of Doctors of Arches and known as Doctors Commons. In 1567 it seems, to use a modern expression, to have been let out in Flats. There were two other occupants, namely, a cousin of the Lady Mountjoy, George Carlton (2), a grandson of Margaret Culpepper (the mother of Joan Leigh), by her second marriage with Richard Welbeck and John Hastings, of Kenthorpe (3), in Lincolnshire, who appears to have been a not very distant relative of the Earl of Huntingdon.

It would seem that by this time Lord Mountjoy had recognised the inroads which he had made in his wife's fortune, and was apprehensive lest there should be no provision for her and her family. He therefore devised a scheme which bore some resemblance to a post-nuptial settlement. First he approached Carlton to know whether he would accept a commission, in other words a trust, for the benefit of Lady Mountjoy. Carlton declined to bear the sole responsibility, but agreed to accept it on condition that John Hastings was joined with him as a co-Trustee. Lord Mountjoy, having received a favourable opinion of the latter from the Earl of Huntingdon and the Earl of Bedford, assented, and the trust was executed in due course.

In addition to this trust, which would appear to comprise all the lands in Dorset and Yorkshire in which Lord Mountjoy had any interest, there was a lease of the principal workhouse for alum at Okeman's house, (also known as Totnam's), in the Parish of Canford, made to four trustees, Thomas Randolfe, George Carlton, Thomas Cotton, and Cotton Gargrave, in trust for Lady Mountjoy and her two sons, then under age. By this time, or possibly a little later, there would appear to have been at least three alum work-houses scattered along the coast from Bournemouth to Poole. In all five names are mentioned, but the same house may occasionally be known under more than one name.

The first building erected cost no more than £5. It was situated in Hampshire, where Boscombe now stands. Alum Chine Road preserves its name, and led to its site. Its first tenant was one Cornelius Stephenson, not improbably

---

(1) Court of Requests, Eliz., 114/56.
(2) See p. 19 ante, George Carlton was the uncle of the better-known Dudley Carlton Lord Dorchester.
(3) It has been suggested by the late Canon C. W. Foster that this should be Kingthorpe, in the Parish of Apley, near Wragby.

the same as Cornelius Stephens, formerly under the allegiance of Spain (1), and therefore a native of the Low Countries, who, in company with others from Liège and neighbouring states, was naturalised on 3rd January, 1562. Later John Mansfield, Richard Leycolt and Clement Draper held it for a term of one hundred years, for which they paid Lord Mountjoy £800 in cash and a rent of £900. Okeman's house, transferred to the trustees (2), was a much more substantial building. It included thirty acres lying between Canford Launde and the sea. A map of the Isle of Purbeck, dated 1585-6, in Hutchins's Dorset (3), shows alum works between Parkstone Church, $1\frac{3}{4}$ miles N. of Havens House and the same distance East of Poole, which corresponds closely with the description of Okeman's house. The other names of alum houses are Darling Chine, Havens House, and Branksea, usually written Brountsey. Lord Mountjoy, writing from Blandford Forum (4) to the Earl of Leicester and Lord Burghley on 8th April, 1572, mentions three houses only, the Merchants house (Darling Chine), the house let to Cornelius Stephenson (Alum Chine), and the third house committed to trustees (Okemans), which was then also under the care of Cornelius Stephenson. Meantime, a new enterprise was started, one fated to be as barren of results as any of its predecessors, but which at least produced a little grist for the Canford Mills. In the sixteenth century the search for precious metals went hand in hand with that for minerals of commercial value. Though gold could not be found in England, at least it could be made here if the necessary science were available.

Many were the pretenders, both native and foreign, to this science, and countless the sums of money expended by both private individuals (5) and the Government in subsidising their efforts. Amongst these pretenders was one William Medley, who, for a short time, succeeded in cozenning statesmen like Burghley and Leicester, a diplomat like Sir Thomas Smith, and a Navigator like Sir Humphrey Gilbert. Sir Thomas Smith (6), sometime Provost of Eton, and for many years Ambassador in France, had been drawn into these speculations through his interest in natural philosophy. Whether he seriously believed that gold could be manufactured may be doubted, but he was satisfied that iron could be converted into the more valuable metal copper, if only the correct procedure were adopted. When we

(1) P.R. 966 (4 Eliz., pt. II., p. ii.).
(2) D.S.P., Eliz. Case H., No. 21. Evidence of George Dickinson.
(3) 5th Edition, vol. i., p. 462.
(4) D.S.P., Eliz., 86/26.
(5) Ashmole Theatrum Chemicum.
(6) Strype's Life of Sir Thomas Smith, p. 160.

41

remember that the name "copperas" was applied indiscriminately (1) to both iron and copper pyrites, and was the principal ingredient in the transmutation, the results professed to be obtained in limited tests were not so very miraculous.

In the year 1571 an association was formed between Sir Thomas Smith, Sir Humphrey Gilbert, and William Medley to transmute iron into copper with the help of vitriol; Sir Thomas described it as a scheme to find primum ens vitrioli. The scene of their operations was to have been Winchelsea (2). Gilbert contributed £100, which Medley soon spent, as he said, in providing and furnishing a house. The qualified success that rewarded their exertions led them to believe that Winchelsea was unsuitable. Medley received another £100 from his co-adventurers, and, finding the "earths" at Poole quite as suitable for his purpose as the vitriol which hitherto they had had to purchase, they took a lease of Okeman's House from the trustees of Lady Mountjoy at a rent of £300 per annum, Sir Thomas entering into a bond of £1,000 for payment thereof.

Two Charters were in due course granted by the Crown (3), the first on the 4th December, 1571, having omitted Medley, the second, in 1575, included him amongst the patentees. Sir Thomas Smith, of Theidon at Mount, in Essex, had, so the recitals ran, through long search in books of art, many vain trials and essays, manifold expenses, and (as the Charter of 1575 alone added) through the industry of William Medley, found out the art of making copper from iron and quicksilver from antimony and lead. As a reward, Sir Thomas, Leicester, Burghley, Gilbert and Medley were incorporated in the Society of New Art, Sir Thomas being the first Governor.

Shortly before the grant of the first Charter, Sir Thomas had to return to his post in France, and left Sir Humphrey to supervise the work. The reports that he received from time to time in reply to his anxious enquiries were most unsatisfactory (4). Nothing was being done. Pray God it be not less than nothing. To save their honesties they must lay out another hundred pounds to Lady Mountjoy. Gilbert was still abused with Medley's words and promises, and was led by the nose like a buffalo (bufle). Medley would do nothing till new privileges were granted. No doubt he

(1) See Selden Society. vol. xxviii., p. 23n.
(2) D.S.P., Eliz., 86/14. Lands 19/45.
(3) P.R., 14 Eliz., pt. 12, and 17 Eliz., pt. 9. See Selden. Society Publn., vol. xxviii., pp. lxii., 20.
(4) S.P. Foreign (1572), No. 146 (13).

resented the omission of his name. Sir Thomas replied by the query: "What getteth My Lord Mountjoy by his privileges" adding that "it was labour and order that bringeth gain, not these foolish privileges."

He then recommended that they should desert copper and quicksilver, and turn their attention to saltpetre and alum, warning Gilbert that Medley, like Geber (1), Ripley and other alchemists, was simply leading him on. By following him they were like young children who seek a lapwing's nest, and when they are almost at it, seeing the old lapwing fluttering hard by them, and crying fitfully (as they think) "Here it is, here it is," they follow her from place to place all round about, till at last, before they be aware, they are over-shoes in the fen or in a slough, and find as many lapwings' nests as horses' nests.

Smith's suggestion then was to abandon their patent and buy that of Lord Mountjoy. But, he added, as some men would not give up their bauble for the Tower of London, he might ask too high a price, certainly more than £20,000, as he valued it at over £2,000 a year.

Meantime Gilbert carried on his negotiations with Lady Mountjoy (2). Counsel were called to advise how far the permission of Lord Mountjoy was necessary, and their opinion was to decide whether the rent was to be £500 or £400.

The works did not remain long at Okeman's House. So far from being led by the nose, Gilbert soon realised the emptiness of the scheme, and that the alluring picture of wealth was not likely to be realised. Relations between the parties were first strained and then resulted in an open breach. By May, 1572, the quarrel was at its height, and Medley appealed to Burghley. His excuses for failure are such as we should expect (3). The "earths" had to lie ten or twelve months unwashed, so that the liquors produced might be of full strength. Time was therefore necessary. He had been desirous to make copperas and alum, but dared not put in practice his best methods lest they should come to the knowledge of Lord Mountjoy. He and his friends went very indirectly about.

The difficulties were increased by lack of money. He would be glad to repay Gilbert, and so to cleanse his hands of such pitch.

(1) Jabir ibn Hayyan of Kufa in Iraq. C. 722-813. See the works of Geber, by Dr. Holmyard.
(2) S.P.D., Eliz., 85/45.
(3) id., 86/14, 44.

He had heard of like mines in Yorkshire and of a well which appeared to come from such a vein. Later, he had within sixty miles of the un-named town from which he wrote his last letter, found plenty of ore and seaweed and thirty acres of land, with a house and everything but utensils provided, at a yearly rent of £20.

The later history of the adventure may be very shortly stated. The works were soon moved to Anglesea, which, presumably, was the locality indicated. Sir Thomas Smith returned from France to undertake for the second time the duties of Secretary of State. He was now inclined to support Medley, who had offered to prove that he could convert six tons of iron into five tons of copper (1), and produce from the liquors in which the boiling took place sufficient alum and copperas to be sold at the then current prices for £10,000. This offer could be tested, and the recommendation was made that application should be made for a new patent to include Medley. This suggestion was made in December, 1574, and, as already stated, the patent was granted the next year (2). But in 1576 the bubble burst, and Medley died, a prisoner for debt, in the Counter.

Meantime the position of Lord Mountjoy had been getting gradually worse, and his debts were accumulating at an enormous rate. John Browne, the mortgagee of Canford, was now suffering from consumption, and was anxious to put his affairs in order before his death. Money lent upon mortgage was not such a simple investment then as it is now, and he preferred to die possessed of ready money. He first begged Mountjoy to redeem, but Mountjoy was quite unable to find the money. We find many appeals to the Queen, both before and after this time, suggesting plans by exchanging his estates for others belonging to the Crown for the relief of his fortune. The Treasurer of the Queen's household, Sir Walter Mildmay, who had to consider them, suspected that their real object was to defraud his creditors. Mountjoy strenuously denied the charge, and maintained that his only object was to pay his debts in full. Then the Trustees, Carlton and Hastings, hit upon a plan which later provoked much criticism and involved them in costly legal proceedings, but which appears to have been a prudent measure.

(1) Lands, 19/45.
(2) P.R., 17 Eliz., pt. 9.

Henry, Earl of Huntingdon, the President of the Council of the North Parts, was a nobleman of great wealth. Though married to Catherine Dudley, sister to the Earl of Leicester, he had no share in the principal mining companies in which his brother-in-law was interested, but it is not likely that he was proof against the fascination which such speculations exercised. The Trustees had themselves entered into a bond guaranteeing the repayment of the Puddleton mortgage to Sir Matthew Arundell upon a date then past, and were liable to be sued upon their guarantee. If the Earl could be induced to purchase from the mortgagees and trustees the Puddleton and Canford estates, workings and all, they would be safe. Eventually the negotiations materialised, and in July, 1570, Mountjoy's interests in Canford (subject to the reservation of his right to dig for alum ore) and Puddleton were transferred to Huntingdon freed from encumbrances (1). It was said later and after her death that Lady Mountjoy approved the transaction, but her husband most certainly did not. He was still pressing an exchange of his mortgaged lands and protesting the sincerity of his motives and his intention to pay every creditor in full. The creditors, on the other hand, who comprised many of Mountjoy's co-adventurers in the Society of Mines Royal, such as Sir Lionel Duckett, Sir Roger Martin, Mr. Byrde, declined to recommend the exchange. It is perhaps hardly necessary to mention that at this period it was difficult for a creditor to satisfy his debt out of the lands of his debtor unless the latter had charged his lands by recognisance under the Statute of Henry VIII., and this Mountjoy had done.

Then, when sanguine as he was, he thought that he had succeeded in persuading the advisers of the Queen to agree to an exchange of lands, he learnt to his surprise that the transfer to Hutingdon had taken place behind his back. He cast the blame for this upon his wife's trustees. "If Carlton and Hastings had performed their trust," he said, "my debts might have been paid and I left so honourable a Baron's living as my father never had, nor the more number of Barons at this time have; which is now far otherwise" (2).

He still continued to press for some assistance. On 4th January, 1578, Sir Walter Mildmay wrote to Burghley (3), then Lord Treasurer, that he had perused the book that concerned Lord Mountjoy's suit (4). After calling attention

(1) Close Rolls, 12 Eliz., pt. 8, 13 Eliz., pt. 13.
(2) D.S.P., Eliz. Add. 13/49.
(3) Harl, 6,992/108.
(4) Probably D.S.P., Eliz. Add. 13/39.

45

to a few points that required careful consideration, he concluded that he saw no inconvenience, but that her Majesty should do graciously to relieve a good nobleman greatly distressed. But nothing came of the appeal, and on 7th August, 1579 (1), Mountjoy, from his lodgings over against the French Church, applied to Sir Julius Cæsar, then in Paris, to be employed in any of his affairs there, a request which met the same fate as his appeal to the Queen.

So long as Lady Mountjoy lived, Lord Huntingdon contented himself with the rents of assize and casual profits arising from Canford and Puddleton (a very poor return upon his investment), and left the alum works alone. But she died in 1577, and the same year a commission of inquiry was directed (2) to ascertain the annual nature of the Queen's tenth share in the three houses at Boscombe, Branksea and Alum Chine reserved to her in the original grant to Cornelius de Vos. This share was put at £9, making the total yearly profit £90. The Queen had parted with her tenth share in Okeman's House to Burghley, who had in turn leased it to Mountjoy, and the latter had passed it on to the tenant, Edward Meade, Citizen and Goldsmith of London, for £100 (3).

It was therefore not included in the inquiry. Later this Edward Meade in February, 1578-9, unsuccessfully petitioned the Queen to grant (4) him her right of preemption of alum and copperas manufactured under the patent. He had paid £800 to put Okeman's house in repair, and received a lease at a rent of £300, but for the first three years the rent was to be devoted to repayment of his outlay and the balance only to be paid to the lessors. It would therefore appear that he must have been tenant shortly after the failure of the attempt to transmute iron into copper.

Alum Chine, as we have seen, was now vested in John Mansfield, Richard Leycolt and Clement Draper. Haven House appears to have been in the possession of Thomas Hampton and two brothers, John and Edward Lane. Thus the houses were all let and apparently in full operation; yet they contributed nothing to the supply of alum which still came into the kingdom from foreign countries, principally from Spain and Civita Vecchia (5). If it is asked how they

(1) B.M., 12,506/242.
(2) Exch. Sp. Com., 710.
(3) S.P., Eliz. Case H., No. 21.
(4) Lands, 27/60.
(5) Lands. 26/14, 44/53.

managed to pay their rents and wages to workmen, the answer is that given by Gerard Malines, who wrote fifty years later (1). They made great quantities of copperas and some alum, apparently very little. But copperas was then sold, so he says, at £30 a ton; £12 10s. od. would be nearer the figure (2), but even this would leave a fair profit. It is therefore not so surprising that there should be quite a competition for these houses.

In 1580 Huntingdon grew tired of waiting for his money. His first step, so far as we can disentangle the very complicated skein of legal proceedings, was to buy up several of the statute debts charged upon the lands of Lord Mountjoy, to obtain judgment and take the necessary steps to get the lands extended. By virtue of the extent he granted a lease to his own nominees, who thus claimed the right to evict the tenants of Lord Mountjoy. In October he made an attempt to get possession of Okeman's House under one of these extents (3). Apparently the tenant, Edward Meade, was quite prepared to assist him so far as he could. Thomas Hampton was concerned in some way that is not quite clear. But here he was attacking the interests of the two young Blounts, William and Charles. On the death of their mother, the trustees Carlton and Hastings held the lease upon trust to pay her debts, and to dispose of the balance for the benefit of the two sons. These latter at once appealed to the Privy Council, who, on 7th October, commanded Meade to forbear doing anything to the prejudice of the young gentlemen, and directed certain Justices of Hampshire and Dorset to sequester Okeman's House and the works. The sequestration was executed on military rather than judicial lines (4). In the afternoon of 12th October these justices, Sir Henry Ashley, John Hastings the trustee and Henry Uvedale, accompanied by the two young Blounts and several others, repaired to Okeman's house, where some thirty or more men were employed in the manufacture of alum and copperas. In the absence of Meade, they called upon his wife to give up possession, which she refused to do. After a fruitless wait the majority departed, leaving a small piquet behind. On the 20th October Sir Henry Ashley and Henry Uvedale returned with about forty more, turned Mrs. Meade out of the house, and handed over the premises to John Poole, who was supposed to be an impartial person, but who,

(1) Lex Mercatoria (1622), p. 269.
(2) Index to Remembrancia Rolls, p. 109.
(3) A.P.C., vol. xii. N.S., p. 228.
(4) Star Ch. Pro. Eliz. M. 2/1.

as Meade affirmed, was in fact supplied with victuals and money by Richard Leycolt, one of the tenants of Alum Chine, under Lord Mountjoy. Meade then filed his bill in the Star Chamber against Ashley and Uvedale. Process was forthwith served upon the two latter out of the Queen's Bench, but was promptly revoked (1) on the 9th November. Two days later there was a complaint that Samuel Meade, the brother of Edward, had re-entered Okeman's with a strong hand.

For the next few months there is an apparent lull. Then the Lanes enter into the picture. They sprang from Walgrave, in Northamptonshire, where they were neighbours of the Treshams, of Rushton (2). They were also related to the Montagues, of Boughton, in the same county (the ancestors of the Dukes of Manchester and Earls of Sandwich), and one of the family, Edward Lane, appears to have been settled for some years in Dorset;he was one of the Jury chosen (3) to value the mines in 1577. On 3rd July, 1581, Edward Lane, who had entered into possession of Okeman's (4), was ordered by the Privy Council to give over possession to Edward Meade, and the latter was to pay his rent within eight days to the two sons of Lord Mountjoy. Apparently, instead of complying with the order, Lane changed sides and took Thomas Hampton with him. Having entered in the interests of Lord Huntingdon, they went over to the enemy. On the 7th August Margaret Greene, widow, and Edward Meade (5) complained to the Privy Council that by an agreement lately made between William and Charles Blount on the one hand, and Edward and John Lane and Thomas Hampton on the other hand, they were dispossessed of the alum works at Canford. But on the 18th September Lord Mountjoy was making a like complaint to the Privy Council against Thomas Hampton (6). At Michaelmas Lord Mountjoy held a conference in the house of Robert Mansell (later Sir Robert Mansell) (7), in Coleman Street, London, with the various parties interested in the mines, namely, John Mansfield, Richard Leycolt, George Dickenson, Henry Smith and Edward Meade. They complained of their loss of possession both of Okeman's and Alum Chine. Lord Mountjoy put the blame upon Thomas Hampton, and referred to an earlier dispute between the latter and Lord Huntingdon, where Hampton had framed so scandalous a

(1) A.P.C., vol. xii. N.S., 66, 261, 264.
(2) Hist. MSS. Commn. Various, vol. iii., pp. 20, 44.
(3) Ex. Sp. Com., No. 710.
(4) A.P.C., vol. xiii. N.S., p. 116.
(5) id., p. 161.
(6) id., p. 213.
(7) D.S.P. Eliz. Case H., No. 21. Evidence of John Mansfield.

bill of complaint against Huntingdon that Mountjoy refused to allow it to be presented. Nothing came of the Conference, and then in November, 1581, James Lord Mountjoy died.

On Lord Mountjoy's death Lord Huntingdon was minded to strengthen his title to Okeman's (1), which was decidedly weak. On the 1st December following, the then trustees, Thomas Randolf, George Carlton, Thomas Cotton and Cotton Gargrave, assigned their lease to two trustees, Richard Branthwaite and Richard Polie, in trust for the Earl of Huntingdon, who covenanted to pay £300 a year in reduction of the debts (amounting to £1,400) of Katherine Lady Mountjoy, and £100 a year equally between William (now Lord) Mountjoy and his brother Charles Blount.

Carlton maintained that prior to this assignment he had offered the lease upon the same terms to William Lord Mountjoy (2), who had refused to accept it. The next stage was to get possession of Okeman's (2). A letter of attorney was made out to William Constantine, of Merle, a tenant of the Earl and former Mayor of Poole, directing him to give possession to certain citizens of London. On St. Stephen's Day he proceeded to serve it, accompanied by a number of serving men, variously stated at ten to thirty, some carrying swords as their custom was, the rest unarmed. As Edward Lane would not suffer them to enter, they drew as near as possible, read the deeds, delivered them to Thomas Jennings, the Earl's servant, and went quietly away.

Thus foiled in the attempt to obtain possession, the Earl's advisers thought fit to indict the Lanes at the General Sessions of the Peace, holden at Blandford, for forcible resistance to a peaceful entry. Under what statute they proceeded is not disclosed by the evidence.

The Blounts replied by a writ of Certiorari to remove the indictment; the Earl retaliated by a writ De procedendo to continue it; writs which seem to have been obtained with greater ease and celerity than now. Only a few days elapsed between St. Stephen's Day and the Sessions on the 20th January, and yet there was time for the issue of the writs and the consultations thereon. John Hilliard, of Bucklands, the clerk of the Peace for Dorset, at once took both writs up to London to consult Mr. Hanham, of the Middle Temple. While on his way he met young Lord Mountjoy in company with his Counsel, William Harris (3). They asked why the

(1) D.S.P. Eliz. 150/78.
(2) D.S.P. Eliz. Case H., No. 20.
(3) Later Serjeant at Law.

49

writ of certiorari had not been returned; Hilliard produced the writ De procedendo; Harris asked to see it; Mountjoy took it from him, put it in his pocket and walked off. The writ was never seen again. None the less, whether on Mr. Hanham's advice or on his own responsibility, Hilliard treated the writ of certiorari as annulled, and the indictment went forward.

The next move is even more surprising, to our minds. Certain of the workmen employed by the Lanes and John Pavie, who acted as Solicitor for Lord Mountjoy, were arrested on the very day of the January Sessions at Blandford by George Michell, of Bridewell, servant to Sir George Carye, Knight Marshall, acting under a warrant from the Privy Council. The fee of £5 was paid by John Mansfield on behalf of Lord Huntingdon, leaving no doubt as to the true authors of the act.

Pavie was acting as Solicitor on behalf of Lord Mountjoy in another case. Lord Howard and the other Justices permitted him to continue to act whilst the evidence was being given, but, notwithstanding his protest, he was arrested before the verdict was given and carried off to Poole, ten miles distant.

Two of the workmen arrested were conveying a cart laden with copperas into Poole. The victims were kept but a few days in custody, some released on bail, others pressed to accept a groat and become the Earl's servants at a week's notice. The delay occasioned by the issue of the writ of certiorari necessitated an adjournment of the indictment, and it was directed to be tried at a Privy Sessions to be holden at Wimbourne, four or five miles from Poole. The arrested workmen, though released from custody, were unable to give evidence, and the Jury, comprised of William Constantine of Merle, and seven other tenants of the Earl, and only four impartial persons found the indictment against the Lanes proved. A writ of restitution was then awarded in the Earl's favour.

About Candlemas, John Dolling, of Salisbury (1), a servant of Edward Lane, was arrested by the Mayor of that Borough at the request of John Mansfield on behalf of the Earl, for having assisted Lane to take possession of Alum Chine. He was imprisoned for ten days, and then released, receiving the Mayor's passport under seal to travel to meet the Earl. He found him at Bagshot, but when he desired to have access to him and to complain of his wrongful imprisonment, Mansfield, who was accompanying the Earl, charged

(1) Sarum, Wiltshire, in the original.

him to return and meet the Earl at Dorchester Assizes, or England would be too hot for him.

On his way to Dorchester he spent a night at Salisbury, was taken out of his bed by the Mayor and his officers, and committed to gaol. After three days he was sent to Poole, a journey of twenty-four miles (nearer twenty-nine), with his legs tied under the horse's belly, his arms pinioned, and a pair of iron manacles on his hands. At Poole he was presented to the Earl. He was afterwards imprisoned for thirty days at the suit of Mansfield and another. His jailor's wife brought him a dish of fish and tried to induce him to confess that Edward Lane had committed a robbery in the North Parts and had victualled certain pirates, assuring him that he would find favour if he would so confess, but he refused, not knowing his master guilty after any such manner.

On the afternoon of the 4th March (the first Sunday in Clean Lent), probably the day after his interview with Dolling, Lord Huntingdon, who had slept the previous night at Poole and had attended church service in the morning, after the sermon went down to Okeman's house attended by two or three of his servants. According to the story which these told, there were no threats, merely expostulation; Huntingdon only advised the Lanes to consider what danger they might incur by working without sufficient warranty. He told John Lane that his brother Edward had taken a strange course, first to set workmen to work in the mines to the Earl's use, and then to continue the work to the use of another man. If in the end it fell out by trial that he was injured by them, the poor men who were working there were not to look for any favour from him. As they were leaving the mines a labourer followed the Earl and told him that if the Earl would forbid him he would work no longer, but the Earl, suspecting a trap, called him a " crafty colt " and refused.

The Earl was also advised to take possession of Okeman's under his suit of restitution, but would not permit its execution lest it should be held to be breach of the order of the Privy Council, at any rate until he had given notice to the last mentioned.

On the other hand, the case for Lord Mountjoy alleged that the Earl had used such threats that the workmen and carriers of fuel did not dare to continue in their employment.

The Assizes were held at Dorchester shortly after this visit.

As far back as the January Sessions the Dorset Justices had endeavoured to reconcile the parties, and had partially succeeded, but ultimately the attempt failed, owing, as it was said, to the obstinacy of Mountjoy. Then in March the Sheriff, at Huntingdon's request (1) armed with the writ of restitution, went to Okeman's, accompanied by a band of men, rather, as he put it, to make show of force than to use any. As the result of this action a further and more successful attempt at reconciliation was made, and the agreed terms were approved by the Privy Council on 5th March, 158½ (2).

All proceedings were stayed. Okeman's house was to remain in the hands of Edward Lane, Haven House in those of Edward Meade, but workmen at the former were to lodge at the latter, though formerly some had slept at the works and others walked from Parkstone, a quarter-of-a-mile distant.

The questions of law were referred to Chief Justice Anderson (of the Common Pleas) and Mr. Justice (afterwards Chief Baron) Periam, rather in the capacity of arbitrators than of Judges. As a preliminary, interrogations were exhibited (3) and depositions taken on 17th May, 1582, by Dr. John Hammond and Matthew Carew, and these afford a fairly complete story of the events. Other depositions were taken by Sir George Rogers, Sir Henry Ashley, and Chr. Ankestil (4), but these were sent to Huntingdon and are not to be found in the Public Record Office.

The interrogatories wandered over every conceivable element in the case, viz., the extents upon the lands, when the statute debts were being enforced, the outstanding third in the Canford estate, the outlawry of Hastings the trustee, the intention of the lawyer who drew the lease to Leycolt (not admitted to be material), the heirship of a half-sister, and other points too numerous to be set down (5). The Judges gave their decision in Easter Term, 1583/4, which turned solely on the construction of the reservation to Lord Mountjoy contained in the mortgage to John Browne.

The Court held that Lord Mountjoy had assigned his whole interest in Okeman's to Richard Leycolt (6) for the term of the lease, but that there was nothing to prevent John and Charles Browne and their assignees (including Huntingdon) from also digging for ore.

(1) Case H., No. 21. Evidence of John Mansfield.
(2) A.P.C., 13/229.
(3) D.S.P. Eliz. Case H., Nos. 20, 21.
(4) A.P.C., 13/718.
(5) D.S.P. Eliz., 155/21, 22. 177/42. 188/22. And see D.S.P., Jas. i., 191/26.
(6) Godbolt 17, Man 308, And 307.

So far this was a judgment in favour of Huntingdon, but the reports make no mention of the exclusive right to dig for alum granted to Lord Mountjoy by his Act of Parliament.

The works at Alum Chine had meantime passed through like vicissitudes. They and the works on Branksea Island were in the possession of Richard Leycolt, John Mansfield, and Clement Draper. The last mentioned was a citizen and ironmonger of London, married to one of the three daughters and co-heiresses of Francis Garton, a small Sussex yeoman and presumably the most substantial of the three. The works had not been successful, they had swallowed up a prodigious amount of capital, sums amounting to over eighteen thousand pounds had been borrowed from various persons upon the bond of Clement Draper.

When bonds to the amount of thousands of pounds were floating in the market, it is almost an anti-climax to learn that one to the amount of £160 only and to secure payment of a sum of £120 should have brought about a downfall of the obligor. Such a bond had, in fact, been given on the 27th September, 1580, by Mansfield and Draper to one William Gryffin, and was not met on maturity.

Gryffin, in accordance with the custom of London, attempted to attach in the Mayor's Court a debt of £110 owing to John Mansfield, but so many delays were interposed that he abandoned that suit and recovered judgment in the King's Bench against Clement Draper, who, in April, 1581, was arrested in execution and confined to Southwark prison. This was the position when in the late summer Huntingdon took steps to obtain possession of Alum Chine and Branksea Island, reference to which has already been made. Notwithstanding the subsequent protests, possession was given without having recourse to the law, probably relying upon verbal promises given by Huntingdon. The precarious position of the works and the imprisonment for debt of one of the partners made his intervention less unwelcome.

There was no great anxiety shown to release Draper. On the 10th November, 1582, the Earl, by way of further security, became bound to Gryfin in the sum of £126 (being the original debt and costs), and delivered to him an amount of copperas estimated to be sufficient to defray the debt. Unfortunately, when it was sold it produced £103 10s. only, leaving £22 10s. still unpaid. Then, on 9th May, 1583 (1), Huntingdon took an assignment of their leases from Leycolt, Mansfield and Draper, and by the deed of assignment covenanted to discharge the debts owing in respect of the

(1) C3, 224/12.

53

works; but this brought no relief to Draper. Huntingdon insisted that by supplying the prescribed quantity of copperas he had fulfilled his obligation, and could not be blamed if the recipients failed to realise sufficient to pay the debt. So far the next thirty years and more at intervals Clement Draper, from his prison in Southwark, appealed for his release. On 22nd April, 1588, he petitioned Sir Christopher Hatton, the Lord Chancellor, for relief against Gryffin, but to no purpose. He was in a good position to pay the small sum still owing, but unless he could be released without payment he preferred to stay in prison.

In 1590 (1) he was still a prisoner, his wife had a dispute with an upholsterer who had sold goods for her to procure food for her husband, and, as she maintained, at a less price than she had authorised.

Two years later, September, 1592 (2), he appealed to the Queen, reminding her " of God's promises to Kings " contained in Wisdom vi., 21, and Isaiah i., 17. He had been in prison twelve years; he blamed the Earl of Huntingdon, John Mansfield, his deputy, and Richard Leycolt. His loss had been £10,000.

But Huntingdon died without paying the balance necessary for his release, and in 1605 he was still in prison and likely to lose a legacy of £100 which his father-in-law left to his wife on condition that within a fixed time he gave a general release to the executors of the will (3). Owing to his imprisonment he learnt the terms of the will too late, and his execution of the release was out of time.

Eventually he was released; the date is not stated, only the circumstances, in some proceedings (4) instituted by his nephew, Robert Draper, in November, 1619. From these it appears that while Clement Draper was content to be in the King's Bench Prison for a debt of £20, his wife was carrying on business and entering into pecuniary transactions of several thousands of pounds.

Sir James Deane was now the creditor; whether in consequence of a fresh transaction or as assignee of the old alum debt is not quite clear, but the latter is more probable, although the pleadings speak of a ten years' imprisonment only, while we have traced twenty-four years. Eventually Sir James Deane fell sick and agreed to accept £20 by four

(1) C3, 223/27.
(2) D.S.P. Eliz., 243/9. Lands, 103/44.
(3) C3, 266/56.
(4) C3, 306/89.

quarterly instalments of £5 each. The question at issue in the proceedings was whether this release was due to Robert Draper, who also claimed remuneration for other services which were not admitted.

Richard Leycolt in like manner enjoyed a compulsory sojourn in Southwark Prison for some months in 1583, no doubt in consequence of losses sustained in the same adventure. Five years later he sued in the Star Chamber (1) John Catesby, the Marshall of the prison, for having extorted £9 from him and others upon the pretext of affording him ease of irons and liberty of the house, and for suffering victuals to be brought into the prison, whereas in fact he made an additional charge of a penny for every piece of boiled meat and twopence for every piece of roast which was supplied to him from outside sources. Leycolt is one of the few connecting links between the Dorset and Yorkshire mines, and we shall renew our acquaintance with him later.

We now return to Okeman's house. Shortly before judgment was given in the case, namely, in November, 1583, an inventory (2) had been taken of its contents at the time of Lord Mountjoy's entry, which affords evidence of the very rudimentary stage of the alum manufacture.

There were fifty-five hogsheads of copperas, partly in casks and partly not. No alum is mentioned, but there was one lead furnace for boiling alum and seven other lead furnaces (one being unserviceable); a beam of wood with thirteen several iron weights amounting in all to 6½ cwt; two " reakes " of turves, one containing four loads and the other ten loads, spoiled with the weather; ten wheelbarrows, three cowles (? coolers) to carry " licour," 11 gonne mowthes (? gun mouths) of old iron, 50 pits of " oarefuel," 4 shouts (? shoots) of timber for lycoure " Lycour " left in the house boiled and congealing and since made into 14 hogsheads, about 100 heaps of " oare " ready digged to lie a seasoning.

The judgment of the Court by no means ended the dispute. On 2nd May, 1586, George Carlton had to defend himself against charges of a breach of trust (3), and his defence to Sir Francis Walsingham, the Secretary of State, follows the lines of his depositions of four years earlier.

The Register book of the Privy Council between the years 1582 and 1585 is lost (4), and there is no record of

(1) S.C.P. Eliz., L. 5/29.
(2) S.P. Eliz., 163/56.
(3) D.S.P. Eliz., 189/1.
(4) A.P.C., 14/134.

intermediate orders (1), but on 29th May, 1586, the Lord Chancellor (Bromley) and the Lord Treasurer (Burghley), after considering a very lengthy statement from Huntingdon (2), called him and Mountjoy before them and signed the final order.

Huntingdon was to have the mines and Okeman's house, but was to pay £6,000 to Mountjoy by instalments terminating at Easter, 1591. Well might Huntingdon complain to Burleigh (19th August, 1587) of his causeless contention with Mountjoy. The suit had cost him what he might rightly term a nemo scit (3).

Yet popular sympathy appears to have been on the side of the Blounts. John Hooker, the brother of Roger Hooker, who acted for so many years as steward to Sir Thomas Chaloner, and later to the widow of Charles Lord Mountjoy (4), brought out an edition of Holinshed's Chronicle in 1586. We have alum, he says, wherein the diligence of one of the greatest favourers of the Commonwealth of England of a subject hath been of late egregiously abused, and even almost with barbarous incivility. Lest there should be any doubt who the subject was, the name of Lord Mountjoy appears in the margin.

The original privilege expired on the 1st April, 1588, and its want of success was no deterent to those who aspired to obtain its renewal. In 1571 the Society of Merchants had petitioned without success to have a reversionary grant (5).

The claims of Lord Huntingdon were the weightiest. He had paid over £20,000 in hard cash. The Canford mines were in his own grounds. Even though the father of Lord Mountjoy would have been entitled to some consideration in that he had consumed his whole estate in experiments, the present Lord had no grounds fit for the work, and was likely to take warning from his father's losses (6). Though alum could not yet be made with a profit, the Earl had some hope of success. Hitherto only a tenth part of the cost of making copperas had been recovered. There were only two other houses that made it, and their product was a cheap mixture, full of sulphur and liable to burn clothes. English copperas had lost its reputation.

(1) S.C.P. Eliz., H. 39/29, an action between Thomas Hampton Edward Lane and John Hastings may refer to this dispute.
(2) D.S.P. Eliz., 188/22.
(3) Hist. M.S.S., Commn. Cecil MSS., 3/224, 275.
(4) See Carew MSS., p. 383.
(5) Lands, 13/42.
(6) S.P.D. Eliz., 244/109. Cecil MSS., 4/290.

Where one of these houses was is uncertain, but the other was almost certainly at Whitstable, in Kent. It was founded by Cornelius Stephenson, who for a short time had been tenant to Lord Mountjoy, and its possession was a source of litigation between several of the persons, Edward Meade and the Lanes, who had previously worked at Canford. It was quite a small concern, and employed some ten or twenty persons, who collected " gouldstones " or sulphur stones off the beach.

William Lord Mountjoy died on 27th June, 1593, and Lord Huntingdon, while President of the Council in the North Parts, followed him on 14th December, 1595.

Charles Lord Mountjoy, who was later created Earl of Devonshire, was far too busy as a soldier in the Low Countries, as a Courtier and as Lord-Lieutenant of Ireland, to trouble his head about the alum trade, but, as will be seen hereafter, his potential rights were respected in subsequent grants. It would rather appear that operations soon ceased at Canford.

George Earl of Huntingdon, who succeeded his brother, filed a bill in 1599 in the Exchequer (2), and amongst other things alleged that one Philip Smith, a debtor to the estate, apparently a subsequent lessee, had betaken himself to prison and there intended by all presumption to end his life.

There is an almost illegible answer (3) of one David Waterhouse (sworn on 5th November, 1608) to a bill of complaint of another Henry Earl of Huntingdon (great-nephew of the Lord President) which leads to the same inference, which is further strengthened by a perusal of some Chancery Proceedings in 1610 (4).

The same Lord Huntingdon was involved in litigation with the Mayor and Burgesses of Poole as the result of an attempt on his part to enclose a portion of Canford Waste and to cause it to be husbanded and manured for getting of corn. The inclosure of commons was not popular at this date, and in his Bill the Earl justified his action partly on the ground that he had left sufficient turbary for the exercise of their rights by those who were entitled as commoners (a small fraction of the inhabitants), and partly by the necessity of providing fuel for his alum works. To the latter the Mayor and Burgesses replied that there were only two houses

(1) S.C.P. Eliz., D4/35, G33/21.
(2) Exch. Depts., 42, Eliz., Easter, No. 14.
(3) Exch. B. and A., Eliz., Dorset, Nos. 121, 122.
(4) C3, H., 276/91.
(5) C2, Jas. i., H. 27/34.

for making alum and copperas built upon the waste some forty-six years previously by James Lord Mountjoy, but for many years they had been suffered to fall into decay.

This closes the history of the Canford Works. We may draw the conclusion that in Dorset as in Ireland, alum was made in small quantities, but that there was absolutely no manufacture of a sufficient quantity to satisfy the needs of the nation.

CHAPTER IV.

THE GUISBOROUGH MINES.

So far, Ireland and Dorset had produced alum in too small a quantity to benefit the trade; Yorkshire was to make a further step forward, but for many years the expenses of manufacture swallowed up any profit that might have been derived therefrom. The tradition that Sir Thomas Chaloner was the first discoverer of alum in Cleveland is very much older than the myth of the Pope's curse. The latter, as we have seen, is but one hundred and fifty years old. The former is based upon the Cott. M.S. Julius F. vi., 453.

What the origin of this document is has never been satisfactorily proved. Evidently in its earlier stage it had neither address nor endorsement. It is inserted at the end of one of the volumes in the Cottonian Library. The Clerk who prepared the Manuscripts for binding and who likewise annotated the three preceding has added the superscription " To Sir Thomas Chaloner as it seems about antiquities in the North part of England "; a description which is not quite accurate, as the alum works take up relatively more space than any of the so called antiquities.

There is a later copy (Lands. 909, No. 126, fol. 450) compiled by or on behalf of Warburton, not free from error, and one that throws no light upon the problem of its origin. Nicholls has published the Julius MS. in his Topographical and Genealogical Magazine, vol. 2, p. 404, and it is also published in the Antiquarian Repertory for 1780. It is signed either H.Tr. or F.Tr.; Nichols and the Editors of the printed calendars of the British Museum read the former, but the latter reading has its adherents.

It is clear from the description of the Bruces of Guisborough as ancestors of the King that it must have been written after March, 1603. Camden, who makes no reference to its subject matter in his 1600 edition of Britannia has evidently had it before his eyes when he prepared the edition of 1607. He must have seen it in the Library of Sir Robert Cotton, who was well acquainted with Sir Thomas Chaloner and in the habit of advising him on questions of etiquette arising out of his duties as governor to Prince Henry (1). It is therefore probable that Cotton got the MS. shortly after it was compiled.

(1) Julius C. III., 83-85.

The authors of the Geology of Yorkshire (1) describe the document as reading like the proposals of some successful (perhaps better, would-be successful) prospector, and suggest the possibility that it was addressed to King James. But there can be little doubt that Sir Robert Cotton's clerk was correct in assuming that it was addressed to Sir Thomas Chaloner.

Whether there was or was not a real person who took the walk through Cleveland and happened by chance upon Thomas Chaloner, late of Lambay, one thing is absolutely clear, namely, that in the main the document is the work of the latter alone. It is written by a scrivener at dictation, and hardly in one day.

There are certain features that go beyond our knowledge of Sir Thomas Chaloner. The writer or dictater was evidently a man of culture. He uses the words of art appropriate to mineral and chemical substances as in the treatise on nitre (2), but he was also alive to the literary movements of the day. His comparison of Stonegate side as a site for a cavalry engagement with the Island of Lippadusa (Lampadusa), where a like combat was described in Orlando Furioso, reminds him of the criticism which a certain Bishop had once made upon Ariosto's poem, namely, that he had appointed a " listes for horsemen where by reason of the sharpnes of rockes footmen coulde scarcely stande." Sir James Harington had published a translation of this poem in 1591, but gave no clue to the identity of the Bishop.

The writer again appears to have travelled extensively; to have visited the copper mines at Manflet (Mansfeld), in Germany; to have accompanied Sir Thomas when the latter travelled to Florence in 1596-7, and his name may possibly be found in the Bacon letters in the Lambeth Library. He was acquainted with mining in Cornwall, and with Lord Mountjoy's alum works.

He was no Yorkshireman, for when he reproduces the dialect word " steanes " for stones, he is careful to add " as they call them in their Northern." When he wishes to describe the abundance of ammonites, he writes " there was, as our countrymen say, no geason." According to the Dialect Dictionary, geason is a word still used in Northamptonshire and other counties to denote scarcity. This affords grounds for the belief that the writer was a neighbour of Sir Thomas Chaloner, who lived for many years at Steeple Claydon, in Bucks.

(1) Professors P. E. Kendall and Wroot, vol. i., p. 361.
(2) See p———ante.

A name that fits the initials F.Tr. is that of Francis Tresham. Letters undoubtedly signed by him are extant amongst the Domestic State Papers, and the signature bears no resemblance to that in the MS. He used a more modern form of the capital F, while the Manuscript is ff if it is not H. But it does not necessarily follow that the final letters were in fact a signature.

The following facts may be noted as bearing upon the question. Rushton, the home of the Treshams, was in Northamptonshire. George Tresham, the great-uncle of Francis, was associated with John Chaloner in Irish mines, and borrowed £33 6s. 8d. at 15 per cent. interest from Sir Thomas Chaloner the elder (1). There was a close family connection between the Treshams of Rushton and the Lanes of Walgrave, whose interest in the Canford mines has already appeared.

Whilst his father, Sir Thomas Tresham, was a prisoner in the Tower and elsewhere, Francis was brought up by the Earl of Worcester, who was interested in mining near Tintern, and who married a sister of Henry, Earl of Huntingdon, one of the many sufferers in the Canford undertaking.

His mother was born Muriel Throckmorton, a relative of Sir Nicholas, who as Ambassador in France and in other official capacities, had been connected with the elder Sir Thomas. If Anthony Wood is correct in stating that Francis was at Oxford, he must have been a contemporary of young Sir Thomas, though not at the same College. They both served the Earl of Essex, Francis from 1593 (2), Sir Thomas at least from 1596. Francis must almost certainly have met Sir James Harington whilst serving with Essex in Ireland, and hence we may have an explanation of his comment on the battle of Lippadusa. Finally, the remark that the grass at Guisborough, though not very long, was so sweet and thick platted that an acre thereof would summer as many beasts as the best grounds in the heart of England, if a trifle too laudatory, was one that might have been made by the son of a Northamptonshire grazier.

It is not suggested that these facts prove more than the possibility that the Unknown, if indeed he ever existed, was Francis Tresham. If further research should confirm this

(1) Lands. 824, fol. 4.
(2) Cal. Dom., State Papers Eliz., 7 April, 1593.

possibility, as Francis Tresham died shortly after the discovery of the Gunpowder Plot, we have an additional factor in fixing the date. But while certain features in the description might well be ascribed to someone like Francis Tresham, who had travelled widely, other parts of the information contained can have been derived from no one but Thomas Chaloner, of Lambay, who, during a twelve-years' residence at Guisborough, had had ample opportunity to make himself acquainted with local tradition, not always quite correctly; in his list of the nobility and gentry who in old days surrounded the Prior of Guisborough, he places first the Percy's, Earls of Northumberland, at Kildale. But though for the preceding century the Earls of Northumberland were owners of Kildale through purchase from the distinct Percy family, who in fact had lived there for four hundred years, the Hall, after their purchase, was always inhabited by a steward and never by a member of the family.

Let us now follow his walk round the Northern confines of Cleveland—a good day's journey if anyone cares to follow his steps. After a full description of the Priory of Guisborough (which he spells " Gisbroughe ") and of the neighbouring country, including Roseberry Topping (an early instance of the acquisition by Oseberry of the intrusive R), with an allusion to the practice which we can feel certain that he reprobated, of quarrying stone from the Abbey walls, we arrive at the Port of Dabhoome, annotated in the margin as Dobham, now swallowed up by Cargo Fleet, and only conjecturable through tracing the outlet of Dobham Beck, which still separates Wilton from Kirkleatham. He then proceeds Eastwards through the Coast towns, with their shells, sand and sea-wrack, which served instead of marl to enrich the neighbouring land, making the good husbands of the low towns fat in the purse and merry at the heart. He passed Redcar, a poor fishertown, of whose inhabitants it might truly be said that they were lavish of their lives when they would hazard twenty or forty miles into the seas in a small trough so thin that the " glimpse " (1) of the sun might be seen through it, yet at 10 or 11 of the clock in the morning, when they came from sea, they would sell their boat's lading for 4s., or if they got a crown would suppose that they had chaffered fair.

Thence he viewed Saltburn mouth, Huntscliffe and Bulfeet gate, told some legends of Whitby and St. Hilda, and returned by Skelton Castle. He sipped the mineral spring

(1) Gleams.

at Cawdkell (near Priestcroft), then famed for healing ulcers and cancers, but now out of fashion; and proceeded to a ford called Slape Wath, where was a new work set up in the hope of making alum and copperas. As God would have it, he lighted in the company of a gentleman, Sir Thomas's kinsman of fair condition, who by much labour and many losses in the Isle of Lambay in Ireland had gotten more than a smattering in the skill of alum works. The kinsman told him (and I think we may take it that from now onward it is the kinsman alone who is speaking) that it was the good fortune of Sir Thomas to discover the alum, for when as about a dozen years since he marked that all the leaves of the trees growing on the sides of the hills were dyed with a sadder green than ordinary, and that the oaks took no deep root though they grew into a greater length, having this strange property that when they were barked there was in a manner no sap but all heart, he concluded that the heat exhalations of the mines caused this difference from trees growing in other places.

He further observed the rarities of the earths and clays, of sundry colours, yellow, white and blue, and of such stones wherewith they beautify marble tables at Florence, of several sorts of freestone, and the unaptness of the ground to freeze, together with the glistening sparkles appearing like glass in the paths by moonshine; all these were just motives to kindle a fancy in him to undertake the search of those hills and rivers; wherein though he failed at the first and could never be resolved by the best mineralogists what kind of stuff might be extracted out of so base a mineral as it appeared by the outward coat, nevertheless after three years' travail and his kinsman's happy interposing himself in the trials thereof, he had now found a gainful reward for his pains and a means to set a number of poor on work.

It other words, all that is suggested is that Sir Thomas noticed certain peculiarities of the soil (which, incidentally, other observers have failed to detect), and that his cousin discovered that these peculiarities were due to the presence of alum shale. We have already seen that Sir Thomas had been too fully occupied during the preceding twelve years to make any trials himself. The Manuscript closes with the declaration that upon Belman Bank there was a place convenient for many houses to work alum, the mine itself extending all along that hill. The charges would be very great and amount to many thousands (a prophecy the accuracy of which was proved later), but to comfort him the writer would not conceal his experience that the alum was as good as the Romish and stronger in setting a colour.

It is therefore obvious that the date of the manuscript falls within the period between the erection of the Slape Wath works and those on Belman bank, shall we say, 1604, a computation quite consistent with that previously given.

Twelve years earlier would fix the kinsman's residence at Guisborough in 1592, shortly after Sir Thomas had been knighted by Henry IV. of France, and the same year (1) that William Ussher, son-in-law of the then Archbishop of Dublin, had secured the Isle of Lambay. What more natural than that Sir Thomas should offer to his impecunious kinsman a home on his Yorkshire Estate when he was turned out of his father's little kingdom? What more natural than that this kinsman should continue those researches that had cost him and his father so dear? But it is practically certain that someone other than himself was the first to put in practice the results of these researches.

Malynes, in his Lex Mercatoria, after referring to Cornelius de Vos, James Lord Mountjoy and his work-master, one Master Lane in the Isle of Purbeck and Dorset who, as he said, manufactured great quantities of copperas and some alum, declared that in 1604 one Master Atherton began to practice the making of alum about Guisborough, with whom one Master Bourchier (later Sir John Bourchier) did join to bring it to some perfection.

At this period the Skelton estate was changing hands. It had devolved upon the three surviving daughters of John Lord Conyers of Hornby Castle, namely, Elizabeth, wife of Sir Thomas Darcy; Ann, wife of Anthony Kempe; and Katherine, second wife of John Atherton. No complete partition seems to have been made at this date; indeed, the Julius manuscript attributes the then ruinous condition of Skelton Castle to the variances between these three daughters and their husbands for the division of their shares, so that each for despite ruined the part of the Castle whereof each was in possession.

But even though there had been no partition of the estate as a whole, John Atherton and his wife Katherine must have been in undisputed possession for some years of the lands upon which these early alum works had been con-

(1) See p. 16 ante.

structed. John Atherton, of Atherton in Lancashire, and of Fryton, Hovingham and Slingsby in Yorkshire had married for his first wife, Elizabeth, daughter of Sir John Byron of Newstead, by whom he had a son named John (1). After her death he married, on 20th April, 1584, Katherine Conyers, by whom he had another son, also called John, who died on the 12th November, 1613, under the age of twenty-one, but leaving a daughter, Anne, who was found by inquisition to have been four years old at her father's death! (2). If this is correct, he must have married at an incredibly early age.

Two years before he died he had, notwithstanding his non-age, together with his wife Anne, entered into a recognizance (3) with his cousin, Sir Conyers Darcy, and Dame Dorothy, his wife, relating to the third part of Hornby Castle, and the transaction had been confirmed by a fine (4). John Atherton, the father, had been in pecuniary difficulties from the date of his second marriage, if not earlier. He had entered into a composition with his creditors in York in 1590 (5). He had been outlawed for debt. His lands in Cleveland, Richmondshire and other places had been extended to satisfy a statute merchant. He was therefore hardly in a position to lay out large sums of money in expensive experiments. There seems, however, little doubt that by some means or other he had raised sufficient to start operations.

The litigation in the course of which the transactions came to light did not begin until 1613, and the principal actor was our old friend Richard Leycolt and not Thomas Chaloner of Lambay. Leycolt filed his bill (6) in Chancery against several defendants; and after tracing the devolution of the patent rights for making alum and copperas from Cornelius de Vowce (Vos), through James Lord Mountjoy, to himself under an agreement, claimed that he had brought the works in Dorset to great perfection, and was the first to make alum out of the " mothers " and " Green liquors " of copperas, a claim which the preceding chapter hardly substantiates.

He then declared that out of a desire of good doing to

(1) Flowers Visitation Harl. Soc., vol. xvi., p. 375n.
(2) Inq. p.m. C.142 347/25.
(3) C.54 (2110), Nos. 122, 124.
(4) Y.A.S. Records, vol. cliii., p. 158.
(5) C.3, 222/19.
(6) C.2 Jas. i., L. 7/39. This file is incorrectly described in the M.S. Index, and contains two quite unconnected sets of papers.

this commonwealth (being his native country) (1), he took a journey at great cost and charges out of Dorset into Yorkshire, where, in the grounds of John Atherton, in the Parish of Skelton, he had tasted and found out divers minerals apt and fit for the making of alum.

There was then a house at Spring Bank, near Mygrave (now Margrove) Park erected but not completed for the manufacture thereof.

On the 15th November, 1603, an agreement was made between John Atherton and Katherine his wife of the one part, and Leycolt of the other, under which the Athertons were, at their own cost, to complete the house and furnish it with the necessary appliances, namely, four furnaces and four pans of lead and iron for boiling alum, coolers of lead for congealing, and convenient cisterns of lead for keeping and saving the " mothers " or strong liquors of alum and copperas. They were also to set up a lead-finer with furnace, a balnium for trial of the earth for alum and copperas, pits, pipes, vessels for draining the earth and making liquors, and all other necessary implements.

Leycolt, on his part, undertook after the first year to make 2½ tons of alum every week. He also undertook to instruct three men, Henry Cowell, of Hornby Castle, Roger Tadcastle, of Mygrave Park, and Oliver Kearsley, of West Haughton (Houghton?), Lancashire, in the art of alum making. He was to be paid £500, of which £250 was to be deducted out of the first profits. The profits were then to be devoted to the repayment to the same Henry Cowell and Roger Tadcastle of the sum of £140 advanced by them, then the wages of the workmen were to be paid, and finally Leycolt was to receive the remaining £250. But if he failed to make 2½ tons a week after the first year his remuneration was to abate £100 for each half-ton of the deficiency.

From this it would appear that the money to start the works had been found by Henry Cowell and Roger Tadcastle. Oliver Kearsley, whose name constantly appears later, and whose descendants are still living in the North Riding, was an ale-house keeper in West Houghton in 1592 and 1602, and was so presented at Manchester Quarter Sessions (2). He had therefore not been long in Yorkshire, and came from a region later (if not also earlier) connected with the alum trade.

(1) It may be that this statement is as untrue as the other allegations in the Bill.
(2) Chetham Society N.S., vol. lxxvii., pp. 50, 80.

Leycolt simply repeated his failure at the Canford works. He never, if the answer to his Bill is to be believed, instructed any one of the three men mentioned; he never made $2\frac{1}{2}$ tons a week or any quantity at all, and consequently there were no profits out of which even the first £250 could be paid.

Then in the month of June, 1604, John Bourchier appeared upon the scene. His grandfather, James, was an illegitimate son of the last Lord Bernners; his father, Sir Ralph (1), who was buried at Barking, in Essex, on the 11th June, 1598, was closely connected with Yorkshire, having been Sheriff in 1580, Member of Parliament for the County from 1588 to 1592, and founder of the family settled for many generations at Beningbrough; his grandson, another Sir John, occasionally confused with his uncle, was the well-known Parliamentarian.

Our John Bourchier is described in legal documents sometimes as of Lambeth, in the County of Surrey, sometimes as of Hanging Grimston, in the County of York, an estate which his father, whose second son he was, had purchased for him in 1575 from Thomas Sackville, Lord Buckhurst, later Earl of Dorset. He seems at an early age to have engaged in trade, and thereby to have made the acquaintance of the London merchants whose names will appear in the next chapter, and who, if we understand aright Leycolt's allegations, had already taken an interest in the works with a view to purchase such alum as might be manufactured.

When John Bourchier first saw the works, the workmen were about to give over, and Leycolt was in despair. Atherton brought with him one day an old gentleman, one Mr. Layne, who, as Bourchier said, "roached" up some alum very fair and good, much fairer than Leycolt could so. Here we get another link with Canford, a glimpse of a member of the Lane family, who, from time to time, tried to get a footing in Yorkshire; which of the members of the family is thus mentioned it would be difficult to say.

Leycolt had boasted that the total cost of the alum house and works would not exceed £400, but his directions proved so inefficient that everything built had to be pulled down and rebuilt. For three years Atherton continued to pay him £40 a year, even though there were no profits, but long before the expiration of that period Bourchier had taken over the principal direction of the work.

(1) Dugdale Visitation of Yorkshire, by J. W. Clay, vol. iv., p. 305.

On the 10th November, 1606 (1), John Atherton and Katherine his wife demised for twenty-one years to John Bourchier three closes called Spring Bank otherwise Lodge Hagg, Wilson's Close, and the Great Carr, all within the Manor of Skelton. These closes have hardly changed their names. They are near Slape Wath, north of the Whitby and Guisborough main road, stretching eastward from Alum Beck Bridge. Spring Bank is now more usually known as Combe Bank; Lodge Hagg is forgotten as an alternative designation.

By another deed of the same date Bourchier covenanted to enlarge the workhouse, to maintain and furnish it with mine and other necessaries for alum making, and to pay to Edward Startcliffe and John Blanch, two servants of John Atherton, for his use twenty marks for each ton of alum made, deducting only the charges of fitting and erecting the workhouse and the other charges incident to the manufacture.

We shall learn in the next chapter how, in consequence of ill success, occasioned, as Bourchier maintained, by dilatory and fruitless operations on Leycolt's part the merchants before mentioned, procured other workmen from beyond the seas. Leycolt was ashamed to stay, and induced Bourchier to give him £30 for his journey South, promising never to trouble the works any more or to demand any other payment. It only remains to say that, notwithstanding this promise, Leycolt, in Michaelmas Term, 1613, filed the bill against John Atherton, Oliver Kearsley, and John Bourchier, alleging that though by his skill, invention and labour he had brought to perfection the making of alum, yet by granting the lease to Bourchier, Atherton had put it out of his power to earn £500. Kearsley naturally replied that he was only a servant and no party to the agreement, while the other two relied upon Leycolt's failure to perform his covenant (2).

But it cannot be denied that the circumstantial account of the origin of the works contained in the pleadings, and the absence of any reference to Thomas Chaloner, do throw a certain amount of doubt upon the claim of the latter to be the first discoverer of alum in Cleveland. There can be no possible doubt that the work at Spring Bank is identical with that described in the Manuscript as being near Slape Wath.

Mention is made in Leycolt's bill of a certificate given by John Atherton to the King, that Leycolt by his skill and

(1) C.3, 326/19.
(2) C.3, Jas. I., L. 7/39.

invention alone had brought to perfection the making of alum. Atherton, in his answer, while denying that the certificate had been correctly stated, admitted that some such certificate had been given.

It is therefore a fair inference that there was some contention upon the question who was the first discoverer of alum in Yorkshire, and as we shall learn later that Thomas Chaloner enjoyed a pension of forty marks a year as a reward for his discovery, we may be satisfied that, notwithstanding the certificate, the evidence in favour of Thomas Chaloner carried the day.

CHAPTER V.

THE FIRST PATENTEES AND FARMERS.

Besides the account in Lex Mercatoria already mentioned, Gerard de Malynes, in a letter (1) to the Lord Treasurer Dorset, undated but evidently written at the end of 1607 or beginning of 1608, relates the early history of the undertaking. Statements made by Malynes cannot always be accepted at their face value, but the main outlines of what follows are fairly correct. According to his story, two years before the date of his letter he was made privy to the intention to move the King for a sole grant of the right to manufacture alum. After many conferences, he had leave to join in the execution thereof, and named as his associates William Turner, William Angell, William Hawses, John Archer, and others. Even though we may not accept the prominent position which Malynes claims for himself in the negotiations, there is no reason to doubt his statement that substantial merchants were supporting the scheme, nor that the names which he gives were correct.

Of these only William Turner was a party to the deeds authenticating the transactions, but William Angell undoubtedly had a pecuniary interest in them, and the so-called Alum Company had many shareholders of whom we know as little as of William Hawses and John Archer. For the most part they were merchants trading to Middleburgh, but they were often associated together in other enterprises.

Malynes proceeds to enumerate the main difficulties involved in procuring the grant from the King, namely, that the discovery of alum was no new invention, but a third or fourth attempt, and that the mineral was base not royal. It was therefore concluded that some great persons eminent in their places should be entreated (upon due consideration) to underprop the same. These great personages, as we shall hereafter see, were Edmund Lord Sheffeild, Sir Thomas Chaloner, and Sir David Foulis.

The opposition to the grant of other subjects having alum mines had next to be overcome. Two names were mentioned, those of Lord Eure and Lord Danvers. It is not quite clear what Lord Eure's interest was. It might have been in Baysdale or in Ingleby Greenhow, which he did not sell to Sir David Foulis until much later. Or, as at this time he was President of the Middle Marches and residing at Ludlow Castle, it might have been in Wales or on the Welsh

(1) Vesp C. xiv., 8.

Border. Dr. Jordan, in his Natural Baths and Mineral Waters (3rd Edn.), p. 57, speaks of alum springs at Okengates, in Shropshire, half-way between Penkridge and Shrewsbury, much used by Shrewsbury dyers, and these may have been the scene of the operations.

Lord Danvers was the son of Sir John Danvers and Elizabeth, daughter and one of the co-heiresses of Lord Latimer, and through her was interested in Danby in Cleveland. The third son of the marriage, John, writing long after the event (1), related that his brother, Lord Danvers, on behalf of his mother, for his Majesty's benefit and the bettering of the alum works in Yorkshire, was " dealt withal " to desist from erecting works upon his own or his mother's land there. These difficulties having been partly surmounted, application was made to the Crown by the three prominent statesmen above mentioned for a grant of exclusive right of manufacture.

Of these three Lord Sheffeild took a closer interest in the works than the other two, but confined himself solely to those on his own lands. He was the third Lord Sheffeild, son of Douglas, daughter of William Howard, of Effingham, who, after the death of her first husband, John Lord Sheffeild, is said to have been privately married to Robert Dudley, Earl of Leicester, and then, when subsequently repudiated by him, to Sir Edward Stafford (2).

Edmund Lord Sheffeild commanded a ship against the Spanish Armada, and for his services on that and other occasions was granted by the Queen, on 28th April, 1592, the Manor of Mulgrave, part of the forfeited estates of Sir Francis Bigot for an estate in tail male. As Lord Lieutenant of Yorkshire, President of the Council in the North parts, and Knight of the Garter, he possessed an influence at Court most valuable in securing a grant of the letters patent.

Sir Thomas Chaloner, as the companion of James I. on his journey South to accept the Crown, and as the Governor of Henry Prince of Wales, was of almost equal influence. He had been persuaded, no doubt by his cousin, to bring into common stock the hill-sides at Spa Wood (then called Newgate) and Belmont Bank.

The third name was that of his brother-in-law, Sir David Foulis, husband of Cordelia, another daughter of Sir William Fleetwood, the Recorder. Although only recently naturalised, he had resided as Ambassador in England for some ten years,

(1) D.S.P., Jas. I., 161/69.
(2) Extinct Peerage of Northern Counties, by J. W. Clay, p. 206.

71

and earned from Burghley the character of being " a base, unworthy, presumptuous body " (1). None the less, he was highly valued by his master, who, on 24th January, 1603 (2), two months before his accession to the English throne, had granted to him as a reward for his services in divers embassies (diversis legationibus) the Manors of Greenhow and Templehurst, the grant being subsequently perfected by a fine enrolled in the following Easter Term (3).

Later, on 15th June, 1608, he purchased the Manors of Ingleby Greenhow and Battersby from Ralph Lord Eure. Till then Ingleby Greenhow and Greenhow had always been in separate ownership. The latter, which lies south-west of the former, and is generally identified with the Camisedale of Domesday Book, was in the possession of the Meynell family until it passed to the Lords Darcy. When Thomas Lord Darcy was beheaded in 1536, in consequence of his share in the Pilgrimage of Grace, it was confiscated and granted to Matthew, Earl of Lennox, and Margaret his wife, grandparents of King James.

Foulis was subsequently created a baronet, a title which only expired with the death of Sir William Foulis, the grandfather of the present Lord De L'Isle and Dudley. There is no evidence that he worked alum on his lands, and the probabilities lead to the contrary inference.

On 5th March, 1605-6, the much desired letters patent were obtained. In order to find employment for the idle and indigent poor (so the purpose of the grant was described), the three patentees, Sheffeild, Chaloner and Foulis were authorised and undertook to work alum within their own lands or within other lands by agreement with the owners thereof, and to manufacture the same as good in quality as any made beyond the seas, and after two years not less than the average yearly quantity imported during the preceding seven years. For twenty-one years from the date of the grant no one other than themselves could dig for alum, but subject to the rights of Charles, Earl of Devonshire. For the first two years of the grant the same average quantity of alum as before might be imported, but afterwards the importation was to cease if the conditions of the grant were duly observed. The better to enforce this prohibition, the patentees, with the assistance of constables, were permitted to search any ship or warehouse.

(1) Cecil M.S.S., vol iv., p. 548.
(2) Scotland adopted the 1st January as the commencement of the year from 1st January, 1600.
(3) Yorks. Arch. Soc. Records, vol. liii., p. 2.
(4) C. 66 (1691), P.R. 3, Jas. I., pt. 19.

It will be seen that there was no mention in this grant of John Bourchier (indeed it was not until the following November that he acquired the lease of Slape Wath works) (1). Possibly it was in consequence of this lease that on 18th December, 1606, the three original patentees surrendered the earlier grant, and on 3rd January, 1606-7 a fresh grant was made to them jointly with John Bourchier.

The rights and privileges granted were set out in slightly fuller language than in the preceding grant, the two years of probation were reckoned from 3rd January, 1606-7; the duration of the grant was extended to thirty-one years, and a yearly rent of £700 was reserved. This rent, in fact, only represented the return that had to be made to the Farmers of Customs in consequence of the reduced amount of alum imported, taking as the average yearly importation four thousand two hundred tons, upon which a Customs duty of 3s. 4d. a ton was to be levied.

Malynes is in error when he asserts (2) that the earlier privilege was for Yorkshire only, and the later for all England, Scotland and Ireland, and also when he implies that two years, during which £33,000 were lost, elapsed between the two letters patent; in fact, there were only ten months.

Charles, Earl of Devonshire, had died in 1606—the last legitimate descendant of Sir Thomas Leigh, " soon and early for his years, but late enough for himself," said John Chamberlain, alluding to his disreputable connection with Penelope Lady Rich, which cast a shadow upon his earlier successful administration in Ireland. His heirs and administrators were substituted for himself in the special reservation contained in the later letters patent.

On the 3rd February, just a month after the grant of the letters patent, the patentees leased their rights for a term of three years to the farmers, William Turner, Nicholas Crispe, Ellis Crispe, William Hinde, and Abraham Chamberlain. The profits, after deduction of the expenses incurred and of interest at the rate of £10 per cent. per annum upon the capital provided by the farmers, were to be distributed as follows :—

One-twentieth part thereof went to such of the patentees as had built workhouses in proportion to the tons of alum respectively made in the several workhouses. The remaining nineteen-twentieths were to be divided into two equal shares, one of which was to be equally sub-divided amongst the patentees and the other amongst the farmers.

(1) Ante p. 68.
(2) Lex Mercatoria Ed., 1622, p. 270, and in Vesp C., xiv., fo. 10.

73

The following had a possible interest in the first twentieth: Lord Sheffeild in respect of Asholme and Sandsend, Sir Thomas Chaloner in respect of Belmont and New Gate Banks, and John Bourchier in respect of Slape Wath.

The so-called farmers were well-known London merchants who were closely connected in business. The first three were original members of the East India Company at the date of its incorporation, on 31st December, 1600 (1). They were all merchant adventurers trading in the Low Countries, and especially at Middleburg.

William Turner, who seems to have been in no way related to John Turner, one of the contractors hereafter mentioned, was a grocer and haberdasher living at Islington. He had a country house at Highway, in Wiltshire, not far from Brook House, where Anne Lady Mountjoy resided, and he married Amy, daughter of Edward Mann, a former Mayor of Poole and Member of Parliament for the Borough. His sister Anne married Thomas Lane, a member of the Walgrave family. He must therefore have had an intimate knowledge of the Canford Alum Works. Nicholas and Ellis Crispe each gave his age in 1625 as 63, describing each other as brother, and therefore presumably were twins. The connection of this family with the Yorkshire alum trade lasted for many years.

The remaining lessees, William Hinde, who died shortly after the commencement of the lease, and Abraham Chamberlain were also interested in trade. The farmers did not themselves manufacture alum, but employed contractors or undertakers; the terms appear to be synonymous. Thomas Chaloner, of Lambay, deposed in the proceedings, to which reference is made later, that he was an undertaker to make alum until the coming of the Dutchmen, and there is no reason to suppose that the lease at first made any alteration in the practice that had previously existed. Richard Leycolt was another undertaker, and so was John Turner, but probably not until after the expiration of the lease. In the same proceedings in January, 1624-5 (2), the last mentioned deposed that he had been employed nineteen years in the manufacture of alum and had been a master workman thirteen years; he must therefore have been employed in 1606. This John Turner was, as has been said, no apparent relation of William Turner. In his evidence he claimed to be the first Englishman to attain the

(1) Colonial (East Indies) papers, No. 281.
(2) E. 154, 22 Jas. I., Hil No. 28.

74

perfect skill of alum making, and also the first that made alum to profit in the kingdom; a not unfair reflection upon Thomas Chaloner. In his pedigree, enrolled by Dugdale (1) in 1660, it is stated that he belonged to the Herefordshire family of that name, but he was appointed in 1619 treasurer of hospitals for the Wapentake of Langbaurgh as John Turner, of Waterford (2). He may therefore have been a son or grandson (he was born in 1580) of one of those who accompanied Robert Record (3) from Wales to Clonmines (in Wexford, but near Waterford), and who had thus been an early associate of John Chaloner and his son Thomas. Two successive entries under date 1562 in the Penshurst Papers, H.W.M.S.S., Commission No. 77, p. 378, may have some bearing on this question:

To the Town of Clonmyne in payment of
Victuals delivered to the Almayne—
Miners .... £151 16s. 10d.
To Paule Torner .... £112 10s. 0d.

But these merely suggest that amongst the English miners there was one with the surname Tornor or Turner. John Turner settled at Kirkleatham, where his family did not die out in the male line until the death of Sir Charles Turner, Bart., in 1804. He purchased the manor from Sir William Bellasis in 1623 (4), but he had previously resided in the township. The intervention of the London merchants was necessary for two purposes, (1) to provide the funds required for carrying on the work, and (2) to dispose of the alum when manufactured. It would appear that besides those who were actual parties to the lease, there were several others who were partners in the scheme.

In the absence of the modern system of banking, it was by no means easy to find cash for payment of wages and for purchase of the necessary materials required in the manufacture. The farmers of customs who kept the taxes which they collected as long as they could in their own lands, and let them out on interest, formed one class of capitalists, and the merchant adventurers who traded in Holland, North-East Europe and the Baltic Sea, formed another class. In the absence of authentic lists of the Merchant Adventurers of London, such as those possessed by the corresponding Societies of Newcastle and York, it is impossible to state definitely who were and who were not members, but it would appear as if all the lessees were such.

(1) Dugdale's Visitation, by J. W. Clay, vol. i., p. 59.
(2) N.R. Records, vol. ii., p. 202.
(3) Ante p. 7.
(4) Y.A.S. Fines, vol. lviii., p. 233.

Besides the actual parties to the lease and those mentioned by Malynes, several other London merchants were interested in the adventure. It will be more convenient to deal with this subject later. The works were not a financial success from the start. If we are to accept the statement of Thomas Chaloner, of Lambay, as implying that he was a sole undertaker, it has been seen that his experiments in Ireland had been on too small a scale to serve as a pattern for a larger undertaking, and Richard Leycolt at Canford had no record of success behind him.

Up to the end of the first completed year after the grant of the letters patent, no less a sum than £20,000 was stated to have been lost, and no objection seems to have been ever taken to the statement. Such a disastrous start called for energetic measures. Malynes, in his letter to the Lord Treasurer, averred that at his charge sixteen Germans were imported to teach the Englishmen. It is not of much importance at whose instigation that came over, but every other notice that we have gives the credit of the importation to William Turner, though it may well be that Malynes, from his continental connections, was in a position to give material assistance in recruiting this labour. Another account gives their number as ten or twelve; they came from Liege, Cologne and the neighbourhood.

Thomas Chaloner was pensioned off; an annuity of forty marks was paid to him for the remainder of his life, and, like most annuitants, he enjoyed length of days. Ostensibly it was a reward for having been the first discoverer of alum (notwithstanding the rival claims of Richard Leycolt), but obviously its object was to sweeten the pill when he was ousted from office. Like his father, John, and unlike his uncle, Francis, he possessed a mild, unresentful disposition. He continued to reside at Guisborough, and spent his days walking down to the works, inspecting the new methods which his supplanters introduced, and not entirely in a spirit of hostile criticism. He was not too great a man to refuse to direct his maid to preserve his urine and sell it at a penny a firkin.

The Germans were only engaged for one year. While we are unable to accept the statement in Stow's Chronicle that they were the first to calcine the ore, there can be no doubt that they improved the quality of the alum, especially by re-melting and refining the black and drossy substance which was found at the bottom of the casks, and so produced

(1) Vesp. C. xiv., No. 7.

a commodity which was much more marketable. But they do not seem to have bettered the financial position. So far from clearing off any part of the debt of £20,000, they actually increased it to £30,000.

This may have been the cause why their engagement was not renewed when the year was up. One of them, Lambert Russell, who had been employed in Lord Sheffeild's works at Sandsend, alone remained. His wages were no higher than those of persons occupying like positions in the associated works.

In Ord's History of Cleveland, p. 80, there is a sketch copied from a painting said to represent Lambert Russell, and to be in the possession of R. Chaloner, Esq., at Long Hull. It is a most interesting picture, now at Gisboro Hall, but there is no evidence that it represents Lambert Russell, and the hypothesis is in the highest degree improbable.

The majority of the German workmen returned to their native land when the year's service terminated. Malynes, in the letter (1) previously described, complained of William Turner having seduced one, but for the reasons given above his complaint is not easy to understand. Another man was, as we shall see, induced to start a rival concern near Hoghton Towers, in Lancashire. At this period the Principality of Liège was in advance of this country in mining experience. M. Thomassin, in his Memoire Statistique du Department de l'Ourthe (2), states that alum was first made there in the 13th century, but his argument is not very convincing.

One of the earliest extant documents at Liège is an exclusive privilege (3) granted in 1580 by Gerard de Groesbeeck, Prince of Liège and Stavelot, to Guillaume Stevart to manufacture alum within his principalities by a special process which he had invented. Penalties amounting to six golden florins for every pound of alum manufactured in competition were imposed. No sooner was this exclusive privilege granted than it was withdrawn, but Stevart was permitted to carry on his business in competition with others. One would like to think that the name conceals a Scotsman (William Stewart), but those who know assert that Stewart is too common a name in Liège to render the suggestion probable.

There are other references in the Archives to alum mines in the neighbourhood in the years 1594 and 1601, namely,

(1) Vesp C., xiv., No. 7.
(2) Bibl in 4to des Bibliophiles Liègeois, pp. 419-424.
(3) Kindly communicated by M. E. Fairon, Conservateur Des Archives de l'Etat à Liège.

at Jehonster, Bouillon, and Cornillon des Liège. From which, if any, of these Lambert Russell and his companions came is now too difficult a problem to solve. Lambert is the name of the Patron Saint of Liège; Russell, i.e., the little red man, is a common surname, and identification is difficult.

A well-known capitalist of Liège, by name Jean Curtius, was, on 20th September, 1595, authorised by Ernest de Bavière, on the advice of his Chambre des Comptes, to work all sorts of minerals in the Chaineux (1) d'Amay, an aluminous district. It is possible that Curtius might have been the agent through whose instrumentality the men were obtained.

It must have been in the very early days of the undertaking that the necessity of a supply of coals was felt. The alum shale was calcined on piles of wood, but the boiling of the alum solutions was best affected with coals.

For this purpose John Bourchier leased from Sir John Hedworth, at a rent of £500, some coal mines situate at Harraton, in the County of Durham. In April, 1603, one Robert Bromley held a lease of these, and others at Pencher, for a term of years at a rent of £300. A little difference between him and his agent, John Whalley, resulted in legal proceedings (2), from which it would appear that the agency continued at Monk Wearmouth till November, 1606.

Robert Bromley, amongst his many activities, was a contractor for Army clothing, and not too honest at that; he eventually got into financial difficulties, was outlawed for debt on 27th October, 1608, and died in September, 1610. This gives us from 1607 to 1610 as the probable date for the lease to John Bourchier.

The coal was brought in keels from Harraton down the Wear to Sunderland, and thence shipped either to Dobham for the Guisborough works or to Whitby for Mulgrave and Sandsend. The site of Dobham has been previously described as the junction of Dobham Beck, in the township of Wilton, with the estuary of the Tees. It was close to, if not identical with, Cawkers Nab, a name which appears in the depositions hereinafter mentioned, and has an interesting history. It first appears in the Guisborough Cartulary as Caldcotes, whose meaning, "cold cottages," is fairly obvious. Caldcotes then becomes Cawkers, and it is always found in these depositions with the addition of Nab-

(1) Chambre de Comptes rendages reg. 72, fol. 211.
(2) C.2, Jas. I., B. 23/7, and see E. 112, Jas. I., Durham 245.

promontory.   In one instance we have Call Cotes Nab. To-day it is known as Cargo Fleet; the outlet of the stream rather than the promontory marking its position.   Possibly the cargoes carried may have caused popular etymology to adopt this form as an explanation of the name (1).

As a result of combining Spring Bank with the mines on the other side of the valley, arrangements previously made for ascertainment of the rent payable by John Bourchier or his assignes became difficult to carry out.   On the 10th April, 1610, John Blanch and John Smith, of Atherton (the latter having succeeded Edward Standcliffe, then deceased, as trustee for his master), released John Bourchier from the covenants contained in the earlier deed, and in lieu thereof John Bourchier covenanted to pay quarterly to the trustees £300 a year (2).

With some possible temporary exceptions the rent was paid during the continuance of the lease.   When the mines were at their worst, the Crown adopted that somewhat shady expedient of buying up some old, undischarged bonds and statutes of a former servant and creditor of John Atherton for debts more than twenty-seven years old, and refusing payment of rent on the ground that John Atherton's possession had ceased.   Witnesses were examined (3), and it would appear that their evidence was accepted to prove that the original debt, so bought up by the Crown, had been long paid.

In any case, we find a warrant directing the arrears to be paid on the 1st May, 1617 (4), which evidently related to the Exchequer suit, and another warrant on 12th August, 1625, directed payment of the rent after the conclusion of the suit against Arthur Ingram (5).

The spiritual needs of the workmen and the education of their children were not neglected.   William Ward, minister at Guisborough, preached at the works in his neighbourhood at a yearly salary of eighty marks, and Richard Leake, minister at Lyth, preached at Asholm and Sandsend at a salary of £40.   Robert Wemys, a Scotsman, and Vicar of Kirkleatham, acted as schoolmaster, and was paid £12 a year.

(1) See Place Names of Yorkshire, N.R., p. 161.   The reference there to a terrier is incorrect.
(2) E. 112, Jas. I., Lanc, 170.
(3) E. 154, 15, Jas. I., Easter, 15.
(4) S.P. Warrants, 18/79.
(5) Cal. S.P.D., 12th Aug., 1625, Car. I., Coll. Sign Man, Car. I., 1/79.   The Calendar incorrectly copies Skelton as Skipton.

CHAPTER VI.

THE LANCASHIRE MINES.

No sooner had the first farmers of the Guisborough Mines started on their work than they found a rival in the field. An unsigned document (1), dated 8th January, 1610-11, is the earliest information that we have. It complains that Sir Richard Haughton (2) had erected an alum works in competition with that of the informers, and was thus endeavouring to overthrow the contract with the Crown. He had also taken away one of their workmen, whom at great expense they had brought from beyond the seas. The Attorney General, Sir Henry Hobert, filed his information (3) against Sir Richard Houghton. Interrogatories were drawn and witnesses examined on the 23rd April, 1612, under a commission issued by Chief Baron Tanfield on the preceding 11th February. Anthony Snyder, the workman in question, was examined on both sides, and his evidence tended to show that he broke no contract by transferring his services to the defendant (4). He was not hired or covenanted to be hired with any other person at such time as he first came to serve Sir Richard. He was born near unto Cologne, in Germany, and with other of his countrymen came to England at the charges and by means of Mr. Turner and other merchants of London, who employed him in alum works in Yorkshire by the space of one year or thereabouts. Afterwards he and certain of his countrymen, being by them no further used, came away from thence, and two of his countrymen returned unto their own country, and he, being ready to go with them, was brought by one Captain Taylor to the defendant.

Sir Richard began to erect a workhouse at Houghton, to make alum, in Whitsuntide, 1609, but made no alum till Christmas following. Up to date, only some five or seven tons of alum were made in all, and the total outlay was some £320. It was evidently a very small affair, but the whittawers and dyers of Bolton, Wigan and Cappul, in Lancashire, found it very useful, and bought the alum so made at cheaper rates than elsewhere. For thirty shillings they claimed that they could buy as much alum as would have

(1) Lands, 152/61.
(2) Rectius Houghton.
(3) The bill cannot be found, only the depositions.
(4) Exch. Depns. 10, Jas. I., Easter No. 8.

cost fifty shillings if brought from a distance. As the alum was sold at 28/- per cwt. evidently the retail price in Lancashire was much higher than the wholesale in London, where alum was then selling at 26/- per cwt.

An attempt was also made without much success to prove that the work was merely a revival of a former experiment. Witnesses deposed to a miner having come from Richmond 49 years previously, which would bring us back to a time prior to the grant to Cornelius de Vos, and a tenant of the defendant deposed to a Keswick man having found an alum mine at Withnell about the year 1584; in each case a predecessor of Sir Richard having directed the search.

The man from Keswick was no doubt one of the miners working under direction of the Hochstatters; it is not so easy to explain the presence of the man from Richmond, but the Swaledale lead mines had been previously opened, and the rule seems to have been " once a miner always a miner " no matter what the mineral sought to be worked. Three stronger grounds of the defence were the following, viz. :—

(1) That Sir Richard had no notice of the letters patent;

(2) that he only worked on his own freehold; and

(3) that alum was a base and not a royal mineral, nor were any royal minerals mixed with it in the seam.

Apparently the case was settled, for on the 22nd June, 1614, Sir Richard was granted the privilege of making alum for twenty-one years (1), and of exporting 500 tons a year.

We find two later references to these alum works in Assheton's Journal (2).

On that memorable visit to Houghton Towers, 16th August, 1617, where tradition (though not Nicholas Assheton) asserts that King James knighted the sirloin of beef, he took the opportunity after the mid-day meal to spend an hour viewing the mines. On his return, the journalist chronicles that he went out stag shooting, that he missed one stag and wounded another so badly in the thighbone that Lord Compton had to finish it off. Whether this bad marksmanship was due to perturbation of mind caused by his inspection of the alum works we are not told,

(1) D.S.P. Jas. i. Grant Book 141/134.
(2) Cheetham Society, Vol. 19, pp. 39, 66.

but the following October one of the Lancashire justices was sent to view the mine.

At a later date, when the prohibition of competing against the privileged mines was no longer in force, another mine was opened on land belonging to the then Sir Richard Houghton.

CHAPTER VII.

STATE OWNERSHIP.

The Lord Treasurer Dorset died on the 19th April, 1608. The adventurers were still losing money. If the prohibition against the importation of foreign alum promised in the letters patent were put in force there was good hope that success would attend the undertaking.

But Salisbury succeeded Dorset as Lord Treasurer, and before he acceded to this request he decided to satisfy himself that the two conditions laid down in the same letters patent had been fulfilled, i.e.: (1) that sufficient alum was being made to meet the needs of dyers and others; and (2) that the price would not exceed that usually paid for foreign alum.

The difficulty was to find competent commissioners to make the necessary investigations. A marked feature of this reign had been the close co-operation between English merchants and those engaged in the collection of Customs. One of the ablest of the latter class was Arthur Ingram, who had been a controller of the customs in the Port of London for many years, and in that capacity had carried out negotiations between the merchants and Salisbury (then Lord Cranborne) in order to obtain tenders for their farm of the customs. He held himself a farm of some of the customs (1), and was closely connected in business with Lionel Cranfield, afterwards Earl of Middlesex, and with other prominent speculators (2). Sir Nicholas Salter held from December 24th, 1604, a lease of the great Customs in conjunction with Francis Jones. It was, therefore, not surprising that Salisbury selected Arthur Ingram and Nicholas Salter to survey the mines. This was Arthur Ingram's first introduction to the alum industry, his connection with which has not added lustre to his name. It was suggested later in some undated interrogatories (3) apparently drafted for the examination of the surveyors, contractors and others in some abortive proceedings to which reference will be made hereafter, that those who were engaged in the manufacture grievously deceived the surveyors, and that the latter were satisfied with a very perfunctory visit.

(1) Farm of the English Customs, R.Hist.S. Publn., 4 series, 1.129.
(2) See Hist. M.S.S. Comm., Various Vol. 8.
(3) D.S.P., Jas. i., 86/117.

The surveyors were to be asked as follows—how many houses did you see at work?—how many pans?—how many boilings?—how much alum was made at each boiling?—what was the cost of making one ton, counting coals, liquor, urine and workmen's wages? The contractors were to be asked—did you not entreat the workmen to make great coolers of alum to show Sir Arthur Ingram and Sir Nicholas Salter, and promise them rewards?—were the workmen directed to work as usual or to choose the best boiling pans and to use small alum and washings in place of " mothers " and " green liquids "? Was not more alum made at one boiling than ever since? Did you not know that the alum cost at least £20 a ton to make, and that you were not able to make in one month a twelfth part of the yearly requirements of the kingdom? Ingram and Salter presented their report, and it certainly erred on the side of optimism, whatever may have been the true answers to the above questions. Unfortunately no answers at all have come to light. The surveyors were satisfied that alum was being made in sufficient quantities and as good as Romish alum, and London Dyers who tried some samples found no fault except with their " greenness " (1), i.e., they required to be kept.

There were five working houses, namely, Slape Wath, Belman Bank, Newgate Bank (which seems to have been on the south side of Spa Wood and at the angle where it joins Wiley Cat), Sandsend, and Assholme in Mulgrave Woods. Each house was provided with four coolers, each capable of producing five cwt. of alum a week or five tons in all (2). This would give 260 tons, producing £5,200 a year if the alum realised £20 a ton.

A few weeks later a much more optimistic estimate was presented. Instead of one boiling a week there were to be four, quadrupling the output at 1,040 tons a year. The cost was estimated at £9 the ton; if £25 were the price realised the net profit would amount to £16,640, or, at £20, £11,440. There was hope that the output would be increased to 2,000 tons, leaving at least a profit of £22,000.

Although the surveyors agreed on their report of the existing conditions, they differed in their recommendations. Ingram (3) advised the King to take the works into his own

<hr>

(1) Not " grossness " as Mr. A. W. Price in his English Patents of Monopoly reads the word.
(2) Lands, 152/50.
(3) Exch. Depns. 22, Jas. i. Hil No. 29, Evidence of Sir John Bourchier and Sir Nicholas Salter.

hands; Salter strongly opposed the suggestion, even to the extent of incurring the displeasure of Salisbury. When the inevitable failure came unkind critics insinuated that Ingram was actuated by a deep laid scheme to draw illicit gains from his intervention in the work. This is possible, but it is more probable that he merely desired to give advice pleasing to his patron. Salisbury, like his father, Burghley, while acquiescing in the system of monopolies, was fully aware of and anxious to avoid the evils which so often resulted therefrom, and, to his mind, as indeed to that of the social reformer to-day, the State could do with impunity what a private individual ought not to do. From the first he felt considerable doubt whether it would be right to allow so important a monopoly to remain in the hands of a subject. The interrogatories to which reference has before been made (1), asked " Had the Earl of Salisbury any promise or reward," as if to imply that he had. But there is not a tittle of evidence to support such an insinuation. Arthur Ingram summarised in his defence to the Privy Council (2) the reasons which actuated Lord Salisbury: (1) That alum was needed for cloth and leather. (2) That our common enemy, the Pope, might be hindered. (3) That £40,000 in money or commodities might be spent at home instead of abroad. (4) That thousands of the poor might be employed, instructed in religion and have their children educated. (5) That there might be many ships employed.

After Salisbury's death, Sir Walter Cope, the Master of the Wards, defended his memory in a tract headed Il di loda la sera, which he paraphrased " The night praiseth the day " (3). The date is fixed by the reference to the petition of the farmers of the alum works then under consideration and opposed by Cope, for a further abatement in rent. What specific charge was laid against Salisbury does not appear, but that vague accusations were flying about is clear from Cope's remarks that the world observed him with all admiration when living, but no sooner was he dead than it loaded his memory with all imputations of corruption.

The position now was as follows: The King was entitled to his yearly rent of £700, the amount allowed to the farmers of the customs. The patentees (Sheffeild, Chaloner, Foulis and Bourchier), who incurred no personal liability as

(1) D.S.P., Jas. I., 86/117.
(2) Lands 152, fol. 51.
(3) Gutch-collectanea curiosa 1/125, printing Tanner M.S.S. 278/505 and Lands 151/104.

such, were entitled to a share in the profits under the contract with the merchants or undertakers, William Turner, Nicholas Crispe, Ellis Crispe and Abraham Chamberlain (William Hinde was then dead), who undertook the whole direction of the work and the sale of the alum when it was manufactured. Finally, there were contractors, who had bargained with the undertakers to manufacture alum for them at various prices, generally less than £10 a ton.

Salisbury was determined that the Crown should acquire the rights of the various persons interested(1); on the 25th April, 1609, he told William Turner plainly that the grant would not stand unless the King was made a party. The hint was sufficient. Ingram, in his defence (2) to the Privy Council, suggested that there was some unwillingness on the part of the merchants to sell; those that had borne the burthen and endured the danger considered that they should reap the comfort. But there seems to have been no such unwillingness on the part of the patentees; the negotiations were completed by articles of agreement on the 6th May, 1609, and confirmed by letters patent on the 29th October following (3).

The parties to the surrender were the Lord Treasurer, the Chancellor of the Exchequer, the patentees and their assigns (for all had dealt with their interests) and the merchants. The principal terms certainly did not err on the side of niggardliness. The merchants or undertakers were to receive £6,044 during each of the years of the original term, to be paid half-yearly as from the 1st May, 1609, and to terminate with a proportionate payment of £1,007 on 1st Jan., 1637-8. This sum represented repayment at £20 per cent. of principal and interest of the sum of £30,000 (taken as the total expenditure to date) in twenty-eight years; a rate of interest which can only be described as extortionately high.

The payments were to be secured by depositing at a warehouse within Red Lion Gate in Watling Street all the alum manufactured within the realm, and the merchants had power of sale on default within fourteen days. The warehouse was formerly in the occupation of Edward Davenant, was rented at £50 a year from the widow of William Williamson, a vinter, and was sub-let for a term at £60 to Mr. Osborne. The patentees were to receive

(1) Exch. Depns. 22, Jas. I., Hil No. 28.
(2) Lands 152.
(3) P.R. 1820, 7, Jas. I., Pt. 32, M. 9, No. 23.

nothing at all for the first seven years of the term, but from the 1st May, 1616, they were to get between them £3,000 for the first year and £6,000 for each of the succeeding years of the original term. Another £1,000 a year was to be paid to the merchants in consideration of their indemnifying the King against the several yearly pensions charged upon the works, comprising £26 13s. 4d. to Thomas Chaloner (of Lambay), £200 to Lord Danvers, £66 13s. 4d. and £40, respectively, to the two preachers at the works, William Ward at Guisborough, and Richard Leake at Lythe, £100 to John Coventry, whose name constantly occurs but whose exact connection is difficult to trace, and £20 to Gerard Malynes. The Schoolmaster, Robert Wemys, though not mentioned was included. He got £12 a year.

In addition to these yearly sums the merchants were to indemnify the King against the payment of all rents, including the twentieth part of the profits reserved to such of the patentees as had alum houses built upon their lands in proportion to the amount of alum made. Having got the works in the possession of the Crown, the next thing done was to lease them. William Turner and John Bourchier applied for the lease, and authority was given to the Lord Treasurer and Chancellor of the Exchequer to enter into the necessary agreement.

The actual lease was granted on the 21st April, 1610, to William Turner, John Bourchier, Richard Bowdler and Thomas Jones. Exactly what the relations were between the lessees was later a matter of dispute (1). There was no question that Bourchier gave Turner a bond for £12,000, as Bourchier maintained merely to secure Turner from loss, and to reimburse such part of his expenditure as failed to come back to him out of the profits. Bowdler and Jones joined for financial reasons.

The lease related back to 24th June, 1609, and extended to the termination of the licence on 1st January, 1637-8 (2). The rent was fixed at £2,000 for the first year, £3,000 for the second, £11,000 for the next five years, and then when the annuities became payable to the patentees £10,000 for the remainder of the term. In addition, the lessees undertook to make all the payments due under the articles of agreement to the patentees, merchants, pensioners and others.

(1) C.2, Jas. I., B. 17/45, 47.
(2) Exch. B. & A. (Jas. I.), London, 1364, Lands 152.

They were to be entitled to certain deductions or defalcations in the rent should alum continue to be imported, a provision which later gave rise to contention.

On the 19th June, 1609, now that the transfer of the works to the Crown had been executed, the long desired proclamation against the importation of foreign alum was issued (1). The grounds for the proclamation were very fully stated. Some good and loving subjects had to their great charge and no less commendation found sundry mines in the County of York for making alum, which they had yielded into the King's hands. They could make sufficient alum for the use of the Kingdom and for exportation. Two of the former managers (2) had been selected to act as factors and agents, who were to provide a sufficient store of alum at reasonable prices in storehouses in the City of London and in every port. Severe penalties were to be imposed upon those who infringed the proclamation.

That this proclamation was constantly disregarded is perfectly clear, and it may be convenient to deal with this question now.

The series of Port Books is, unfortunately, too incomplete to enable us to put entire reliance upon their contents, but the evidence which they afford is not without value.

On 8th June, 1609 (3), the Griffin of Amsterdam (Claus Jacobson—master) imported for George Pease into Kingston-upon-Hull two thousand pounds (say one ton) of alum, worth £20. In all during that month about one-hundred and twenty-eight-and-a-half hundredweight were imported from Holland of the value of some £128 10s. 0d.

From the end of June, when the proclamation may be assumed to be well-known, no more importations of foreign alum into the Port of Hull are recorded.

But this does not necessarily mean that these importations ceased. In the early part of the year 1611 (4), an information was filed against several persons alleging that they imported alum at high prices, whereas England was served at reasonable prices from the Yorkshire works. In fact, as we have seen, the opposite was the case—the

(1) Proc. Coll. p. 209.
(2) Probably William Turner and John Bourchier were meant.
(3) Exch. K. R. Port Books, 312/6.
(4) Exch. B. & A., Jas. I., York No. 1213.

object of the proclamation was to enable English alum to be sold at £25 a ton whilst foreign alum had previously cost £20 only. The following charges were made. In April, 1610, Thomas Saltmarshe, Master of the George of Hull, carried 60 barrels of alum from Stade in Germany, and Martin Jefferson brought two little barrels of alum not above £8 in value in the Hare, also of Hull. Emanuel Fenton, searcher at Hull, seized these. Bartholomew Harwood transported in the Pleasure of Hull four little barrels of alum, which were discharged at the Crane Staith in the City of York.

The first two parcels may have been those mentioned to have been seized in Hull in some accounts (1) to which we shall have occasion later to refer. No date is given for the seizure, but it was prior to November, 1612, and the costs of the same together with the charges of searching, unloading, housing, cellarage, casks, cooperage and shipping to the order of the lessees of the alum works in London amounted to £50 4s. 4d. Thomas Ferrers, deputy to the farmers of the customs in the Port of Hull, is there said to have seized the alum, but this does not exclude the possibility that Emanuel Fenton acted under his orders.

How much foreign alum was actually imported is a question difficult to answer. So far as records of the legal proceedings relating thereto afford evidence the amounts were exceedingly small, but they extend over a considerable period. As the scheme for the finance of the works provided for the sale of alum at home at the price of £25 a ton, and abroad at the price of £15, a good profit remained when English alum was bought in a foreign market and brought home to compete with the untravelled article. It was therefore necessary to issue a second proclamation, dated 10th October, 1614, which prohibited the return of English alum after it had been sold abroad.

Again, it was difficult in many cases to ascertain who were the actual importers in this unlawful trade, more especially as the alum was often imported in the name of poor mariners unable to pay the value. A third proclamation was therefore issued on the 16th March, 1617-18 extending the penalties of the earlier proclamation to buyers, sellers and shippers of the prohibited merchandise.

There are several cases where informations were filed both in the Court of Exchequer and in the Star Chamber

(1) A.O.1, 2486/348.

against these delinquents, but it would rather appear that no final judgment was given. It was sought to justify the proceedings by the proposition that for the best profit of the realm all native merchandise was put under the power and prerogative of the King to be disposed to the greatest good of the Commonwealth, and could not be exported into foreign countries or imported thence without special licence.

In 1620 there was a charge against some hundred or more offenders of having imported in all four thousand tons. The occasions were separate and the delinquents came from different towns—Ralph Wall of Westchester, Richard Harryson of Southwark, Henry Boot of Newcastle, and Nathaniel Waterhouse of Leeds.

Two bills (1) were filed in the Exchequer to which the defendants by their Counsel, John Bridgeman, pleaded they could not be compelled to confess. The Attorney General then filed bills (2) in the Star Chamber against the same defendants and they pleaded that a suit to the same effect was pending in the Court of Exchequer.

Again, in 1622, when Sir Thomas Coventry was Attorney General he filed a like bill (3) against over two hundred persons, of whom fifty-seven were named in the bill, and some hundred-and-sixty in a schedule. Three of the defendants confessed the purchase of a hogshead of alum weighing five hundredweight, but as they paid the market price of 25/6 per cwt. they had every reason to believe that it was lawfully sold.

In 1639 commissions (4) sat at Guisborough and Penrith to enquire whence came some small quantities of alum which had been sold in Kendal, Penrith, and Carlisle by Scottish carriers, who brought it on horseback. It was proved conclusively that none of the carriers had bought any alum from the Yorkshire works, but they maintained that they had bought it in Edinburgh, and as many merchants of that City had imported alum from Yorkshire they had every reason to believe that it was in order. It was white, and therefore either English or Luke (i.e., from Liège) and not Romish. An attempt was made to trace some white alum imported

(1) Exch. B. & A., Jac. I., London 1347, 1348.
(2) Star Ch. Proc., Jas. I., 32/7 and 30/18.
(3) Exch. B. & A., Jac I., London 1466.
(4) Exch. Depn. by commissioners 11/12, Car i., Hil. 17, 12 Car 1 . . . . . 22 and 39.

from Holland to Seville in Spain and thence to England, but without success.

But serious though the importation of foreign alum was, the question of finance was far more serious. In any case, it would have been a difficult task to pay the wages of the workmen engaged in manufacturing many hundreds of tons which could not be sold for many months. It was still more difficult when the experimental stage had not been passed and when expenditure of a capital nature was intermingled with that more correctly appropriate to revenue.

The purchase by the Crown had been on generous terms, the undertakers were to be re-imbursed the whole of their outlay, and had they received cash payment they would have had a sufficiency of working capital. But this would have been impossible, there was but little cash in the Treasury, and the essence of the scheme which recommended it to the King was that nothing was to be paid out of the Treasury and that all the payments were to be made out of the proceeds of the sale of alum. It therefore became imperative to enlist the services of many other merchants.

Whether there was a deed of association specifying the interests in the concern of all parties it is impossible to say. The probabilities that such was the case are very great; on the other hand, had it existed, one would expect to find some reference to it.

William Turner, Sir Thomas Jones, Richard Bowdler and Sir John Bourchier were certainly members of the Alum Company, as it was called, in that they were lessees from the Crown, but there were several others, such as William Essington, Robert Barlow and Francis Greenhouse, who appear to have been liable for its debts.

Whether William Megges who was both father-in-law and brother-in-law to Richard Bowdler, was also a partner was a debatable question.

Richard Bowdler had for many years resided and carried on business at Middleburg (1), where he still had agents and factors; one of whom was his former apprentice George

(1) D.S.P., Jac. 1. 120/78b. It was probably the father of this Richard Bowdler who was a resident in Middleburg and contributed to a loan to the Earl of Leicester on 12th July, 1586, see State Papers Foreign. He himself would have been only 12 years old at that date.

Morgan. In October, 1609, six months before the lease was executed, the company appointed this George Morgan as its agent in Middleburg to borrow money on its behalf on bills of exchange.

According to Morgan's story, the appointment was most disastrous to him. By the 23rd May, 1612, his accounts showed that the company owed on these bills £37,794 4s. 7d. Flemish currency, or £22,600 sterling, of which £6,251 10s. 2d. Flemish, or £3,460 sterling (1), was owing to Morgan personally, and for the remainder he was liable on the bills of exchange, no less that £14,900 being due to Peter Courteen. Morgan's accounts were not admitted; his suits with Bowdler, Megges and others occupy many folios, and after being submitted to arbitration and the award set aside by the Lord Chancellor were eventually decided by the House of Lords.

Even this did not settle the matter. As late as 1662 George Morgan was relating his woes to the King and Council and making one more desperate attempt to get repayment of his alleged debt (2). But there seems to have been no dispute as to the sum of money, £22,600, raised in Holland, transmitted to England and spent upon the alum works.

Shortly before this time it had been decided to combine the works in Dorset with those in Yorkshire. The Canford works existed as a name, but had apparently been abandoned; works had, however, been opened near Kimmeridge on the opposite side of the Isle of Purbeck by Sir William Clavell.

Hutchin's Dorset, 3rd Edn., 1, 155, gives the credit of the discovery that Kimmeridge was full of alum mines to James Lord Mountjoy, who was the custodian of the Forest of Purbeck (3), but the details that the author gives are too inaccurate to support his statement. Sir William Clavell was minded to erect four houses, each with forty pans, sufficient to make five hundred tons a year and to construct a pier into the sea. Hutchin's Dorset I., 556, declares that the Pier was constructed at a cost of £4,000, but patient

(1) The two equations appear to be inconsistent. The first gives the English pound equal to 33s. 5d. Flemish, the second to 36s. 1d. Flemish.
(2) D.S.P., Chas. II., 66/146.
(3) See C.3, 13/105.

search has failed to detect any trace of alum shipped thence to London.

We do find record of alum shipped from Yorkshire: The Port Books (1) give the names of at least three ships engaged in the trade in 1611 and 1612: the Allomes Ann of Whitby, Master Luke Fox; the Ann Garratt of Coatham, Master Wm. Fish; and the Fortune of Guisborough, Master John Holland, were bringing coal from Sunderland and carrying alum to London: the Allomes Ann twice 55 tons on 19th February, 1611/2 and 30th April, 1612; the Ann Garratt 11 tons on 24th May, and again the Allomes Ann 47 tons on 6th August and 60 tons on 4th December, 1612.

There are no corresponding entries extant for Coatham, but this does not necessarily mean that there were no such shipments. On 6th November, 1611 (2) the Phenix of Gisburrowe carried from London thirty-three tan hides for the use of the alum works free from duty by the authority of the Lord Treasurer, and the natural inference is that she was on her return voyage after carrying alum to London.

With the help of the Alum Company the lessees duly paid £5,000 as the rent up to 16th October, 1611, and also paid £9,000 to the merchants in accordance with their lease (3), but meantime their position became worse. They applied to Lord Salisbury for some modification of the lease, basing their application on the illicit importation of foreign alum (some of which was imported under the name of copperas and Seville oil—Civill oil) and the competition of Lancashire mines (4).

Though neither cause was considered sufficient, their financial position must have been notorious, and the request was granted. As from 16th October, 1611 (5), the rent for the third and susequent years was to be reduced from £11,000 to £8,000, and after June, 1616 (when the payments to patentees should have commenced) to £7,000, but there were to be no " defalcations " for foreign alum imported.

October came and passed. No rent was paid nor were funds available for that purpose. The lessees again appealed to the Lord Treasurer. Considerable time passed

(1) E. 190 Port Books, 187/5/6.
(2) Id. 16/7
(3) Exch. B. & A., Jac. I., London, 1364.
(4) Lands 152/61.
(5) See recital in P.R. 2007, No. 1 (11 Jac. I., Pt. 30).

in negotiations; Salisbury was by no means disposed to grant the relief asked (1). Finally, on the 20th May, 1612, the Alum Company failed. Four days later Salisbury died. In the words of Arthur Ingram " it pleased God to call my Lord Treasurer." For some time no successor was appointed, and the negotiations were continued with the Lords Commissioners of the Treasury.

The only hope for the works lay in that temporary expedient known as a grant of protection by which creditors were restrained from suing. On the 31st May, 1612, just a week after Salisbury's death, protection for six months was granted to the members (2) of the Alum Company mentioned on page 91 ante, on the ground that they had disbursed £40,000 on the alum works since the commencement of the lease. The grant recited that they had no intention to defraud any man of his just and due debts. If the figure, £40,000, is correct not much more than half the capital had been raised in Holland, but without an accurate account of the sales of alum the figures cannot be verified.

The protection was subsequently renewed for another six months, from 21st November, 1612, and then finally for six months from 13th August, 1613 (3).

William Turner presented his accounts on the 20th July, 1612 (4). It may be presumed that these related only to the period from 24th June, 1609 to 26th April, 1612, but there is such a sparseness of material dates that it is impossible to speak with certainty. If this presumption is correct, during a little less than three years 1,936 tons of alum had been made at all the Yorkshire works at a cost of £42,216 15s. 3d. spent at the works, and £16,474 16s. 2d. spent in materials purchased elsewhere and sent down to the works, in freight of ships, urine and other necessaries, in all £58,691 11s. 5d. —or, approximately, £30 a ton—i.e., half as much again as the market price (£20) of foreign alum.

In addition they paid over £2,000 to Sir William Clavell for the Dorset works, £5,000 to the King as rent, and £15,010 for annuities, the greater part of which no doubt came back to themselves, for it is probable that Nicholas Crispe, Ellis Crispe and Abraham Chamberlain, as well as William Turner, were interested in the Alum

(1) D.S.P., Jac I., 120/78B.
(2) P.R. 1965, No. 28 (10 Jac I., 23 Pt. 1).
(3) P.R. 1948, No. 11 (10 Jac. I., Pt 6); P.R. 1982, No. 5 (11 Jac. I., Pt. 5).
(4) Lands 152/97.

Company.   Of the alum manufactured, the greater part, 1,746 tons, was sold at home at £23 a ton, and the remaining 190 tons sold abroad at £15.   There was about £1,000 received from the sale of coals, leaving the enormous deficit of £36,732 18s. 1d., in other words, they lost about £19 upon every ton manufactured and sold.

Meantime, the question of continuing the works was being very carefully considered.   The 26th April, 1612, was taken as the date of the first relinquishment of the works (1), which possibly meant that no money was paid by the farmers after that date, but it certainly does not mean that all arrears were settled up to that date, and somehow alum continued to be made.

It is a probable assumption that the contractors made alum for the farmers at a fixed price, but it is quite certain that after the so-called relinquishment they brought in their accounts of expenditure in which they merely claimed salaries.   These accounts show (2) no break in the continuity of working.

Turner next made an offer on behalf of his co-lessees ; that they would carry on and pay all disbursements if their rent were reduced to £1,000 a year for some years, and then when better times came on raised to £4,000 (3).   He calculated that there were some 400 workmen besides 300 more employed in shipping and coal-mining ; in all some 2,000 persons (including their wives and children) depending upon the work (4).

Arthur Ingram declared that he recommended the acceptance of this offer, but that Sir Walter Cope, the Master of the Wards, out of respect for the late Lord Treasurer, opposed it.

The Lords Commissioners of the Treasury were anxious lest the failure of the business should cast the burden of the annuities on the King's Purse.   They therefore arranged with Turner to support the works for another sixteen days from the 23rd July, and appointed a commission of four, viz. : —Robert Johnson (an Alderman of London), William Canning, John Farmer and Thomas Foxall, to survey and report.   These Commissioners issued their certificate on

(1) A.O.1, 2486/348.
(2) A.O.3, 1243/3.
(3) Lands, 152/52.
(4) id. 152/86.

28th August, 1612 (1).   Reckoning each of the six Yorkshire houses capable of producing 166 tons a year, or 1,000 tons in all, with £24 a ton average selling price and £13 10s. a ton average manufacturing price, they estimated a balance of about £10,000—not too large a margin for payment of annuities of £7,000, shortly to be increased to £13,000, and to provide £700 as the annual abatement to the farmers of the customs.

This being the state of affairs, it became necessary to come to some decision, and the Privy Council determined to accept a surrender of the lease and to purchase the interests of the several parties.   Sir Walter Cope, Arthur Ingram and Robert Johnson were appointed Commissioners to negotiate for the purchase, and they agreed to pay the following sums (2):—

To the Merchants, five years' purchase of their annuity of £6,044	£30,220	o	o
To the Farmers in lieu of £44,000 disbursed	£30,000	o	o
Four years' interest at £10 per cent. on the latter sum	£12,000	o	o
Freights and other disbursements	£5,280	o	o
	£77,500	o	o

This sum was to be paid in four years by means of alum. During that period seven thousand five hundred tons were to be manufactured, of which four thousand tons were to be sold at home at £25 a ton, and three thousand five hundred for sale abroad at £15.   After deduction of £10 a ton for the cost of manufacture this was to leave the required sum of £77,500.

We have already seen the results of this system under which competition in foreign markets reduced the price to £15 a ton, while the prohibition against importation, imperfectly maintained though it was, enabled the makers to obtain £25 at home.

The heads of the agreement having been settled it was only a question of time before the necessary deeds (3) were executed.   On 27th April, 1613, the King entered into a

(1) Lands 152, p. 109.
(2) D.S.P., Ja. I., 74/20.
(3) Recited in P.R. 2007, m.1 (II. Jac. I., Pt. 30).

Covenant to pay William Turner, Nicholas Crispe, Ellis Crispe and Abraham Chamberlain the sum of £37,400 (1), to be provided as follows:—

Every year for four successive years one thousand tons of alum were to be delivered at Dyce Key or at some other Key between the Custom House and London Bridge, and were to be sold at £25 a ton in gross and 26s. per cwt. retail. Out of the proceeds of sale the merchants could deduct £9,350 in reduction of their own debt, £10,000, or £10 a ton, for manufacture, and £2,000, or £2 a ton for freight. The balance, £3,650, was to be paid to the King.

Then on 31st May, 1613, another indenture (2) was executed by which Sir John Bourchier, William Turner, Richard Bowdler and Thomas Jones surrendered their tenancy and obtained a full discharge from all their obligations under the lease of 16th October, 1611. They also handed over the lease that they had taken of the coal mines at Harraton for the purpose of the works. The sums agreed to be re-imbursed were to be satisfied in the following manner:—Sir John Bourchier and his partners were to receive the four thousand tons of alum for home vent previously mentioned and to deliver them to the merchants.

The three thousand five hundred tons for foreign vent were to be delivered to agents for sale at £15 a ton, of which £10 was to be paid to the King for the cost of manufacture, and £5 to Sir John Bourchier and his partners. Any loss between loading on ship board and discharging on the quay was to be borne by the King who also covenanted to pay £15 for every ton of the four thousand for home vent, and £5 for every ton of the three thousand five hundred for foreign vent that should be lacking.

Had this scheme been carried out the whole debt to the merchants would have been settled in four years, and that to the farmers substantially reduced, but needless to say even this modified scheme was not carried out.

During this period Arthur Ingram was gradually consolidating his position. He appears to have taken advantage of the knowledge that he gained whilst surveying the works to secure a part interest in them. He was not punished for this irregular act, but as it interfered with the scheme of the lease, he was induced to surrender

(1) This included the sum for freight and other expenses.
(2) P.R. 2007, m.1 (11 Jac. I., Pt. 30).

it, and to accept in lieu thereof a year's pension of £200 for the remainder of the term of thirty-one years payable in the first instance out of the alum rents (1). The grant was dated 20th February, 1610-1. In March, 1612-3, he was appointed Secretary to the Council in the North parts of which Sheffeild was still President, and his brother William Ingram was appointed his Deputy.

There is an undated letter (2) to which attention should be called, though its effect is not quite obvious. It is written by one R. Lane (a pencil note of much later date adds Richard), who claimed kinship with Sir Edward Montagu (later Lord Montagu), and stated that he lived in Aldersgate Street at the sign of the Pig and Capon next to the Recorder (then Henry Montagu and afterwards Earl of Manchester). He was, therefore, one of the Lanes of Walgrave, whose connection with the Alum trade we have already seen (3). According to his story, he had been employed by the person to whom his letter was addressed to manufacture, with the help of a German named Fredericke at the Savoy, alum from stone brought out of the North, and had succeeded in making it at a cost of £9 a ton without sea coal, wood or urine. He also declared that Mr. Tapsell, a kinsman of Arthur Ingram, and therefore William Tapsfield, whom we shall meet later, and his servant Wade had watched the process, thought that they had discovered the secret, but failed to reproduce it in Yorkshire. Lord Salisbury had also unsuccessfully tried to obtain the secret.

The letter ends with a reference to Mr. " Gerrat Malynes," a Dutch merchant, who had men continually in the North to search out the dealings in the works, and who was ready to confirm Lane's statements. Unfortunately, our knowledge of Gerard Malynes does not give much value to this confirmation. The reference to Lord Salisbury makes one inclined to infer that the letter was written shortly after his death, but how long after it is difficult to guess. Not much credence need be given to the statements contained in it.

(1) P.R. 1888, 8 Jas. I., Pt. 50, No. 1.
(2) D.S.P., Jas. I., 75/68.
(3) P. 48 ante.

CHAPTER VIII.

THE STATE AS ALUM MANUFACTURER.

The negotiations that resulted in the surrender of the works to the Crown took some time, nor is the sequence of events quite clear. Arthur Ingram alleged that he and Alderman Robert Johnson, who were appointed Commissioners to manage the undertaking on behalf of the King, rode down to the works (1); they found a great number of poor people crying out with bitter exclamations for money due to them for their wages which they had first to see satisfied, work was stopped through lack of coals, urine and other necessaries, which they had to supply, and the decays in the houses had to be repaired. They then let the houses to contractors who had previously worked them and who undertook to make and supply alum at a fixed price per ton. The statement was correct in its main outlines, coloured to enhance the services which Ingram claimed to have rendered.

There is no period of which we have fuller details than that which immediately succeeded the abandonment of the work by the farmers. Previously the master of the works had been Richard Willis, who resided at the Old Bailey. The continuance of his services was requisitioned, and he rendered three accounts for the period from 26th April, 1612, to 27th March, 1613, when Thomas Carpenter succeeded him. One of these is in the form of a book, and contains the names of every workman employed about the work with the rate of his wage and period of employment, and also detailed entries of every receipt and payment (2). The other two are identical, filed in the Audit office and Pipe office, respectively, and contain the summary merely which was passed on audit (3). Although 20th May has been given as the date of the failure of the Alum Company, Willis registered the first relinquishment of the mines as having happened on the 26th April. He himself did not act as paymaster until the 29th August (the day following the date of the report by Johnson, Fermor, Foxall and Canning) (4), and it is marvellous to notice that for eighteen weeks the works were carried on without any paymaster. During those weeks there were twenty-six day-tale labourers

(1) Lands 152/49.
(2 A.O.3, 1243/3.
(3) A.O.1, 3486/348. P.O. 3381.
(4) See p. 96 ante.

99

at Belmont Bank with a total of 450½ days' work between them at wages of 8d. and 6d. a day; a considerable quantity of piece work was also performed there at a total cost of £234 2s. 3d.; the various operations of manufacture were in full force, and yet, until the report was accepted the chances of the workmen being paid their wages must have seemed very remote.

The activity of the other works at Newgate Bank, Slape Wath, Mulgrave and Sandsend was in like proportion, except so far as work was delayed by necessary repairs.

There were two groups of mines: (a) Those near Guisborough—Belman Bank, Newgate Bank and Slape Wath—over which Maurice Long exercised a general supervision, and (b) those near Whitby on Lord Sheffeild's estate at Mulgrave and Sandsend, managed by his Steward, Richard Haslam.

Under Maurice Long, whose salary was £30 per annum, the following workmasters were employed:—At Belman Bank upper house, George Powell, £25 a year; lower house, Richard Southworth, 30s. a month. At Newgate Bank, John Turner, £40, and at Slape Wath, a Frenchman, John Babe, £24. At the last-mentioned place our old friend Oliver Kearsley acted as Overseer and Clerk of the Works at a yearly salary of £30.

In the Whitby Group the Workmasters were James Langtoft at Mulgrave and Gideon Adcham at Sandsend, each 10s. weekly; Lambert Russell, for overseeing and disposing of the work in the Holmes, calcining and making the liquors at Sandsend, received 6s. weekly.

Richard Willis stayed in Yorkshire from 29th August to 22nd September, then returned to London with Oliver Kearsley, where they remained till 21st November; their expenses in London and on the journey for the eight weeks and five days amounting to £14 18s. 4d. They spent their time there soliciting money for clearing the arrears. The debts on the 29th August totalled £2,602 1s. 4d., principally wages to overseers, labourers and workmen. The accounts do not show when and how these were paid. Arthur Ingram declared (1) that he raised £2,300 through his brother, Sir William, at York, and was subsequently repaid out of monies supplied by the Treasury. The first sum paid out of the Treasury was £1,000 directed on 7th September

(1) Lands 152/54.

1612, to be issued to William Turner for the alum mines (1), but apparently issued by Sir Fras. Egioke in the Easter Term following, and duly accounted for by Johnson (2).

The inference from the accounts is that no serious attempt was made to pay the outstanding wages until the early part of December. On 25th November, Willis and Thomas Carpenter, his successor, who had returned with him from London four days previously, made a journey to Yarm with three other men to receive £400 from Humphrey Wharton of Gilling Wood. The next month Alderman Francis Jones sent them a bill of exchange for £1,000, of which the balance of £800, after deducting the old debt of £50 4s. 4d. (3), was paid by Thomas Ferrers at Hull, where he acted as Deputy Collector of Customs, and the remaining £200 was paid at York. It cost no less than £6 17s. 2d. in the expenses of the escort detailed to guard the money paid at Hull.

The manufacturers had evidently under-estimated the corrosive effect of the liquors, and it had become necessary to make preparations for renewing such of the furnaces and pans as were worn out. The materials for such renewal had been ordered and, notwithstanding the failure of the Alum Company, were duly delivered. In all, some eleven or twelve tons of bar iron were purchased from the Lealholm Forge in Danby of Sir Francis Hildesley at £16 the ton. Sir Francis, a member of a Berkshire family, had married for his first wife the co-heiress of the Bulmers of Wilton and widow of Francis Cholmley of Whitby (4), but this gives us no assistance in tracing his connection with Danby. At p. 48 of the Yorkshire Arch. Journal, Vol. 8, Canon Atkinson gives a list of forty-eight mediaeval iron furnaces in the vicinity of Danby, three of which were at Lealholm.

The payment of a shilling to a guide to direct the draughtsmen in the night to Danby is duly recorded.

So far as coal was concerned a somewhat similar state of affairs obtained. The freight for 1,218½ chalders of Harraton coal from Sunderland to Coatham at 4s. 9d. a chalder was owing to the masters of nine vessels, all of

(1) P.S. File 34/7.
(2) A.O.1, 2486/349.
(3) See p. 89 ante.
(4) See her description at page 10 of Sir Hugh Cholmley's memoirs.

whom bore Flemish names, though one ship was described as of Sunderland. The remainder belonged to Harling (Haarlem), Flushing, Amsterdam and Anchusen (Enkhuizen). The chalders so carried were reckoned by keel measure of 54 bushels; when led to the works 1,895½ chalders were paid for, and the list of the loads proves conclusively that these were reckoned by land measure of 36 bushels. The cost of leading was 5s. a chalder.

The method of manufacturing appears to have been the following:—Both day-tale labourers and piece-workers were employed in baring the rock and clearing away the rubbish, which cost from 1d. to 2d. a cubic yard (1), and also in digging the mine, breaking it into small pieces and barrowing it into the calcining heaps from 2d. to 4d. The wages of the day-tale labourers varied from 6d. to 8d. These latter were not employed every day as such, but sometimes we find the same man working one day at one task, and the next at another, and the third day at a daily rate. Carts with one horse at 10d. a day and coops (or waggons) with two or three yoke of oxen at 2s. 6d. conveyed the shale from the rock to the calcining heaps when, as in the case of the lower house at Belman Bank, the distance was too far for the barrow.

Georgius Agricola De Re Metallica (Ed. Hoover), Book xii., pp. 568, 569, described the aluminous rock as first roasted in a furnace similar to a limekiln. At the bottom of the kiln a vaulted fireplace was made. When the calcined matter was cool it was drawn out, piled in heaps, 50ft. x 8ft. x 4ft., and sprinkled for forty days with water. There is no trace in the accounts of any such calcining kilns: the method of calcining seems to have been similar to that employed in the Guisborough alum works in 1854 (2).

In the first place shale was calcined in heaps composed of alternate layers of brushwood and shale, the base being two hundred feet square and the layers rising in the form of a pyramid to a height of eighty or ninety feet. The heap was set on fire as soon as it reached the height of four feet, and subsequently the piling and calcining processes went on

(1) The phrase in the accounts is square. In Tracts and Table books of English Weights and Measures, p. 2, Camden Miscellany, Vol. xv., superficial feet are *pedes constratos*, solid feet, *pedes quadratos*.

(2) A Visitors Guide to the Guisborough Alum Works, p. 30, and see Young's History of Whitby, Vol. 2, p. 812.

simultaneously. In later times (1) these often lasted eight or nine months, and produced some 100,000 solid cubic yards from which one would expect 800 tons of alum.

So far as one can judge from the accounts, the calcining heaps were not so large as these. Calcining grates are mentioned and priced at 30s., implying that their weight was not more than 2 cwts. If these were the grates upon which the first layer of brushwood and whins was laid, the suggestion is that instead of one large pile there were several small. The payment of £4 15s. to John Wicliff and eleven others in the Spring of 1612/3 for levelling a calcining place to make it higher, the dimensions being thirty yards long, nineteen wide and two-and-a-half deep, leads to the same inference (2).

Cleveland was not so well wooded then as now, but there was enough on the Skelton estate to make up for the deficiency round Guisborough. During the period reviewed wood for the works was corded in Skelton Park and Howl O' Hay (written Hollough Hay) and Rocke Bank. Some rough calculations give four cords to a ton of alum or thereabouts. The cost of cording varied at 8d., 9d. and 11d. a cord, leading was extra at 2s. 6d. or 3s.

A little later difficulties arose. Mr. James Bellasis, who apparently resided at Skelton Castle and managed the property on behalf of Sir Conyers Darcy, his nephew by marriage, refused to allow any more wood to be corded in Skelton Park. Henry Trim, the Clerk of the Works, had to spend 14s. in a journey to Hornby Castle to interview Sir Conyers. He was successful in his application, but only upon payment of a further rent of £24 a year. One great difficulty that must have presented itself in the absence of scientific instruments was to regulate the heat of the calcining heaps. Too rapid combustion was checked by plastering the sides with moist earth. Here the experience of Lambert Russell would be of most value. The chemistry of the subject is thus explained in the Geology of Yorkshire (3). In the process of burning the iron pyrites ($Fe S_2$) found in the alum shale loses one half of its sulphur as sulphur dioxide (SO_2) and becomes a black sulphide of iron ($Fe S$) which, absorbing more oxygen and water from

(1) Ure's Dictionary of Arts, 7 Ed., Vol. i., p. 111.
(2) A.O.3, 1243/3, m. 99.
(3) By P. F. Kendall and H. E. Wroot, Vo. i., pp. 358-363.

the atmosphere, changes to green vitriol or sulphate of iron ($Fe\ SO_4 7H_2O$). In the presence of abundant oxygen and at a high temperature the sulphate becomes more highly oxidised and transfers sulphuric acid to the clay which is also present, and the alumina from which is then more or less completely converted into sulphate of alumina. Other reactions might also obtain at temperatures such as would prevail in the ignited shale heaps (1). The object was to attain a temperature at which $Al_2(So_4)_3$ (Aluminium sulphate) was stable and $Fe_2(SO_4)_3$ liable to be decomposed, leaving Fe_2O_3 insoluble, and SO_3 free to attack more alumina in the shale. This temperature is between 450 degrees-550 degrees. Raised beyond this limit the aluminium sulphate is decomposed, and resolved back into clay (alumina) and sulphuric anhydride $(Al_2\ (SO_4)_3 = Al_2O_3 + 3SO_3$

As, however, the heap cools the sulphuric anhydride so formed would re-act with the alumina in the clay more readily than with the ferric oxide, and again form aluminium sulphate. Hence the importance of the " mellowing " which in reality meant a gradual cooling to permit this last re-action to take place, and in practice was effected by permitting a sufficient time to elapse in order to promote the absorbtion of oxygen by the calcined heap.

When this stage was reached the next process was to steep the calcined shale in pits full of water in order to extract the sulphate of alumina from the waste siliceous matter. From a survey made in 1625 (2) we can derive some idea of the development of these pits. The oldest were described as of wood and out of repair; the later as having stone sides and deal floors—their dimensions being 26 to 29 feet long, 12 feet broad and 3 feet deep. The Visitors Guide before mentioned, describes them in 1854 as stone built cisterns 18 yards long, 5 yards broad, 32 inches deep at the deep end, and 20 inches at the shallow, measurements which give 65 cubic yards of calcined mine as the contents of each.

After the pits were filled with mine water was poured over them, which, after standing for twenty-four hours was run off into a cistern, whence this liquor was conveyed into a second set of pits containing dry mine. The process was

(1) Communicated by Mr. H. N. Wilson.
(2) E.154, 22, Jas. I., Hil. No. 28.

repeated until the liquor acquired the necessary specific gravity. In later times the hydrometer was introduced and a specific gravity from 1.13 to 1.19 acquired.

The authors of The Geology of Yorkshire state (1) that the required specific gravity was determined by floating an egg in the liquid, which they describe as the alum makers secret. But Dr. Young, in his History of Whitby, uses this phrase to describe a bottle which determined the specific gravity, as follows (2):—A bottle containing one-third-of-a-pint was filled with distilled or clear spring water and weighed, a leaden weight, called the counter or water weight, which exactly balanced it being ascertained. The bottle was then weighed dry and empty, and with small shot added balanced against the counter weight. Finally, it was filled with the liquid and weighed for the third time against the counter weight, but on this occasion the small shot necessary was put in the same scale as the latter. If the first quantity of shot is treated as 80 pennyweights and the same amount had to be added on the third occasion the specific gravity would be 2. If only one pennyweight were necessary the specific gravity would be 1.0125. Dr. Edward Jordan (who later was unfortunate enough to enter into a contract to make alum) in a letter in which he excused his ill-success, claimed that in " heightening of liquors " his workmen had wrought them from five to ten pennyworths, apparently implying that he had raised the specific gravity from 1.0625 to 1.125.

There are no notices of any such bottles in the accounts, but assay dishes, also called proof dishes, and purchased from time to time at 4d. each, or 3s. 6d. the dozen, probably served the same purpose.

Another letter in which Dr. Jordan claimed that he made use of an assay glass and did not depend upon " scotches and notches or dishes," suggests that the amount of liquid contained in the dish was marked by a notch. Possibly the Doctor was the true inventor of the bottle.

The pitmen whose duty it was to empty (or teem) the pits of washed mine and fill them with fresh mine were always paid by piece work. The usual payment was 2s. 6d. a pit, but varied between 2s. and 3s. 6d. The Liquorman, who undertook to regulate the density of the liquor, usually received 11d. a day. When the liquor had reached the

(1) p. 360.
(2) Vol. 2, p. 814.

required density it was mixed with the "mothers" (a term to be explained later) and boiled for twenty-four hours over a furnace in lead pans, 9ft. x 5ft. x 2ft. 6in. These pans (varying in number from eight to fifteen) rested upon iron supports. Eight pans required 8 fodder of lead at £12 each, 6 ton of wrought iron at £14 a ton, and 6 ton of cast iron at £8 a ton; bringing the cost of each pan and its supporters to £28 10s. The pans were left continuously on the boil every morning, their contents were run off into settlers, where they were mixed with the urine or other alkaline lee. To every eight pans there were three settlers composed of two fodders of lead between them. They cost £12 13s. 4d. each for material and making.

Having remained in the settler about two hours to deposit the sediment, the liquor was conveyed thence to coolers, where it was stirred for some time, and then left to crystallise. The coolers were considerably smaller than the settlers, ten coolers went to one settler, they were made of deal plank and cost about 25s. each. The liquors were left in the coolers for four days, the liquid portion, which was called the "mothers," was then drawn off in order to be pumped into the pans as previously described. The crystals of alum, which chiefly adhered to the sides of the cooler were collected and put into a tub, where they were washed with water and then conveyed into bins with holes in the bottom to allow the water to pass through—the "dreyning" tubs of the survey.

Next the alum was again dissolved in water and boiled a second time, the saturated liquid being poured into "roaching" casks to crystallise again. After standing about sixteen days holes were bored in the casks to allow the residuary liquor to pass into the receptacles, where it could be preserved for use as "mothers and green liquors." The scrapings and foul alum at the bottom of the casks should next be broken off to undergo a second purification, while the clean alum only was ready for the market. This extra precaution, introduced by the "Dutchmen," was not always observed after their departure. When the second crystallisation had taken place the process was complete; the alum was taken from the roaching casks and laid in the storehouse for export. All this work of boiling the liquors, roaching the alum and attending to the fires day and night was the duty of the housemen, one of whom received 5s. a week and the rest 8d. and 9d. a day. The number of housemen at work on any one day in any one house is not easy to discover from the accounts, there would appear to be not less than six and not more than twelve. As several received sixty-three days pay in nine weeks, obviously work proceeded on a Sunday. In addition to the staff employed in the manufacture of alum, there were bricklayers and masons receiving up to 16d., coopers up to 12d., smiths up to 8½d. a day.

The accounts throw much light on the difficulties involved in the work. In the month of August, 1612, a very serious flood took place; ten men had to work through the night to save the buildings at Slape Wath, timber and wood were carried down-stream. It took two draughts two days each to lead them back.

To build the new furnaces, stone was got from the " old Abbey " on more than one occasion. No doubt it was an old practice. The writer of the Cottonian MS in praising the freestone of the district declared that one could dig stone at an easier rate out of the quarry than pull it out of the Abbey walls. The refuse or slam was a constant source of annoyance. Bridges had to be contrived to carry it away lest it should obstruct the highway. Some years after the date of these accounts the then lessees of Slape Wath were indicted on several occasions for this very offence (1). In these indictments Canon Atkinson noticed that slam is translated amircum, and his informants defined it as the " slimy " stuff that was deposited in the pans in which the alum liquor was left to settle after being boiled, i.e., in what are in the accounts called settlers.

Notwithstanding the bankrupt and derelict condition of the works, 129 tons 11 cwts. appear to have been manufactured at the Guisborough group of houses and 47 tons 7 cwts. at the Whitby group (or in all 176 tons 18 cwts.) during the eighteen weeks that elapsed between the failure of the Alum Company and the arrival of Willis; i.e., nearly 10 tons a week. During the following nine weeks up to October 31st, when the King was treated as having taken possession, only 41 tons 12 cwts. were made at all the mines, or less than five tons a week, but Willis was back in London most of this time, and the arrears of wages due to the

(1) North Riding Records, Vol. 5, pp. 65, 68, 104, 154, 169.

workmen were still unpaid.   Out of the former total of 176 tons 18 cwts. of alum so made only 31 tons 10 cwts. remained in store on 29th August (1), the proceeds of sale of the balance cannot be traced.

At Coatham the Harraton coals were brought from Sunderland in five Flemish ships, carrying from 26 to 19 chalders apiece. They were chartered through a Fleming called Garrett Adrianson; in all there were 333 chalders carried in seventeen voyages to Coatham.

The Allomes Amye of Whitby, Master Luke Fox, a well-known Whitby Mariner, who commanded in succession many vessels of that Port, brought 23 tons of urine from London and transported thither on her return voyage 28 tons 18 cwts. of alum.   At Whitby the local vessels had a larger share of the trade than at Sunderland.   Richard Harrison, master of the Fortune, carried four freights of 22 chalders each of Harraton coals.   William Williamson, Master of the Amity, 18 chalders, and William Browne, Master of the Harry, two freights of 25 chalders each.   Paul Hayes, Master of the Unicorn of Haarlem, chartered by the same Garratt Adrianson, carried 58 chalders in three freights.

The work at Harraton continued.   For November and December, 1612, £173 16s. 1d. was paid to the two workmasters there, Ralph and John Nattress, for working, getting and leading from the pits to the staithes 802¼ chalders by keel measure at 4s. 4d. per chalder (abating 4d. in the whole).   But difficulties were arising.   Thomas Carpenter and Richard Willis spent six days there, from 16th to 22nd December, supervising the work, and on the 29th following sent down two men with six pump horses for the water engine.   Nevertheless £143 2s. 4d. was paid to the same workmasters for 660½ chalders won during the three months, being at the same rate and 2d. over.

Robert Johnson and his three colleagues had estimated the cost of 166 tons of alum at £2,193 17s. 8d. (2), including 1,000 chalders of sea-coal at 13s. 4d., 10 tons of urine a week £300, 60 workmen daily at 8d. for 300 days £600, 18 carts and drivers £100, 300 loads of wood £75, and several other expenses.   It cannot be said that this estimate was unduly optimistic.   The conditions at the various works varied to such an extent that it is quite

(1) A.O.1, 2486/349.
(2) Lands 152/109.

impossible to lay down a fixed quantity of necessaries for each ton, but, with the exception of Slape Wath, the accounts do not show a wide divergence from the estimate.

At Slape Wath only 8 tons 6 cwts. were produced, at a total cost for wages alone of £180 13s. 8d., but here three new furnaces and eight new pans had to be constructed and the boiling was therefore in arrear. But the estimate took no account of the rents, and these were by no means small. In the case of Slape Wath they were crushing. The yearly rent to the assignees of John Atherton has been stated at £300, but, in addition, Roger Tadcastle let Springbank at £20, James Shepherd charged 10s. a year for a way-leave through Waterfall, and John Bransby £1 for land for clay pits and tile yards. Mention has already been made of the charge made on behalf of Sir Conyers Darcy for permission to cord wood from Skelton Park.

No rent was charged for the site of any other of the houses, but in most cases easements were required over adjoining lands for which payments had to be made. Part of Guisborough Old Park was laid to Newgate Bank, and compensation of £1 a year was paid to the tenant (one Crake succeeded by John Bransby), and Robert Lincoln received a like sum for a portion of the Gilse laid to Belman Bank. Lord Sheffeild and his tenants received several rents and payments in respect of land occupied for the purpose of the works. George Poskett (? Postgate) £1 10s. for Growman (Grosmont) close, where the roof of the workhouse was framed and the timbers laid; Lord Sheffeild £14 a year for Horse Rails Springs and Asholmes, but the farmers let out agistments and so reduced the net cost.

On 12th February, 1612-3 (1) Thomas Carpenter rode post to London from Northallerton, whither he had been escorted the previous day by Willis and two others. He was met at Helmsley on 22nd March and escorted back to Guisborough the next day (2). The commissioners, Sir Arthur Ingram, Robert Johnson, Foxall and Garway, came North in the same month, and remained there five weeks. It was no doubt to this journey that Ingram referred when he alleged (3) that he rode down to the works and made the necessary arrangements for carrying them on. They now appointed Carpenter as paymaster at his former salary of

(1) A.O.3, 1243/3.
(2) A.O.1, 2486/349.
(3) Ante p. 99.

£100, while Willis was continued as his assistant at £133 6s. 8d. (also unchanged); both salaries were paid up to Christmas, 1614 (1). Carpenter took over from Willis on the 28th March, 1613, just one month before the agreement was executed fixing the compensation payable to William Turner and his partners (2). His first care was, as Ingram stated, to contract for the manufacture of alum at a fixed rate. He soon succeeded in letting the houses at Belmont and Newgate Banks as from 1st May to a partnership of four, all of whom were at the time engaged in the works, namely, Maurice Long, John Crispe, John Turner and George Powell. There were two houses at the former and one at the latter; for the three years ending 1st April, 1616, they contracted to manufacture every year in each of these three houses 500 tons of alum at £9 15s. a ton, or 1,500 tons a year in all. They received £100 earnest money, and materials for the improvement and upkeep of the works, amounting with carriage and other incidental expenses to £2,450. These materials consisted of fifteen tons of bar iron (part from Danby at £16 and part from Kent at £14 18s.), over twenty tons of cast iron mostly from Kent at £8 to £6 a ton in the form of supporters and puncheons, fifteen fodders of lead at £14 10s., and, in addition, fifteen boiling pans, five furnaces, four settlers, seventeen steeping pits, six receptories, thirty-four coolers, one mother cistern, one water cistern, and four-hundred-and-eighty deal boards (3).

They paid the King 9s. a chalder for three hundred chalders, three quarters, five bushells and three pecks of coal, and they also received on loan five hundred chalders (which cost the King 5s. a chalder for land carriage from Coatham to the works) on condition that they left an equal quantity in stock at the expiration of their contract.

To defray the cost of these materials and to pay the arrears due to the workmen and other necessary expenses recourse was had to the King's Revenue. Including a sum of £3,000 received from the farmers of the customs, £13,100 was paid out of the issues of the exchequer for the alum works in the North and West. No alum at all was received from the Dorset works. The three houses at Belmont Bank and Newgate Bank instead of producing

(1) A.O.1, 2486/350.
(2) Ante p. 97.
(3) i.e., four long hundreds of six score.

1,500 tons a year only produced 766 tons 1 cwt. up to 31st January, 1614-5, for which the contractors were entitled to receive £7,468 19s. 9d.

Slape Wath being, as we have seen, the earliest of the houses and the most expensive to work, was much more difficult to let. It was managed directly for a further period of 363 days until 25th March, 1614, during which time only 56 tons 5 cwts. of alum were produced. The cost per ton must have been enormous. Carpenter showed in his accounts an expenditure of £1,033 8s. upon various items of manufacture. In addition there were other payments, such as the rent of £300 to the assignees of John Atherton and the other subsidiary rents, the cost of getting and delivering at Coatham 789 chalders of coal, the proportion of Sir John Hedworth's rent of £500 applicable to the same, and the cost of delivering the alum in London.

From 24th March, 1614, these works were let to Dr. Edward Jordan. This unfortunate physician was born at High Halden in the County of Kent in 1569 (1); educated at Oxford, probably at Hart Hall, took his degree of M.D. at Padua about 1591; admitted licentiate of the College of Physicians 7th November, 1595 and fellow 22nd December, 1597. He appears to have been more interested in science than in his own profession, although he claimed that he enjoyed a large practice in London.

On 8th June, 1608, he obtained (2) a patent for twenty-one years for a process of extracting silver from lead ores; when the lease to Turner, Bourchier, Bowdler and Jones finally failed he turned his attention to alum. It is probable that he was one of the associates of the Earl of Southampton, who on the 12th Jan., 1609-10 (3), entered into an arrangement (never actually carried out) with William Turner with the sanction of the then Lord High Treasurer, Lord Salisbury, for the making of alum. But whether this be so or not, there can be no doubt that in 1613 (4) Dr. Jordan made a distinct offer to farm the whole of the alum works and to deliver alum at £8 a ton. He was prepared to offer as security for the performance of his contract bonds to the value of £17,000, guaranteed by Lord

(1) Roll of Royal College of Physicians, i., 113.
(2) Grant Book (1608), p. 35.
(3) Lands, 152/69.
(4) Lands, 166/175.

Southampton, Sir Henry Nevill, Sir Robert Killegrewe and Sir Herbert Croft. Sir William Twysden was another of his backers.

He maintained that the Privy Council had advised the King to accept his offer and that Sir Arthur Ingram put a spoke in his wheel. Ingram denied the allegation, but, as we have seen, other arrangements were made in the majority of the works. Then, on 8th March, 1613-4, he contracted to make alum at Slape Wath, not at £8, but at £9 10s. a ton. He undertook to furnish and complete the house before 25th June, 1614, for which purpose he was allowed a sum of £450. But by the 31st January, 1614-5, only 71 tons of alum were produced. Dr. Jordan had abandoned his practice in London at a fortnight's notice, and had moved his family down to Guisborough. Here he intended to put his theory into practice. Briefly they were the following: The use of chalk instead of urine to neutralise the acidity of the solution; the replacement of coal by peat for the furnaces; raising the specific gravity of the liquor before boiling. His improved assay glass has been mentioned above (1). His estimate of the cost of making a ton of alum was as follows:—

	£	s.	d.
Calcining of mine	1	0	0
Six pits at 2s. 6d.	0	15	0
Liquorman	0	4	0
Wood for calcining	0	3	0
Chalk	0	2	0
House work	0	18	0
Repairs	0	10	0
Fuel (if good coal)	4	4	0
	£7	16	0

He much under-estimated the cost of repairs. His adventure, so far from fulfilling his expectations, resulted in disaster (2).

He had hoped to obtain the services of a workman whom he described as Black Dick from Purbeck. The same nickname is to be found in the Ingram papers for the joint

(1) Ante p. 105.
(2) S.P.D., Jas I., 84/3.

overseer at Slape Wath in 1619, and referred to Richard Southworth or Richard Atwater, both of whom worked in the isle of Purbeck (1).

Failing in this hope he succeeded in engaging from Asholme the workmaster, James Langtoft, who, as previously stated (2), was there employed as workmaster at a weekly salary of 10s. Differences of opinion soon arose between them; he accused Langtoft of committing wilful damage either of his own malice or at the instigation of others, of disobedience to orders and of wasting mine, liquors and "mothers." Langtoft left, whether compulsorily or voluntarily we know not, and was at once engaged in another house, probably Newgate Bank. Indeed he was still an alum worker in 1637 (3). Were the records of the Wapentake Court at Guisborough in existence we might find some allusion to the dispute. Dr. Jordan lamented that there was no warden, as in the "tin business" (4), in whose heart true honour would overbalance profit, and who would decide disputes between contractors and their workmen, instead of leaving them to the Wapentake Court, where some wilful and wrangling fellow, better acquainted with the country and practice of the Courts than others, would only for molestation try his skill and show his stomach.

Besides difficulties with his workmen, the Doctor was unfortunate in his season. The summer of 1614 was, so he tells us, exceptionally dry, and water for steeping the mine scarce. It was followed by an early and hard winter. In York (5) snow fell on 16th January and lasted until 7th March following. The water was frozen, and equally difficult to obtain; a deep covering of snow stopped boring of the rock and getting the shale.

Under these circumstances, Ingram claimed the right to cancel the lease on the ground of failure to make the stipulated quantity of alum. He was then himself negotiating for the lease, of which we shall read in the next chapter. The doctor maintained that Ingram was merely seeking his own advantage. For a Commissioner to negotiate for a lease to himself is a transaction which lends itself to suspicion, but so far as we can see there was no prospect that Dr. Jordan could carry out his undertaking.

(1) Hist. Mss. Comm. Various, Vol. 8.
(2) A.O.3, 1243/3.
(3) E.178 (13, Chas. I.), 5789.
(4) A reference to the Stannaries Court in Cornwall.
(5) Drake Eboracum i., 256.

He retired to Bath, where he ended his days after the publication of his work on natural Baths and Mineral Waters. In this book (3 Ed., p. 57) he thus refers to his unfortunate experiences—" and now I come to alum *(indignum vox ipsa jubet renovare dolorem),* the greatest debtor I have, and I the best benefactor to it, as shall appear when I shall think fit to publish the artifice thereof." If he did think fit so to do, his publication is not to be found in the British Museum, but enough appears in the State Papers and accounts to enable us to reconstruct his story.

He, like John Chaloner, was steeped in the literature of the subject. In the treatise before mentioned, and in his letters (1) preserved amongst the State Papers we get a list of the principal alum mines at home and abroad. He mentions Camforth in Dorset (obviously Canford), Gwyder in Carnarvonshire, the Isle of Wight, and alum springs in Shropshire at Okengate used by Shrewsbury dyers. Abroad he praises the works of the Turks at Capsilar, of the Pope at Tolfa, and of the Emperor in Hungary and Bohemia (Bœmerland).

We will now turn to the Whitby Group. Mulgrave and Sandsend were let as from 1st November, 1613. The direct maintenance therefore of Thomas Carpenter only extended from 28th March to 31st October—say seven months. During that period Mulgrave sent 65 tons of alum to London and Sandsend 61 tons 3 cwts.; in all 126 tons 3 cwts. Omitting, as before, items of expenditure borne by the Commissioners, Carpenter paid out £883 18s. 7d. at the former and £708 15s. 2d. at the latter. Among other items, we note £29 paid to carpenters for making " jewels " for the bearing of liquor troughs over the beck (2).

The constant repairs to the works and the necessary provision of materials for the same were no doubt a temptation to the countryside. At the Quarter Sessions holden at Helmsley on the 8th July, 1613, a man was presented for stealing a piece of iron weighing one stone from the " officina vel forgium Dno (Dni?) Regis apud Mowgrave Angl. vocat' allom mines " (3).

The negotiations for letting the Mulgrave and Sandsend works entailed many journeys, not only to Mulgrave but also to Normanby, Lord Sheffeild's other seat in Lincolnshire. Eventually the lessees (4) were Richard Haslam and George

(1) D.S.P., Jas. I., 84/2, 3.
(2) Cp. N.R. Records, Vol. 3, p. 24, and Dialect Dictionary S.V
(3) N.R. Records, Vol. 2, p. 22.
(4) A.O.3, 1243/3, fol. 36.

Weatherell, the former the Steward at Mulgrave who had previously acted as overseer and governor of the works there, the latter holding an official position at Normanby.. It is by no means improbable that they acted on behalf of Lord Sheffeild, who had always shown a much more intensive interest in the work than either of the other two original patentees. Up to 31st January, 1614-5, 286 tons 18 cwts. were manufactured under this lease, for which the lessees were paid £8 15s. a ton, but from the sum of £2,510 7s. 6d. so due £301 14s. was deducted in respect of 431 chalders of additional coal delivered out of store at 14s.

Meantime the position at Harraton was getting worse. After Carpenter's visit in December, 1612, up to April 8th, 1613, 564 chalders were carried down to Sunderland in five " streams of keels," and from the latter date to 31st January, 1614-5, 4,864 chalders were worked at Harraton (1), but at some intermediate period the mines were drowned out.

An action was tried at Durham Assizes, referred to as " Porter's extent," and ended on 28th July, 1613, which most probably had some bearing on the matter. A week earlier William Wilson had been sent down from London to Durham to act as staithsman at a yearly salary of £66 13s. 4d., and he so acted up to Christmas, 1614. Meantime coal in small quantities was purchased from Coquet Island, Lumley, Tees, Pencher and Westworth Collieries. Then, on 20th October, 1613 (2), the Privy Council directed Sir George Selby, Timothy Draper, Henry Madeson and Martin Haliman to assist Wilson. They were to appoint viewers of the works underground, to satisfy the debts and settle the rates of wages of the keelmen. Sir George Selby was Governor of the Hostman's Company of Newcastle-on-Tyne in 1612 (3), and Draper and Madeson two important members of the same. The Crown paid the rent of £500 for a year-and-a-half after the assignment by Bourchier; then as the coal mines continued drowned no rent was paid for more than eighteen months. Finally arrangements were made under which Bourchier, ever ready to take up any speculation, agreed in consideration of a sum of £2,100 to discharge the arrears, then amounting to £840, to take over the coal mines at Harraton and the Staithes and Staith houses at Wearmouth, together with all necessary utensils and to pay the rent for the next fifteen

(1) A.O.1, 2486/350.
(2) A.P.C., 1613, p. 229.
(3) Surtees Society, Vol. 105 passim.

years. This arrangement soon gave rise to legal proceedings (1). There were some eleven keels used in conveying the coals from Harraton to Wearmouth. When the works were subsequently leased, as we shall learn in the next chapter, to Ingram, Freeman and Lowe, the two latter (Ingram seems not to have joined them) maintained that these keels passed by the lease and remained in their possession until "hollantide, being the Feast of All Saints." Shortly afterwards Bourchier claimed them, and attempted to enforce his right before the Lord President and Council of the North, of which body Ingram was the Secretary. He alleged that soon after the flooding of the mines they lay abandoned as unserviceable until after he made his bargain with the Crown. He obtained an order for their possession and sold four of them to Sir William Lambton. Then in February, 1616-7, Freeman and Lowe filed a bill in the Exchequer Chamber to maintain their rights, alleging that the Lord President and his Council had no jurisdiction in the matter. They obtained an interim injunction (2), and the proceedings were transferred from York to the Exchequer Chamber, where they appear to have died a natural death.

It is now possible to review the situation during the period with which this chapter deals. In all, Robert Johnson, as Commissioner, received from the Exchequer by means of Privy Seal Warrants £13,100, and Arthur Ingram £2,900, making a total of £16,000 (3).

The alum manufactured and in store amounted to 1,635 tons 16 cwts. Almost the whole of this was sent by sea to London, not entirely without risk, as is shown by an entry of 27lbs. of gunpowder at 10d. the lb. delivered to the master of the Phenix, laden with alum to London, for defence against pirates on the coast (4). 1,460 tons 18 cwts. 24 lbs. were treated as sold to William Turner and his partners at £25 a ton, but in reality they only paid £12 a ton and deducted £13, or a total of £18,991, from their original debt of £37,400. 110 tons 12 cwts. 2 qrs. and 14 lbs. were sold to two merchants, John Fermor and Thomas Foxall, whose names have appeared before, part at £25 and the remainder at £24 11s. 8d. Over 6 tons 17 cwts. was lost in seventeen voyages between 18th March,

(1) Exch. B. & A., Durham 238.
(2) Exch. Decrees, Series iv., 2/116.
(3) A.O.1, 2486/349.
(4) A.O.1, 2486/350.

1612-3, and 30th January, 1614-5.   The price paid by
Fermor and Foxall and the balance paid by William Turner
and his partners were expended in the manufacture.
Approximately, each ton cost £22 and was sold for £25,
but inasmuch as the sale price was artificial and the result
of the restriction on import, it would be true to say that the
net gain of £3,000, being the difference between the
reduction of the debt to the merchants and the amount
issued from the Exchequer, was, in fact, paid by dyers and
other customers, who had to pay an exorbitant price for an
inferior article.

CHAPTER IX.

SIR ARTHUR INGRAM AS JOINT LESSEE.

On the 11th July, 1614, the white wand of the Lord High Treasurer was entrusted to the Earl of Suffolk (1). By this time it was clear that the constant drain upon a depleted exchequer could not continue. Including disbursements and liabilities for future payments more than £50,000 were at stake. Calculations showed that the King could make no alum at a less price than £18 a ton, the merchants who formerly worked the mines made none under £20, and, indeed, as we have seen, £22 represented the actual cost to the King for the past few months. Suffolk therefore took counsel with Ingram, who at that time held a farm of the customs of Ireland conjointly with Martin Freeman, George Lowe and Richard Gothorp, and who induced Freeman and Lowe to join with him in taking a lease of the works. Articles of agreement (2) (not enrolled) were executed on the 22nd February, 1614-5, by virtue of a Privy Seal of the same date addressed to Suffolk, and the then Chancellor of the Exchequer, Sir Fulke Greville (later Lord Brooke). The conditions were much less onerous than those contained in the lease to Turner, Bowdler and Jones. The term was to commence on 1st April, 1615, and to last twenty-one years to the expiration of the patent. The lessees were to receive £10,000 to put the work into thorough repair and to provide new workhouses. They agreed to make 1,200 tons the first year, 1,500 tons the second, and 1,800 tons in the third and subsequent years. They were to receive £10 a ton for the making of the alum so made, a thousand tons were intended for home sale at £25 a ton, and the balance for foreign sale at £15. They incurred a penalty of £13 for each ton that fell short of the prescribed quantity for home sale, and of £5 for each ton in like manner deficient for foreign sale.

So far from showing an increase of production under this contract, there was actually a decrease. In the year ended 31st March, 1616, only 674 tons, and in the following year only 575 tons were made. The deficiencies together amounted to 1,451 tons, and the corresponding penalties to £13,263, i.e., more than the contract price payable at £10 a ton for the 1,249 tons actually made.

(1) D.S.P., Jas. I., 111/17.
(2) Recited in P.R. 2112, m. 28. C.R., 2332.

A contract had already been made with certain persons (Christopher Thornton and John Havelock) to build a new workhouse at Selby Hagg, not far from the present site of North Skelton Station (1), for £2,000, and an additional house at Mulgrave for £900. The lessees undertook to adopt this contract, and out of the £10,000 to make the stipulated payments besides other necessary expenditure upon the works. The contracts with Maurice Long, John Crispe, John Turner and George Powell to manufacture alum had still some months to run, and were adopted by the lessees. Dr. Edward Jordan was evicted from Slape Wath at the end of 1615, and John Turner took his place. The profit to the lessees consisted of the difference between £10 a ton and the varying sums paid to the contractors for the manufacture, after defraying the necessary costs of repair and maintenance. So far the arrangements appeared to be in the best interests of the Exchequer under the difficult circumstances, but there were others to which very serious objection could be and was taken.

First of all, there was the position of William Turner and his partners in the original lease. The sum of £30,220 covenanted to be paid to them as composition for the annuity of £6,044 was very considerably in arrear; interest at £10 per cent. was running on, and soon mounted up (2). The alum supplied under the contract helped to extinguish part of the debt for disbursements, but the total amount owing was nearer £40,000 than £30,000, and the chances of its repayment seemed remote. Then, on the 3rd March, 1614-5, Suffolk gave orders for striking tallies upon the farmers of the customs for payment of £30,000 to Turner. Four months later, on 14th July, 1615, Sir Francis Hildesley, whom we have previously seen supplying iron to the works (3), William Turner and John Reeve were appointed agents for sale, overseers and controllers of the alum works for life at a yearly salary of £766 13s. 4d., with an allowance of forty shillings for every ton conveyed to London.

It was not until four years later that the circumstances leading up to these two transactions were thoroughly brought to light. The Countess of Suffolk was accused of having received £1,900 from William Turner as the price of the former, and a sum variously stated as £1,500 and

(1) Shown on Ord's Map of Cleveland.
(2) D.S.P., Jas., 111/17.
(3) p. 101 ante.

£1,000 from Hildesley as the price of the latter. In their essentials the charges were not denied, but Suffolk attempted to prove his ignorance (1). He declared that it was not until June, 1616, that he heard of the gifts being made to his wife by Turner and Hildesley, that he at once caused them to be returned and entered into a new contract of agency. The Court of Star Chamber did not accept this story (2). It found that when the abuses in the alum trade were brought in question before the Commission hereafter described and these matters amongst others were likely to be discovered, the Countess wrote several letters (produced in Court), by which it appeared that she offered Turner a bill to repay him so that he might swear that he gave nothing. Then when the matter was ended she was to give back the bill, and the Earl, as a member of the Commission, was to see that Turner was not put on his oath in any disgraceful manner. After his examination was over, Turner, who had got his money back, sent to her £500, for which her servant, Daniel Bales, gave a bill dated 9th November, 1616, payable the following Christmas. It might be convenient here to follow out this part of the story.

In Easter Term, 1622, Turner sued Bales on the bill in the King's Bench. Bales, giving his address at Audley End in Essex (the Earl's house), then applied for an injunction in chancery staying the action (3). He alleged that William Turner, whom he described as salter, had run himself out of £36,600 in making alum in the King's mines. The Earl, having pity and compassion of Turner's great loss and undoing, the rather for that his endeavours to compass the said works were worthy and for the good of the State and the Realm, though by his improvidence he did " stick in the middest for want of ability " made suit to the King that Turner might be recompensed. The King hearkened to the Earl's solicitations and gave orders that the moneys should be paid out of the Treasury. This was done, and Turner left £500 with some person for the Earl's use. But for as much as the Earl, when he understood thereof, was not fully satisfied whether he might in conscience justify the acceptation of such a reward for his labour and travail in Turner's behalf (for his Lordship was always of himself very generous and of a tender conscience that way), he commanded Bales to give Turner on his behalf

(1) D.S.P., Jas. I., 111/17.
(2) English Historical Review, xiii., p. 720.
(3) C.2, Jas. I., B. 32/10.

this bill of debt for repayment of £500, nevertheless upon these terms, that the Earl would think and consider better of the nature of that gift, and if he might afterwards be persuaded that he had deserved that sum in recompense of his travail and charitable help that he would take the whole or part as he should in conscience think just and righteous.

The bill then went on to allege that Bales executed the bond and someone else delivered it to Turner; that afterwards the Earl, knowing that he had by his just and charitable solicitation and travail saved Turner from utter undoing and raised him to good wealth, resolved to accept the £500 and required Turner to re-deliver the bond to Bales. But instead of complying with this request Turner, being as it seemed endued with a most ungrateful and dishonest mind retained the speciality and put the same in suit.

The bill then argued that the Earl, being Bales's lord and master, did relieve Turner in his distress by his noble and charitable solicitation and travail, and that rewards for the services of that kind were fit to be given and might with honour be taken; for the King (though of extraordinary insight and despatch in his princely affairs) yet being born of man, could not understand the suits and necessities of his people but by the solicitations and means of his great officers who attended him for that purpose. Finally, the bill asked for relief in equity on the grounds that travail, painstaking and attendance deserved recompense in a generous, righteous and due proportion, especially as the Earl had at first out of the tenderness of his conscience refused to accept the sum, and as Bales himself never received a penny of the money.

It is only fair to add, even though we attribute little credence to the denial, that Turner in his answer sworn 3rd July, 1622, denied that he had paid Suffolk any reward or bribe, or that Suffolk in any way assisted him to get payment of the sum received, which he declared was £32,000 only, and paid so slowly as to cause a loss of £10,000 in interest. He maintained that the £500 was a loan merely.

It is not easy to trace what became of the alum manufactured during the two years 1615 and 1616. Commerce could hardly have dispensed with the annual output of six-hundred-and-fifty tons, and it is therefore obvious that it must have been sold in the ordinary way upon the market. Robert Johnson brought in supplemented accounts up to 30th November, 1615 (1), winding up his agency and showing a further delivery on account to William Turner and the other representative members of the Alum Company of over 260 tons, valued at £3,388 13s., in respect of their composition. It is not likely that William Turner, when he associated himself with Francis Hildesley in the agency as from July, 1615, overlooked his own interests, and as the net proceeds of the manufactured alum would balance approximately the amount left owing, it is not an unfair inference that this happened.

So far as the patentees were concerned, Sir Thomas Chaloner died, as we have seen, in November, 1615, and no payment was due to arise until the following 1st April. Some seven years later (2) Sir John Bourchier declared that, in his opinion, eleven or twelve thousand pounds were paid to the patentees, but the greater part of this went to Sheffeild. Both Chaloner and Foulis settled their share in the annuities. So far as part of Chaloner's share was concerned his brother-in-law, Sir William Fleetwood, was by the original agreement of 6th May, 1609, to receive on behalf of Chaloner's children by his first wife £500 on 1st May, 1617, and thereafter £1,000 a year up to 3rd January, 1636-7.

A certificate given in 1637 to James Chaloner, one of the surviving six children of Sir Thomas's first marriage, by the Auditor, Sir Robert Pye (3) proved that all his father's estate had received on this account was the first payment of £500 and £750 for nine months up to 1st February, 1636/7. At this time James had got an assignment of his share from the Trustee to enable him to prosecute his claim. His arrears were said to amount to £3,291 13s. 4d., a calculation that does not quite correspond with the certificate, but is not very far out.

The year 1616 was a very important period in the history of the industry. On the 11th April in language inscribed on the Patent Rolls (4) the King had been given to understand that the alum works, which in appearance should have brought in a large revenue to his coffers, had proved not only fruitless but very chargeable through the many pensions, the defalcations to the farmers of the

(1) A.O.1, 2487/352, 353.
(2) Exch. Deptn. 22, Jas. I., Hil. No. 29.
(3) P.S.O.2, No. 108.
(4) C.66, 2090 m.3, 14 Jas. I., Pt. I.

customs, the charge of reparations, the rewards for the relief of decayed agents therein employed, and other payments issuing out of the Treasury. The charges would include the payment to patentees due to commence on the 1st May, the yearly sum of £700 allowed to the farmers of customs as compensation for loss of duty on imported alum, and the pension of forty marks to Thomas Chaloner of Lambay. A commission was therefore granted to George, Archbishop of Canterbury (1), the Earl of Ellesmere, L.C., the Earl of Suffolk, L.H.T., Edward Earl of Worcester, and others to settle the alum business. They were authorised to call before them the patentees, contractors, agents and dealers, to examine them on oath, to consider the cause of granting payments, the prevention of the importation of foreign alum, the number of houses to be erected, the best means of working and selling the alum, and various other matters. The Attorney General and the two auditors of imprests, Francis Gofton and Richard Sutton, were ordered to assist the commission.

We may assume that the undated set of interrogatories, to which reference has been previously made (2), was drafted in connection with this commission. The answers, if they ever existed, have not come to light, and Mr. Price (3) appears to be quite correct in his deduction that the inquiry dragged on bringing to light a considerable amount of information, but without arriving at any satisfactory solution. There is a reference in an exchequer bill (4) to a certificate of the Commission finding the prevalence of smuggling alum, but no such certificate has yet been discovered in the Public Record Office. Similarly other findings may have vanished. One very valuable document (5) undoubtedly owes its existence to the Commission. Arthur Ingram had been summoned to appear, but was unable through sickness to obey the summons. He therefore sent in a full history of the affair, extracts from which have already appeared in earlier pages. It is endorsed in the handwriting of Sir Julius Caesar, then Master of the Rolls, " Sir Arthur Ingram's declaration of the proceedings of the alum business 1 June, 1616 ": he adds the commentary *nul hombre seguro in este mundo*—no-one is safe in this world—alluding to Ingram's position in the

(1) George Abbot.
(2) Ante p. 83.
(3) English Patents of Monopoly, p. 91.
(4) E.112, London, 1348.
(5) Lands, 152/149.

world of finance, probably a paraphrase of the comment (1) which Sancho Panza made when his master suffered dire indignities at the hands of the Yanguesian carriers through the misbehaviour of Rocinante " no hay cosa segura in este vida." Four days later, 5th June 1616, a pass was issued to enable Sir Arthur to repair to Spa in Germany to make trial of the waters for the recovery of his health (2). Thither he was to be accompanied by Sir John Gibson of Welburn, who was later to be associated with the alum works. It was no doubt one consequence of this commission that the accounts of Richard Willis and Thomas Carpenter as paymasters, and of Robert Johnson, an agent, were audited on the 10th March, 1616-7.

Notwithstanding the pendency of the commission, and the searchlight which it cast upon the transactions, Arthur Ingram succeeded in obtaining a very important modification of the terms of his lease. The penalties for deficiencies in the amount of alum manufactured amounted to a far larger sum than he cared to lose. He had now succeeded in finding some optimists who were anxious to experiment where he had failed, and who were willing to take a sublease upon condition of making the stipulated quantity of alum at the price of £9 per ton. These optimists were Sir John Brooke, and his co-lessees in the original lease, Thomas Russell and George Lowe. The moving spirit in the triumvirate was Thomas Russell. He had an idea that by using little shallow stoving pans, 6 inches deep, the evaporation would be more rapid, and a greater quantity of alum produced in a given time. He was also one of the principal and earliest advocates of the use of kelp in place of urine.

It was therefore necessary to clear off the accumulation of arrears under the old lease and make a fresh start. Later (4) it was charged against Ingram that he had " such extraordinary inwardness and power " with Suffolk that the latter was induced without any warrant from the King to surrender to Ingram the original articles of February, 1614-5, and thus deprive the Attorney General of the power of suing for breach of the conditions. There can be little doubt from an examination of many cases that the pecuniary

(1) Don Quixote, Pt. 1, chapter xv.
(2) A.P.C. (1616), p. 571.
(3) A.O.1, 2486-7/248-352.   P.O., 3381/1-8.
(4) E.112, Jas. I., York, 1760.

relations between Ingram and Suffolk and the debts due by the latter to the former were quite sufficient to raise suspicion. On the other hand, it was distinctly proved that alum manufactured up to the stipulated quantity would have been difficult to sell.

This being the state of affairs the articles were surrendered, and on 7th January, 1616-7, the same alum works in Yorkshire and Dorset were leased to the same tenants from the 5th April following for nineteen years. Lest there should be any mistake this time the deed was enrolled both on the Patent and also on the Close Rolls (1). The lessees were to make 1,800 tons a year, of which 1,000 tons were destined for sale at home and 800 tons abroad. The penalties for short workings were the same as before, namely, £13 for every ton deficient in the quantity for home sale and £5 for every ton deficient in quantity for abroad. But the agents for sale were to weigh the alum at the end of every month at the alum houses, and pay the sum of ten pounds within twenty-eight days thereafter for every ton manufactured and so weighed. In default of such payment the lessees had power to sell the alum to their best advantage, deduct the cost of manufacture, and account for the balance. The schedule to the deed gives an inventory of the furniture of an alum house.

The boiling pans were of lead set in furnaces of brick. To every fifteen pans there were thirty coolers of deal plank, three settlers of lead, three cisterns of stone for " mothers " with a reasonable quantity of " mothers " for three months work, sixteen steeping pits, one great or two small cisterns for urine, three receptories with pumps and troughs, five hundred chalders of coal of land measure according to the measure of the several localities, twenty tons of urine or its equivalent, calcined mine for three months work, one stone cistern for water, pixes, hammers, barrows, etc. There was power to collect sea-weed, sea-wrack, sea-oare or kelpe, to burn it and use the ashes in place of urine should it be thought desirable.

A week later, on the 14th January, 1616-7, another deed (2) was executed, likewise enrolled on both the Patent and Close Rolls, under which Sir Thomas Bludder, Sir Arthur Ingram and Martin Freeman agreed to take 800 tons

(1) C.66, 2112 m 28, 14 Jas. I., Pt. 16   C.54, 2322, No. 4,
        14 Jas. I., Pt. 39.
(2) C.66, 2105, No. 5, 14 Jas. I., Pt. 16. C.54, 2322, Pt. 3
        (14 Jas. I., Pt. 39).

of alum every year for seven years at £24 a ton. The alum was to be weighed at the works and to be conveyed to storehouses in London. The price was to be paid as follows:—£10 a ton was to be paid to the lessees under the preceding deed, £2 retained to liquidate the cost of transport, and the remaining £12 was to be paid at the Receipt of the Exchequer. The agents were authorised to re-sell the alum at 26s. a cwt. Under this arrangement the Crown eventually received £67,200, which assisted in reducing the debit balance standing due upon the works. Martin Freeman died shortly after the deeds were executed.

A selection from the Ingram papers has been printed by the Historical Manuscripts Commissions (1), which throws a good deal of light upon the difficulties of the situation. The three sub-lessees held the works from 2nd April, 1617, to 2nd April, 1619, under their contract to make 1,800 tons of alum every year at £9 a ton. During these two years Lowe maintained (2) that he spent no less a sum than £29,826, of which £18,900 was actually disbursed by his factors, Richard Wynne and William Baynes at the works.

Thomas Russell was not successful in the improvements which he inaugurated. His little shallow stoving pans were a complete failure, and the use of kelp did not at first conduce to a greater production of alum. To make pans of the required size he melted and re-cast the large boiling pans, and so threw a great expense upon Ingram when the sub-lease expired, and the earlier methods of working were restored. By September, 1617, after six months experience, it was quite clear that all was not well. Lowe was at Guisborough, and wrote on 11th September to Ingram. Things were much out of order; houses had fallen down at Belmont Bank; little alum was being made; no more with kelp than before with urine; the previous year a boiling with kelp lees produced a ton; this year not above 4 cwts.

During the remainder of that year Lowe's anxieties increased. By the following January he realised that there was no possibility of making 1,800 tons in the twelve months. He earnestly besought Ingram to spend £5,000 in putting the houses into repair, and replacing the large old-fashioned pans. If this were done it might, he thought, be possible to make 800 tons at Belmont Bank, Newgate Bank and Slape Wath, 100 tons at Selby Hagg, and 300 tons at Mulgrave and Sandsend, or even to increase these

(1) Misc. No. 8.
(2) Exch. Depns., 22 Jas. I., Hil. No. 29, Evidence of Lowe.

figures to 1,400 tons in all. The cost would have to be raised to £9 5s. a ton. Russell's small round pans, he maintained, were useless, they only came off once in the twenty-four hours, and were twice as expensive as the old style.

The condition of the workmen at this time was terrible. A multitude of " poor snakes, tattered and naked, ready to starve for want of food and clothes." Some were unpaid for three months, others for four; they could get no credit for their food and drink. Some were arrested in Lowe's sight for their diet and carried to prison. Every day they laboured for nothing but tickets, which they could only set before their wives and children when asked for food.

As this letter brought no relief, he wrote again three days later. Russell owed £1,500 to workmen, pensioners and others. He tried to get Lowe to advance this sum so that he might continue his experiment of making alum at a price of £6 a ton by means of his small stoving pans. But Lowe absolutely refused to advance another farthing, and eventually it was agreed that Russell should surrender the houses at Guisborough and Skelton to Lowe, and should confine himself to Mulgrave and Sandsend where it would appear that Lord Sheffeild still retained confidence in him.

But then arose the usual dispute on taking over. Russell maintained that Lowe took over mine calcined by Oliver Kearsley to the value of £600, urine to the value of £200, and 40 tons of alum. But whether this were true or not, the workmen took matters into their own hands, Lowe offered pay for the last month, but it was hardly likely that they would be satisfied with that small fraction of their arrears. They would neither work themselves nor suffer others to work. In modern language, they struck. Meantime, Lowe placed John Turner at Newgate Bank, George Powell with Richard Wynne at Belmont Bank, and Oliver Kearsley with Black Dick (Richard Southworth or Richard Atwater) at Slape Wath.

When four years earlier £10,000 had been granted to Arthur Ingram for repairs, one of the terms of the grant had been that he was not to be compelled to give an account of his expenditure. Later accusations were made that a large part of this advance was unexpended. It is unlikely that these accusations were to any great extent true, having regard to the fact that George Lowe and Arthur Ingram were at arms length, but it was common ground between the parties that at this date £2,000 was unexpended, and this was just the sum that would have been most useful at this stage. Russell went so far as to write to the Archbishop of Canterbury's Commission on this very point; he excused this action to Ingram on the ground that he wrote at the instigation of Lowe. Lowe, he declared, had flown at him like a bear robbed of her whelps, though Lowe had only to act the part of a Steward and Eater while Russell himself was the Cook. If Lowe had kept faith with him the alum would neither have failed in quantity nor cost of manufacture. In the end Lowe would find that his great roaring against Russell would be but like a raging billow against a rock dissolving in its own froth.

As a result of these quarrels the under-lease to Brooke, Russell and Lowe was surrendered, and Lowe surrendered at the same time his interest in the principal lease to Ingram, who was now treated as the sole lessee.

During the two years that the sub-lease was in existence, in place of 1,800 tons only an average of 600 tons was made each year (1). What was far worse was the waste and destruction of the fittings in the works. At Belmont Bank, in place of 24 great pans there were only 7; at Slape Wath, in place of 12, only 6; at Newgate Bank, in place of 18, only 3 or 4; at Mulgrave, in place of 20, only 7; and at Sandsend, in place of 13, only 3.

There were, it is true, a certain number of small pans, melted out of the large, but these were of no use except to melt again. Russell had a scheme of raising money by melting the large pans into sows of lead and selling them in France, but Sir William Chaloner, who, after the death of his father Sir Thomas, took a keen interest in the works and saw his share of the annuity as patentee jeopardised, prevailed upon the Lords of the Treasury to stop his action (1).

The reference to the arrears due to pensioners enables us to date a most pathetic letter from Thomas Chaloner (of Lambay) to the Privy Council attributed in the Calendar of State Papers (but without any valid reason) to 1615, a date which is very difficult to reconcile with known facts (2). He describes himself as Thomas Chaloner, gent., and therefore clearly distinguishes himself from his cousin, Sir Thomas Chaloner, though it may be that the cause of the attribution of 1615 as the date was the death of the latter in that year.

(1) Exch. Depns. 22, Jas. I., Hil. No. 28, Evidence of Oliver Kearsley.
(2) S.P.D., Jas. I., 80/41.

The petitioner claimed that by the expense of a great part of his estate and of his younger years in many chargeable trials of sundry minerals (alluding no doubt to his share in his father's experiments in the Isle of Lambay) he had discovered the Yorkshire alum mines, in respect whereof the first undertakers had granted to him and Lord Salisbury had confirmed the pension of forty marks. This had been duly paid up to the preceding mid-summer since which time two quarters had been incurred, and a third at hand, but the then farmers refused to pay it, and so had driven the poor petitioner, being an aged gentleman, of about 72 years old, to travel on foot above 200 miles for relief.

For reasons that will appear later one is inclined to date the petition March, 1618. If so one must admit that the pilgrimage had no immediate result. On the 21st April, 1619, Lord Sheffeild wrote (1) from his house in St. Mark's Lane to Sir Julius Caesar imploring his aid for his chaplain Mr. Leake, who had been (so he said) settled at Lythe, near Mulgrave, at the beginning of the alum business by himself and the other patentees, and had a stipend of 100 marks per annum given to him for the preaching of the Word of God to that people who, in those times, had scarcely the knowledge of God in a saving manner. This stipend was twelve months in arrear, and he had made eight fruitless journeys to London to get payment. He was again there. A similar request was made on behalf of Mr. Ward, described as an honest, painful preacher, who had been settled upon like terms at Guisborough.

Sheffeild had now reached a crisis in his career. On February 14th, 1618-9 (2) Thomas Wynn wrote to Carlton that he had surrendered the Presidency of the North to Emanuel Lord Scrope, and wished to command the combined English and Dutch Fleet against the pirates, but the Dutch would not have an English Admiral. A month later the same correspondent announced that Lord Sheffeild had married a Scotch wench of sixteen, the daughter of Sir William Irwin.

But notwithstanding this change in his position, his influence was still strong enough to secure a favourable reply to the petitioners. On 25th July, 1619, a warrant (3) was granted in favour of Leake and Ward, but with no mention of Thomas Chaloner. But this omission was

(1) B.M. 12496/174.
(2) S.P. Dom., Jas. I.
(3) Warrants, x., 70.

rectified when the Privy Seal was finally issued on the 9th December following (1). This document, after tracing the origin of the three pensions of 100 marks to William Ward, £40 to Richard Leake (disregarding the attempted increase to 100 marks), and £26 13s. 4d. to Thomas Chaloner, gentleman, " who first found out and discovered the alum mines in those parts," mentioned that they had been unpaid for the space of two-years-and-a-quarter ended at Michaelmas then last past, and commanded the farmers and contractors to make the necessary payments in future together with arrears.

From this it is obvious that the last preceding payment had been on 24th June, 1617, and as Thomas Chaloner wrote his letter when two quarters were overdue and a third at hand, he must have written it in March, 1617-8, and not in 1615 as alleged in the Calendar of State Papers.

This date also fits in better with his age. In 1624, in his deposition, he gave his age as 76, an age which agrees with that stated in a letter dated 4th September, 1563, from his Aunt Ellen Saunders to his uncle Sir Thomas Chaloner, where she describes him as of school age. If this is correct he could only have been 70 and not 72 when he wrote to the Privy Council in March, 1618. But if the true date of that letter is 1615 the difficulties of reconciling the ages are considerably increased. It is interesting to note that, like all pensioners, Thomas Chaloner enjoyed a long life. His pension was mentioned as still payable in 1625 (2), and on 6th February, 1633-4, there is to be found a receipt (3) (not improbably the last) by him of the sum of £6 13s. 4d. at the hands of John Turner at Newgate Bank on behalf of the alum farmers due to him at the following Lady Day. The signature, though shaky, is not unlike those in the Irish State Papers (4). He could not have been far short of 86 years old when he signed his name.

(1) P.S.O., 2/42.
(2) P.R.1., Ch. I., pt. 13.
(3) S.P., Ch. I., 260/28.
(4) Ante p. 16.

CHAPTER X.

ARTHUR INGRAM AS SOLE LESSEE.

In later years, when serious charges were brought against him, Arthur Ingram claimed great credit that he took over the works when Russell's schemes failed, and thus exposed himself to a risk which, in the opinion of his friends, would sooner or later bring ruin upon him. It is difficult to see what other option he had. True it was a novel contract, but its construction is clear enough to us and apparently also to the lawyers of that day.

We have first the agreement for a lease for twenty-one years; this had been surrendered and for the moment may be put out of our minds. But it is replaced by a lease for nineteen years from 1st April, 1617, with a clear and definite covenant to produce eighteen hundred tons of alum every year. Martin Freeman was now dead, and George Lowe had lost every penny that he had, or so he said. Whatever rights the Crown might have had against the executors of Martin Freeman and against Lowe, the covenant was most certainly enforceable against Ingram. Nor was it any answer to say that he had contracted with Sir John Brooke, Thomas Russell and George Lowe to make the prescribed quantity and that the failure was theirs. He none the less remained liable on his covenant and his only remedy would have been to sue his sub-contractors for their breach of contract. Influenced, it may be, by these considerations, or more probably by the hope that he would succeed where others had failed, he arranged that Lowe should release his interest and the sub-contractors surrender the works. The King at the same time advanced a further sum of £1,000 to enable him to clear off debts owing by the last mentioned.

His entry into the works coincided with the fall of the Lord Treasurer. The year 1619 was fatal to Suffolk. The accumulated weight of the charges against him overwhelmed him and it is a marvel that so many years should elapse before the thundercloud burst. Reference has already (1) been made to those charges which concerned Francis Hildesley and William Turner. Many others had no relation to the alum business, but one of the most important embraced the contract with Ingram. It was a charge often to be repeated; namely, that he delivered to Sir John Bingley for cancellation the articles of February, 1614-5, and failed to remit for collection to the Remembrancers Office at the Exchequer the debt incurred by the lessees in respect of

(1) Ante p. 120.

deficiencies (1). By way of defence, or it may be extenuation, Suffolk retailed his services. He asserted that when he came to be Lord Treasurer in February, 1614-5, he took into due consideration His Majesty's Revenue in the alum works, and finding disbursements and security given to a joint total of £50,000, and yet that the same were still unproductive, and being informed that no alum was made under £18 a ton, and that the merchants who formerly held the lease made none under £20, he thought it best to demise the alum works at some certain rate. Divers persons, when approached, refused to deal therein. At last Ingram, Freeman and Lowe took them at £10 a ton for twenty-one years. Liberty was reserved to himself and the Chancellor of the Exchequer to increase or diminish the quantity of alum that should be vented. The Articles and Bond were delivered to Sir John Bingley instead of to the King's Remembrancer, because there was some ambiguity in them. For the output of the first year ended February, 1615-6, namely, 674 tons, the King received £8,763, and for the second year, 575 tons 17 cwts., £8,060, which was much more profitable than ever before. He perceived that if a greater quantity of alum was made it would have lain as a dead stock, and to avoid loss and to advance the revenue he treated with Ingram, who entered into a contract on the part of himself, Sir Thomas Bludder and Martin Freeman to take 800 tons each year at £12, so that the King had at least £9,600 a year, and more if more could be vented.

The result of the trial is a matter of history. The judgment of the Star Chamber was given on 13th November, 1619. The Earl was found guilty on all charges, and was fined £30,000. Sir John Bingley, whose association with the Earl was confined to receipt of the articles, £4,000 (2).

At the same time Suffolk was deprived of his office as Treasurer, which after being in commission for some months was conferred on the Lord Chief Justice of the King's Bench, Sir Henry Montagu (created Viscount Mandeville and subsequently Earl of Manchester); the same Mr. Recorder with whom the unidentified R. Lane claimed kinship. Lord Mandeville's known probity precludes any suspicious dealing on his part, but he soon was deprived of office through losing the favour of Buckingham (3), and replaced by Lionel Cranfield on Michaelmas Day, 1621.

(1) D.S.P., Jas. I., 111/17.
(2) Id., 111/18 ; English Hist. Review xiii., 617.
(3) Clarendon History of the Rebellion.

It must have been, therefore, during Lord Mandeville's treasurership that the final lease to Ingram, from 3rd September, 1621, for thirteen years, was negotiated, but his close connection with Cranfield would naturally lead Ingram to expect that the change would thoroughly establish his position.   If he had any such hopes he was doomed to disappointment.   The new Treasurer, whom three years earlier Suffolk had scorned to accept as his Sub-Treasurer, telling the King that he would resolutely resign his staff rather than be matched and yoked with a prentice of London (1), after holding the highest position in the State, after being advanced to the Peerage as Earl of Middlesex, was only destined to enjoy his honours a little longer than two years, and in April, 1624, had to meet charges of bribery which were to result in his disgrace, and rendered any further hope of assistance from him impossible.

As soon as Ingram took possession of the works his first task was to repair the deficiencies caused by Russell's useless schemes.   According to the evidence of one of his workmen, Richard Wynne, he spent £3,200 before the following Michaelmas, but this no doubt included £2,000 still in hand from the grant of £10,000 by the Crown and the later advance of £1,000, leaving only £200 for him to find.   A more steady output resulted.   From 1st April, 1619, to September, 1620, 1,800 tons were made, of which 1,351 tons 12 cwts. were made before 1st April, 1620: in the next four years ended 1st April, 1624, 4,600 tons were made, and from that date to 5th September, 1624, 660 tons. There was, therefore, each year ample to supply the agents (of whom he was one) with the 800 tons contracted to be taken, but the output was far below the stipulated quantity. His excuse was that there was no market for the overplus. It was all that he could do to sell 800 tons at home ; it was impossible except upon very rare occasions to sell any abroad at a profit.

As he was allowed £10 for each ton manufactured, and only paid his contractors £8 10s., he gained thirty shillings (assuming that his overhead charges were not increased by the increase of output), and therefore it was to his interest to make as great a quantity as possible.   But he maintained that the agents for sale did not pay for the manufacture as promptly as the contract provided.   For the first 800 tons he was himself one of these agents, but beyond that figure other agents were employed who could only pay by means of monies released from the sales of alum.

(1) S.P. 14, 89/39.

Sir Francis Hildesley, William Turner and John Reade, as we have seen (1), held the agency until the disclosures which eventually ended in Suffolk's trial rendered it advisable that they should resign the appointment, and the resignation was confirmed by a Deed of Surrender dated 4th June, 1619 (2). What sales had been effected during the four years it is difficult to ascertain. The Deed contained a simple statement that the King had been duly paid by Hildesley, Turner and Reade for all alum, and that the accounts stood even. There was a general release on both sides. On the 14th July following, the right to carry alum from the works to London was granted to Arthur Ingram and George Lowe at a fee of £200 (in place of £766 13s. 4d.) and 40s. a ton. They undertook to pay £10 for the manufacture of any ton of alum lost at sea, purloined or wasted before delivery, the King bearing the loss of its profit-value.

About the same time, in July, 1619 (3), Sheffeild made an offer to take 1,000 tons for sale abroad at £15 a ton (of which he was to pay £10 to the makers). He had succeeded in getting a lump sum down of £500, part of his share as a patentee in the stipulated annuity of £6,000, but apart from this his arrears amounted to £4,500, and he saw little prospect of getting anything more. It is difficult to see how his scheme was to be carried out. As he himself said, no merchant would venture upon it. £10 for the manufacture, £2 carriage to London, £1 for forbearance of money (i.e., interest on outlay) and £5 the price brought the total to £18, considerably more than the alum would fetch in the foreign market. In any case, his offer was not accepted, and in lieu thereof the following plan was adopted:—In December, 1619 (4), Robert Johnson and William Essington were appointed for their joint lives and the life of the survivor agents and overseers with very full powers of sale ,especially abroad) of all alum manufactured in excess of the quantity of 800 tons. They were to pay £10 a ton for the manufacture, and were allowed 40s. a ton for carriage. Their salary was to be fixed by the Lords Commissioners of the Treasury. Though Suffolk had ceased to be Treasurer, Sir Henry Montagu had not yet been appointed. The deed of appointment recited the varied history of the works up to that date; amongst other matters,

(1) Ante p. 119.
(2) C.54, 2418, No. 18 (17 Jas. I., Pt. 25).
(3) Lands, 165/296.
(4) C., 54, 2407.

that the composition of £37,400 to the first farmers had been paid, and certain sums towards the annuities to the patentees whereby it appeared that the works, if well managed, might still be profitable to the King and Commonwealth. It was regretted that notwithstanding several proclamations the importation of foreign alum continued through the remissness and negligence of officers in several parts of the Kingdom, and through the boldness of such merchants and mariners as dared to run into the contempt of the King's commandment. In consequence, English alum, though in goodness and quality sufficient to serve the whole land, could not be uttered or vented but lay unsold (1).

The accounts of Robert Johnson and William Essington were not vouched until 19th July, 1633 (2), though their agency terminated on 29th February, 1627-8. Robert Johnson was dead, and his daughter, Martha Midleton, and her husband, Timothy Midleton, represented his estate. From these accounts we learn that during the years 1620 and 1621 a total amount of 818 tons was sold abroad. There is no trace of any additional amount (beyond the 800 tons) being produced and sold in 1622. Then on 1st April, 1623 (3), an order was issued that for the time being no more alum should be manufactured for exportation to the Low Countries or other foreign parts on the ground that there was no sale for it. The contract for the sale of 800 tons expired on 1st April, 1624, but before that date the condition of the works was such as to give rise to considerable criticism. The men had never been paid with any regularity; the most that they could hope was to receive some corn or beef, the price for which at a rate much above that obtaining in the local market was ultimately deducted from their pay.

Both centres, Guisborough and Whitby, sinned equally in this respect; Guisborough under John Turner (of Kirkleatham) and Whitby under William Tappsfield (a kinsman of Arthur Ingram) and Richard Haslam, the steward of Lord Sheffeild, but it was from the latter quarter that the first protests emanated.

Some six weeks before Whitsuntide, 1622, three of the workmen at Sandsend, exasperated at their treatment, warned Tappsfield, when he told them that they should

(1) C.R.54, 2407, No. 10, 17 Jas. I., pt. 14.
(2) A.O.1, 2487/354.
(3) Conway's Letter Book, p. 44.

starve before he gave them money or provisions, that they would complain to the King and the Council. " Complain to the King and to the Devil if you wish," was his reply. Thereupon the workmen (including Lambert Russell, the so-called Dutchman) went to London and presented their petition which, as one of them said, he left with some gentleman to be delivered to the King and Council, and he *thought* that it had been delivered. No such petition is calendared in the State Papers or indexed in the minutes of the Privy Council. Some of the party returned on the Thursday in Whitsun week. There was a pay-day shortly afterwards. Tappsfield, seeing the workman whom he took to be the ringleader in the payhouse, as the pay was being distributed, asked him if he had brought a whip or a scourge for him ; he replied, " Neither " ; had he brought a letter, " he had not." Tappsfield then said that as he had gone to London for his own pleasure he should now go for Tappsfield's, and proceeded to distribute the pay due to him amongst Tappsfield, Haslam and other creditors for debts alleged to be due, but would give no reckoning.

But if there is no record preserved of the visit of these alum workers to London, several letters are to be found from Sir John Bourchier leading up to the grand climax.

Towards the end of 1623 Bourchier made another attempt to get the alum works into his hands, and to combine in one patent the manufacture of alum and soap. To further this project, he wrote a string of letters, some dated and some undated, but all evidently belonging to this period (1). For the most part he confined himself to accusations which had been made on several previous occasions.

The works were worse fitted and furnished than when they first came into the King's hands, notwithstanding the advance of £10,000 wherewith to repair them. Instead of 1,000 tons for home sale only 800 tons were made, through which reduction the King lost £2,600.

Ingram had refused offers of sub-contractors to make alum at £8 10s., therefore he must make it at a cheaper rate, and the £10 a ton which he receives is exorbitant. He must at least save £2,700 on 1,800 tons. His carriage, for which he gets 40s. a ton, only costs 20s., therefore, on the 800 tons carried he makes £800.

(1) D.S.P., Jas. I., 161/70, 71 ; 155/25.

Instead of selling the alum at £24 a ton he usually realised £26, from which he derived £1,600. Later, on 12th July, 1624 (1), Bourchier returned to the charge. He seems to have discovered a deed (not apparently enrolled) of the 14th February, 1621-2, by which the works were on the surrender of an earlier grant leased to Ingram for 13 years from the preceding 1st September with the intention of releasing him from all consequences of the breach of former covenants. Even if this was its effect, Bourchier maintained that penalties were still due under the later deed—namely, for failure to make the additional 200 tons for three years at £13, i.e., £7,800, and 800 tons for export at £5 until 1st April, 1623 (when the order to cease making alum for export was given), i.e., £6,000, or £13,800 in all. If the larger claim could be sustained, Ingram had gained £50,500 unlawfully, and, in addition, was liable to pay £65,950 for alum unmade, for carriage and for money advanced. The letter next asked for an investigation into the truth of the report that the poor workmen in the country, whose wages were brought down so low that they could hardly live, often had to wait seven or eight months, and then commonly were paid in ill corn and bad meat at excessive rates, whereby divers were said to have been starved to death. A result which reflected no honour upon the King and prevented God's blessing.

To these charges Ingram replied in the August or September following (2). He was originally only one of three partners, Martin Freeman and George Lowe being the other two, and therefore he could only be liable for one-third. When the works were desperate, Martin Freeman being dead and George Lowe refusing to meddle any more, he, at the hazard of his estate, undertook them alone, and brought them to such a good pass that the quantity required could then be made at such reasonable rates as to leave him a yearly profit of £3,000. The value of this for the remainder of the term was near £20,000. At the present time his accounts would show that he was £6,000 out of pocket. He was the only loser through the failure to make the stipulated quantity of alum which, if made, could not be sold. When his term of seven years for the sale of alum in the Kingdom was over there were 1,200 and more tons unsold, for which he had paid the King over £14,000, and yet some question was made as to whether he could have liberty to sell the same. No reply was made to the charges of ill-treatment towards the workmen.

(1) D.S.P., Jas. I., 169/54.
(2) D.S.P., Jas. I., 172/13.

Sir John Bourchier for his part did not make much progress in his application to combine the soap and alum patents. Conway (Secretary of State) described in August, 1623, the soap business as likely to prove the same as other projects, namely, glorious in show, difficult to effect, and of little profit in the end. The State Papers contain later references to offers from Bourchier to pay £2,000 a year to Conway out of the soap and alum combination, which may have induced him to look with more favourable eyes upon the project, but which was insufficient to carry the matter to its desired end.

Meantime, as will be seen in the next chapter, the Attorney General had felt compelled to intervene, and evidence was being prepared, the cumulative effect of which was to cast lasting discredit on Sir Arthur Ingram.

CHAPTER XI.

A COMMISSION OF INQUIRY.

In Michaelmas Term, 1623, the Attorney General, Sir Thomas Coventry, filed a Bill in the Court of Exchequer (1) and set out in full the transactions which have been related in the earlier chapters. In particular he relied upon the articles for a lease for 21 years from 1st April, 1615, and the payment of £10,000 for repairs, which brought the total cost to the King to £60,000. The deficiencies under the articles were stated to be 526 tons the first and 925 tons the second year, which at the appropriate penalties (751 tons at £13 and 700 tons at £5) amounted to £13,263. But Ingram, desiring to be disburthened thereof and having, so the bill alleged, extraordinary inwardness and power with the Earl of Suffolk, procured the latter to give a warrant for delivery up of the said articles and thus the Attorney General, through failure to produce the articles, was unable to sue at law for the debt of £13,263. This, as we have seen, had been one of the charges against Suffolk (2).

Further penalties were claimed under the substituted lease of 7th January, 1616-7, amounting to £6,600 a year upon the footing that in place of 1,800 tons no more than 800 tons a year were produced, showing a deficiency of 200 tons for home vent, and of 800 tons for foreign vent.

The lessees were also charged with having made a great quantity of alum badly roached and unmerchantable, which was transported abroad and brought great discredit upon the trade. The information made no charge against Ingram in respect of his neglect to pay his workmen or of their having been forced to take corn in lieu of money at prices considerably above those obtaining in the market.

Judging from the correspondence (2), Ingram was not very anxious that a legal decision should be reached, and made several offers of surrender with a view to stay the proceedings, but at first these offers were not accepted.

Eventually it was he who made the first move in the litigation. On Tuesday, 30th November, 1624, his Counsel, Sergt. Thomas Crewe, moved apparently *ex-parte* for a commission to examine witnesses in Hamburg, Amsterdam and Rouen (3). The motion was adjourned for the

(1) E.112, York, 1760.
(2) D.S.P., Jas. I., 172/10.
(3) Exch. Decrees and Orders. Series ii., Vol. 37, pp. 104, 108.

attendance of the Attorney General, and the same day a consent order was made for five commissions, namely, in London, Yorkshire, Rouen, Middleburg and Amsterdam. Other commissions were also to be taken out to examine the Earl of Suffolk, Lord Wotton, and such witnesses as could not fitly travel.

Before any commission sat under this order, Sir David Foulis and Sir Thomas Postumus Hoby took an Inquisition at Stokesley on 7th January, 1624-5 (1). The Jury, composed of well-known and substantial freeholders, such as Thomas Pilley (of Commondale), Henry Marwood, Thomas Layton and others, found that Sir Arthur Ingram was possessed of the seven workhouses of which we have so often heard, described as in the Parishes of Skelton, Guisborough, and Lythe, for the residue of a term commencing on 2nd September, 1621, and terminating on the 2nd April, 1635, worth £100 a year. They valued the lease at £530 a year and added that the commissioners had seized the same into the hands of the King.

The London and Yorkshire commissions were duly taken a week later, and are to be found in the Record Office (2). The commission to examine witnesses in Rouen was addressed to Humphrey Hall, Thos. Cockeram, Richard Lymbray and John Tottell, Merchants, but it was returned unexecuted with an endorsement dated 3rd March, 1625, *stilo novo,* and signed by all four commissioners to the effect that they were informed by Counsel learned in the laws of France that they could not administer an oath in Rouen without incurring *crimen læsæ majestatis* (3). The costs of this abortive commission came to £43.

It may be that the commission to the Low Countries was dropped on like grounds, though instances can be found of commissions executed in those countries. We learn from the accounts (4) of the agents that a commissioner of the name of William Allen was sent in 1625 to examine witnesses in Flushing, Middleburg and Amsterdam, and that his charges came to £60, but there are no other references to the matter. Nor does it appear that the evidences of Lords Suffolk and Wotton were ever taken on commission.

(1) E.178, 7119.
(2) Exch. Depns., Hil. 22, Jas I., Nos. 28 and 29.
(3) Exch. Depns. 22, Jas. I., Easter, No. 12.
(4) A.O.1, 2487/354.

The commissions in London and Yorkshire were executed simultaneously. That in Yorkshire was held at Guisborough on 13th January, 1624-5 (1). Apparently the custom was for either party to nominate two commissioners; those representing the Attorney General were the *custos rotulorum*, Sir Thomas Postumus Hoby (of Hackness), who had already assisted in taking the inquisition at Stokesley, and John Legard; those representing Ingram were his subcontractor, Maurice Long, and Thomas Pilley, of Commondale, who had served on the Jury at Stokesley the preceding week. The London Commissioners, who sat at the Grocers' Hall on the 14th January, 1624-5 (2), and following days, were Sir Richard Sutton, Sir John Gibson, Christopher Wandesford and Abraham Jacob. As the King was charged in the Agent's accounts (3) with £9 12s. 6d., being one half the diet and other provisions provided for the Commissioners at Grocers' Hall by William Bowyer, Vintner, it is probable that the costs of the commission were equally shared between the two parties.

The interrogatories in the two commissions were not identical. Those in Yorkshire related to the quantity and condition of the alum manufactured, the number of workmen employed, the state of repair of the houses and utensils, and the payment of the workmen.

Those at London went into the early history of the business, and were framed to show the great losses which the King had sustained through following the advice of Ingram.

The workmen were fully examined. A few of them claimed to have worked since the opening of the mines, indeed, the names of several witnesses are found in Richard Willis's detailed account as employed in 1612 (4).

So far as related to the conditions of the alum the principal charge was that instead of cutting off five or six inches of the foul and drossy alum at the bottom of the roaching casks for a second boiling and washing the remainder before putting it in the storehouse, in some cases the whole contents of the casks were taken straight into the storehouse without washing. Needless to say, the workmen differed as to the effect—one considered that

(1) ut Supra, No. 28.
(2) ut Supra, No. 29.
(3) A.O.1, 2487/354.
(4) A.O.3, 1243/3.

washed alum was more " eyely (1) than the other but little better for profit." Although, as one would naturally expect, the evidence of the workmen dealing with seven houses many miles apart varied to a wide extent, the charge that no foul or drossy alum was cut off the bottom of the casks failed to be proved. Thomas Chaloner, the original discoverer, stated (2) that he had often gone into the houses to see the alum manufactured but limited himself to the opinion that the workmen did not cut off so much of the drossy bottoms as the " Dutchmen " used to cut. Lambert Russell again, one of the sole survivors of the German alum workers, is another witness on whom we can rely. He complains that there was not so much washing of alum as there used to be, and that there were nitre and copperas mixed with the alum, which would have been dissolved had the proper washings taken place, but his evidence also does not go far enough.

As Sir John Bourchier, a disappointed candidate, was the instigator of the charges, it is only natural that they were exaggerated, but there can be no doubt that much alum was sold, especially abroad, in so foul a condition as to reflect little credit upon the industry. So far as home sales were concerned, most of the dyers who were called declared that the alum was as good as it ever had been. Mr. Bell, tanner, of Thirsk, and Mr. Becke, of York, were reported to have been quite satisfied with it.

The accounts show that fourteen tons of foul alum were returned from Amsterdam to London and refined in the Strand during thirteen weeks in January, February and March, 1622-3 at a cost of £59 14s., producing 10 tons 10 cwts. 1 qr. 24 lbs. of good alum. To explain the dirty condition of quantities of the alum the majority of the witnesses blamed the carriage from the works to the sea and to London. A great part was carried in open waggons, exposed to the rain and liable to be splashed as the horses tramped through the mire. Other part was carried in the sacks which had conveyed the coals to the works. Whilst the alum lay upon the floor of the storehouse workmen with muddy boots tramped upon it, and it suffered the same fate when laid on board the ship which was to take it to London.

But there was yet another cause from which it suffered. The two qualities of alum known in the trade were distinguished as white and red alum. The white came

(1) Dialect Dict. gives " eyable " in this sense.
(2) This is where his age of 76 appears.

from Liege (Luk) and England, and the red from Italy. As Luk alum oversold English alum it was thought good to " Romish " it, i.e., to dye it to make it appear like Roman alum. The custom was referred to in a letter which Richard Wynne wrote from Guisborough to his employer Ingram at Westminster (1). For " redding " alum, he said, the houses there were so out of case by long standing idle that they had much ado to fit them in the old course, and he suggested that it would be much better to make all coloured alum at Mulgrave.

The ingredient used was cochineal. There is no reference to any such purchase until we get to the accounts of Robert Johnson and William Essington extending from the 12th December, 1619, to the last day of February, 1627-8, unfortunately without any more precise date. There is 2s. 6d. charged for " red colour " to colour alum, and also the freight from Dieppe to London of 340 lbs. of cochineal (£2 13s. 8d.) and of a barrel of the same from Dieppe to Dover 13s. 8d., and from Dover to London 15s. 8d.

The material itself appears to have been taken in exchange for alum. The evidence tended to show that at least for the previous five years John Crispe practised this method of colouring the alum at Cargo Fleet (Cawkers Nab). The alum had to be broken into small pieces, and it was suggested that it was the siftings of this small coloured alum that mixed with the uncoloured and caused the latter to appear dirty.

A far more serious charge against Ingram's administration of the works was the treatment by his agents of the workmen employed. Instances of every form of mal-practice were given in evidence; such as those methods of extortion which later led to the passing of the Truck Acts; irregular payment of wages; unjust refusals to pay the wages fixed by previous agreement; compelling the workmen to take bad corn at excessive rates, and the like.

The irregular payment of wages was almost a necessity. In the absence of a local bank, prepared to allow a substantial overdraft and ready to honour any cheque up to that amount, the provision of cash was not an easy matter. Arthur Ingram, as a farmer of taxes, was one of the capitalists of the day: he held in his hands or in those

(1) Ingram's papers, Hist. M.S.S., Comm. Various, Vol. 8, p. 24.

of his collectors the taxes which were collected and was in no immediate hurry to pay them into the Treasury. But even with this advantage it was not so easy to get money down to a distant place like Guisborough. Escorts had to be provided, it was not safe to travel alone and unarmed, silver had to be exchanged into gold for convenience of carriage and then back into silver for convenience of payment. Journeys were made to the principal fairs and other places, Beverley, Hull, Bawtry and Scarborough, where bills of exchange drawn upon the farmers of customs could be discounted. The agents for sale of 800 tons, Bludder and Ingram, were to pay at the end of each month £10 for every ton manufactured during such month, but it was quite clear that this obligation was never faithfully observed. An instance of the difficulty of obtaining working capital occurs in the accounts of Johnson and Essington. The agents were arrested at the suit of Peter Balles, a servant of the Earl of Suffolk, and therefore possibly a relation of Daniel Bales (1), previously described. They were so utterly bereft of their credit that they could not borrow even £100 upon their bonds. They had more alum upon their hands than could be sold abroad, and yet under their appointment had to pay for the manufacture of more. They therefore purchased upon credit a parcel of indigo from the East India Company for £3,000. But when they attempted to turn it into cash they lost £300 by the transaction and for this amount they claimed credit (2).

The pays took place at very irregular intervals of some eight or nine months, not on the same day in all the works. As it was quite impossible for the men to subsist on hope only, the system of imprests sprang up, a system which gave rise to many abuses.

Charges of extortion in connection therewith concerned John Turner of Kirkleatham at the Guisborough and Skelton Mines, William Tapsfield and Richard Haslam at Mulgrave and Sandsend. All three gave voluminous evidence at the inquiry, but no opportunity was given to any one of them to deny the serious charges. The workmen went between the dates of pay to one or other of these and asked for an advance of part of their wages. In many cases they met with a refusal, but the majority were offered corn, beef, mutton or other produce of inferior quality, measured by unfair measures, and at extortionate prices.

(1) It is hardly necessary to state that the difference in spelling the name is of no consequence.

(2) A.O.1, 2487/354

144

A few workmen expressed themselves as quite satisfied with their bargains, but most were exceedingly dissatisfied. The following gave evidence of their dissatisfaction:—

Ralphe Rochite *alias* Launde of Kirkleatham, who carried coals from Coatham to the mines, was, in the year 1622, sued for his rent. He went to John Turner and Richard Wynne (1) and asked for some of his behind-pay— 20 marks in all (£13 6s. 8d.). He could get no money, but was forced to take 16 bushels of rye at 6s. and could only re-sell to raise the rent at 5s. 8d., 5s. 6d. and 5s. 4d. a bushel. The following year he had to take 16 bushels of peas at 6s.: part he used himself, but some three or four bushels he sold in Guisborough market for fourteen groats and two pence (4s. 10d.) a bushel. At Michaelmas, 1623, he had three bushels of white wheat at 6s. 8d., and the same of red at 6s.: most he used, but he sold a bushel of white at 5s. 2d. and a bushel of red at 4s. 8d. At Midsummer, 1624, he had to take 20 bushels of red wheat at 6s., some of which he sold within two days in Redcar at 4s. 10d.

The last pea-seed time (i.e., 1624) he had seven bushels of the " hinder-ends " of peas at 3s. 8d. He used them himself because they were " grown " and he could have got little for them. Once, when he had earned ten shillings by carrying kelp to the alum works, and asked the kelp man for it, the latter told him that John Turner had detained the money. He met Turner on horseback and told him that it was hard that a poor man should labour and not get one penny of money a whole summer to supply his need withal, and should have nothing but hard pennyworths. Whereupon Turner rode away, having first called him a rogue, and declared that he and his wife and children should starve before they should get one penny or pennyworth from him.

If the workmen bought their corn elsewhere they were made to suffer. Marmaduke Holden, who had been working at Newgate Bank when William Turner and his partners were in occupation of the mines, bought some corn of Maurice Long, his former master. For this he was, as he calls it, snubbed by Mrs. John Turner, the daughter of Robert Coulthirst, a man of property in the neighbourhood. This same Holden alleged that he owed but tenpence to Francis Barley, who kept an ale-house in Guisborough, and bought his malt from Turner. Barley gave Holden's

(1) These were brothers-in-law. Each married a daughter of Robert Coulthirst of Upleatham.

reckoning to be ten groats (3s. 4d.), Turner supplied sufficient malt to that amount to Barley and stopped it off Holden's wages. When Holden would have taken proceedings in the Lords' Court at Guisborough, Turner threatened that if he sued Barley he would be turned out of the works. Thereupon he did surcease his suit and durst never since seek for remedy.

Robert Massam, a skinner in Guisborough, knew that Turner bought barley in Malton market after May-day when the best barley was selling at 2s. a bushel; he himself that summer bought barley at Malton at 14s. the quarter. Turner retailed it to two workmen at 14d. the peck Guisborough measure, which was five Malton pecks to the bushel (1). The carriage of every four bushels of barley from Malton to Guisborough usually cost 2s. Massam himself retailed his barley in Guisborough at 9d. and 10d. the peck.

Ralph Clarke of Danby had earned money carrying urine but could not get paid. Turner offered him corn and gave him fourteen bushels of malt, Guisborough measure hard and sharp at five shillings each. Clarke owed George Fairweather for a mare which he had bought and gave him four bushels of the same malt at four shillings, and Fairweather re-sold at eleven groats (3s. 8d.). At Christmas last he had three bushels of beans of Turner at 3s. each, but he could have bought as good for eight groats (2s. 8d.) At the same time he had of him two bushels of red wheat at 4s., of which he made no complaint, but last summer he had to take one bushel of barley at 4s. to re-sell in Guisborough market for ten groats. He never had corn of him, but he could have bought the like corn cheaper in the market. Before Michaelmas last he was constrained to deliver his corn on the ground some shorne (2) and some unshorne to creditors for payment of his debts.

In the winter of 1623, when he and his family were ready to famish from want of pay, he bargained with Turner for four bushels of oats at 2s. 6d. He carried his sacks to Turner's house and left them there to be filled. Owing to a heavy fall of snow he could not come for a fortnight, and then found the oats were sold to someone else. Nevertheless, when pay day came, Turner stopped ten shillings of his pay, and though he promised to look into the matter Clarke could get no recompense.

(1) Apparently a Guisborough peck=1¼ Malton pecks.
(2) i.e., reaped, cp. Burns "Robin shur in hairst."

Richard Shawter, a urine man of Guisborough, only the previous April was forced to take a quarter of malt off Turner at 5s. a bushel. He sold six bushels to enable him to buy other provisions, and could only get 3s. 4d., the price that he had seen paid for a similar sample in Guisborough market. Afterwards he was forced to take ten pecks of peas off Turner, measured by Turner's own measure, at 4s. a bushel. As they were white and mouldy he could only get 3s. for one bushel and eight groats for another. He sold the bushel for 3s. to a man to whom he owed money for his shoes. After measuring out the bushels by the market bushel, there only remained one-and-a-half pecks instead of two. He once got a mett (1) of oats and a bushel of peas from Maurice Long in lieu of wages at market prices. When later he went to Turner for wheat and other corn the latter in anger told him to get his corn where he had got it before for good pennyworths, and declared that he should starve before he got corn of him. Owing to non-payment of wages, his house, which had cost him £25, was all but forfeited for £12 10s. (probably borrowed on mortgage). George Powell, one of the sub-contractors, allowed him half-a-ton of alum on credit which saved the situation.

He had a long haggle about the price of carriage of urine; as he declined to carry it for less than 10s. a ton Turner agreed, and Shawter saw the price entered in the Clerk's Book. But Turner, when he heard that he had complained of the mouldy peas, refused on that account to pay more than 9s. Once when he had earned 4s. for a week's work baring the rock, in company with one Dakins Storke, a great resorter to the ale-house, Turner refused to pay the amount due on the ground that Storke had drunk it.

Francis Porritt, of Guisborough, a pitman at Newgate Bank, likewise had corn of Turner at rates dearer by sixteen pence, twelve pence and eight pence in the bushel than the market rates. On the average he earned £8 in each of the last four years, but the most in any one year that he received in cash was 40s. He was forced to take the rest in hard pennyworths of corn or cheese. He often asked Turner for a ticket showing the amount of wages due to him upon which he could have got victuals, but Turner always refused, asking him if he meant to beggar him, by which words he implied that he should take no victuals upon trust of other than himself. Porrit did not dare to press for a ticket lest he should be discharged, and was therefore forced

(1) Two bushels.

to sell the clothes wherein he and his wife did lie, the clothes off their backs and their pewter dishes at under-values. Henry Buck, another pitman at Newgate Bank, had a like tale. Besides corn at these dear rates he was forced to take cheeses at 20d., 19d. and 14d., to the amount of £1 2s. 2d. When he offered a fourteen penny cheese for eight pennyworth of bread he failed to get it, and yet these fourteen penny cheese were the best pennyworths of all.

Matthew Ward deposed on both sides. Although a tanner by trade he carried coals from Cargo Fleet to Guisborough, and, in addition, kept an ale-house where six of the workmen boarded. As they could get no pay he could get no lodging money. Therefore, during the eighteen months previous to mid-summer, 1624, between one pay-day and the next he had to buy from Turner 40 quarters of malt at 5s. the bushel, when he could have bought like malt at 4s. for ready money in the open market. Obviously, what happened was that he got the malt and paid nothing. The workmen made over to him so much of their pay in satisfaction for their board, and Turner treated them as paid to that extent, but whether he or the workmen bore the loss his evidence does not disclose. Luke Fox, the well-known ship's captain (1), who was constantly employed in carrying alum to London, and other materials back, told of two ships which carried alum to Amsterdam and brought back to Tappsfield at Whitby, one ship ten and the other twenty-two lasts (2) of white rye. Part was sent to Turner by way of the Tees, and part stored at Whitby. Nearly all the rye was sold to workmen at 6s. the bushel, land measure, which was half-a-peck less in the bushel than water measure, and by these means Tappsfield gained £60. Luke Fox himself adventured six lasts of white rye in one of the ships, and by selling at 6s. the bushel water measure made twelve pence a bushel after paying freight, customs and all other charges. Ralph Church, the searcher at the Custom House, Stockton, tells a similar tale, which may refer to the same transaction or to another. An Englishman named Thomas Jesopp, living at Amsterdam, brought into the Tees a ship laden with white rye, and stored 70 quarters in a granary at Cawker's Nab, when the country was in great need. Some small quantity was sold at 5s. the bushel, Stockton measure, but John Turner bought up the remainder and carried it from Cawker's Nab to his own house at

(1) See D.N.B., 20/21.
(2) Last=ten-quarters.

Kirkleatham, whence he was reported by credible persons to have retailed the same to workmen and labourers at 16 groats (5s. 4d.) the bushel by a measure defective to the extent of a quarter-of-a-peck.

We shall also read later of another version of the same or a similar transaction (1).

The consequences of this irregular pay were too obvious to need statement. One of the workmen, William Grayson, from want of pay and maintenance grew so weak and feeble that he was discharged from the works and forced to beg in the country. Another workman declared that sometimes for two days, sometimes for three days they were without bread in the house, and his children were fain to follow the plough and gather roots for their sustenance. Less corn was brought into the market, as John Turner sold all that he had to the labourers at the alum works and to the alehouse keepers at Guisborough in return for deductions from the arrears of wages due to the workmen.

Cuthbert Corney, a member of an old Guisborough family, describing himself as gentleman, acted as paymaster to the workmen during 1617 and 1618 at the entreaty of Thomas Russell. He disbursed £65 15s. 7d. to poor workmen in great want out of his own money, but Ingram refused to repay the same or to pay him his salary as paymaster, amounting to £40. He often heard the poor workmen complain that they could not get their wages from John Turner and were forced to take dear corn in bad condition and with short measure: Corn which they took for 5s. they had to sell for 3s. 4d.

Thomas Dickinson, then bailiff of the Wapentake Court at Guisborough, told how he had to take in execution the goods of a urine carrier called William Sowerby to satisfy a judgment due to John Horsley, amounting with costs to 23s. 4d. Sowerby went to Turner and asked for part of his wages then due, but he could only get a quarter of malt, which he had to take as worth 40s. He sold one bushel and brought the remaining seven to Dickinson. Turner refused to buy them back at 3s. 4d. (which could have cleared the debt), but eventually Horsley took them over at 3s. 5d. About the same time Dickinson's wife bought like malt at 2s. 8d. the bushel.

Conditions at Asholm and Sandsend were as bad. James Pouse, a rockman at Sandsend, often asked William Tappsfield and Richard Haslam for money for imprests

(1) post p. 156.

between pay day. Sometimes he and other workmen got money, at other times they were enforced to take corn at rates dearer than those in the market by tenpence and twelvepence in the bushel. Sometimes they had to take beef at dearer rates than if they bought it with ready money in the market. Seldom or never could they know the prices until the pay day; they were glad to take the same at any rate to relieve their necessities. Sometimes they were forced to sell the same corn which they took for 6s. a bushel for fourteen groats (4s. 8d.) in Whitby market soon after it had been received.

Roger Alleley, another rockman, had a like experience. Corn which cost him five shillings a bushel he sold at a shilling a peck immediately afterwards. He and other poor workmen at Mulgrave had to take beef at dearer rates than those obtaining in the market. During 1624 he sent his wife to Richard Haslam to ask for either wages or half-a-bushel of corn. She got neither, and was told by Haslam that if her husband would bring a ticket from the clerk of the works he would be paid what was due to him and be discharged. Three days later he was discharged, but no wages paid to him; after a week's unemployment he was re-engaged through the good offices of the Clerk, George Appleby.

Before Tappsfield's management, the workmen could get provisions on credit at reasonable rates, but since they were hardly trusted at all. Francis Greg, another workman, who lived at Goldsborough, deposed that during the preceding five years, between one pay-day and another, he had constantly taken corn from Tappsfield and Haslam dearer by tenpence in every bushel than the market rate. He formerly owned five cows and had to sell four from want of pay to relieve his necessities.

In the spring of 1624 he bought a cow on trust for four marks to supply himself, his wife and three children. If his wages had been paid in cash and not in dear penny-worths he could have bought as good a cow for seven nobles.

Mention has previously been made of the circumstances under which some weeks before Whitsuntide, 1622, certain of the workmen went to London with a petition of complaint. Lambert Russell, who accompanied them, gave evidence thereon and also on the question of hard bargains. He bought a bushel of rye and two bushels of oats, each at 2s. 6d. a bushel, from Richard Haslam when the market price for either was five groats (1s. 8d.). Many poor workmen were beggared and forced to sell their beds and their kyne to maintain themselves, because they could not get the pay due to them.

When Ingram first took over alone the manufacture of alum he bargained with Lambert Russell to pay him fifteen shillings a pit (1) for calcined mine, and gave him twenty shillings as a God's penny to bind the bargain. It was agreed that Russell might choose such partners as he pleased. Afterwards Ingram turned over the making of alum to Tappsfield and his partners.

When more than half the bargain had been performed, Russell asked Tappsfield to advance him £5 as part of his gains over and above his wages. Tappsfield refused, but offered to buy all Russell's share of the clear gains for £13, threatening him that if he declined to take it he should have nothing, but should lose his favour. Russell's share was two-sixth parts of half the clear gains, which half he estimated at £150, making his share £50, but he was forced to sell it for £13 and give an acquittance for the rest.

Two of his partners, the above-mentioned Leonard Greg and Christopher Thomson, completed the bargain but could get no clear gains beyond their wages.

When he went up to London in 1622 with Leonard Greg to exhibit the petition for the arrears of his wages, which then amounted to £3 7s., his wife was brought to bed, and sent her son George to Tappsfield desiring him to let her have part of these arrears. He refused unless Russell would seal a " general acquittance for ever coming any more on his back." Russell did not himself return from London until St. Stephen's Day, 1622, and he was kept out of the works until 24th March, 1622-3.

He had an old debt owing by Thomas Russell to him and his two partners of £600 for deliveries of calcined mine and liquor. Ingram agreed to pay £400 in settlement of this, but still owed £34 of it. Francis Duck, of Hutton Mulgrave, was one of these partners, and he also complained in similar language of the promise and failure to pay the balance of £34. That the liquor had to be of the strength of eighteen pennyweights is an interesting detail, and supports the view that the specific gravity had to be ascertained with some degree of accuracy (2). Francis

(1) This must surely include getting and calcining the mine as well "preparing it in the pits."

(2) See p. 105 ante.

Duck had his own story of oppressive dealing to tell. He and seven other workmen at Mulgrave took as part of their wages two fat stots or steers for £5 2s. from Richard Haslam, and they were to give back the two tongues. Tappsfield saw the stots hanging and calculated they cost eight shillings a quarter. Had their wages been paid punctually they could have bought in the market as good beef at five shillings and sixpence the quarter. When their wages were four or five months in arrear Haslam and Tappsfield would only pay them for three months after deducting imprests, and carry forward the rest to the next pay day.

Thomas Brough of Lythe, a houseman at Sandsend, who had started as a young man of twenty in 1608 and worked ever since was another victim. In April, 1619, he had saved sufficient to buy two cows, ten sheep, two beds and two pewter " dubblers," but he had been compelled to sell all in order to relieve his old mother, his wife and two children. He had now little or no credit with his neighbours, whereas formerly he could be trusted for any necessaries that he wished to buy.

In 1623, Griffin Jones (the clerk) told him and the other workmen at Sandsend, from Tappsfield, that one of them would have to be dismissed unless all agreed to take a penny a day less wages. They went in a body to expostulate and found Tappsfield in the chamber of Roger Beckwith, the clerk of the works. The spokesman, Thomas Sawer, then one of the housemen, declared that they would not consent to have their wages abated, for they had but eightpence a day and had to find themselves. This would have been little enough for the work had it been punctually paid, but it was too little by reason of the badness of their pay. Tappsfield asked " Who said so?" Sawer said " All." Then Tappsfield came fiercely and shook Sawer and Brough by the shoulders. The rest ran away in fear, one of them, Wilson, leaped down a " pair of stairs " and was in hazard to have received hurt, but as it fell out, received none.

Annexed to the Yorkshire depositions is a very full survey of the state of the alum works. Instructions to make the survey were sent by the Lord Treasurer and the Chancellor of the Exchequer to Sir David Foulis and Sir Thomas Posthumus Hoby, who gave the necessary directions to William Chapman of Hackness, John Crispe,

Thomas Rakestraw of Northcote, Guisborough, carpenter, and Symon Lambert, plumber, who had worked for nineteen years in the alum houses at Guisborough and Skelton.

There is first an inventory of such utensils as still remained there, and this was followed by an estimate of the cost of replacing those that were deficient and of baring the rock amounting to the sum of £6,908 17s. 10d. No further references to the suit have been found in the volume of the Exchequer Decrees and Orders, but the matter seems to have passed from the Courts to the Council Chamber.

Chamberlain wrote to Dudley Carlton (1) in the preceding August that Ingram, who owed £50,000, had been brought up from Yorkshire to answer the charges, but it was not until after the depositions had been taken that any strong measures were taken against him. Then, in February, he and Bourchier were ordered to keep to their houses, but the restraint was removed after a few days (2).

(1) Cal. S.P., Jac., 1623-5, p. 360.
(2) Conway's Letter Book. S.P. 14/214, p. 192.

CHAPTER XII.

THE CIVIL WAR DRAWS NEAR.

Two months after the examination of witnesses in London and Yorkshire, namely, on 27th March, 1625, King James died. He had gained nothing or very little by the purchase of the alum works, but there was now the possibility of his successor receiving a fixed rent and incurring no further outlay. Arthur Ingram's connection was to cease, he was quite prepared to surrender the remainder of his lease, and all that he was now concerned to secure was an advantageous settlement of the claim against him in respect of the deficiencies which he had to make good when his surrender took effect.

In other directions he was out of favour. A new commission was being issued for the Council of the North, and though no attempt was made to deprive him of his office as Secretary, his name was omitted from the number of councillors. Eventually, through the good offices of the Duke of Buckingham, he was allowed to pay a sum of money to cover his liability (1), and on 25th December, 1625, his discharge (including that of George Lowe) was granted (2). In the following April his name was included as one of the Council with the not very candid explanation that it had been accidentally omitted from the new commission.

On the 13th of the same month a fresh proclamation was issued in much the same language as before, prohibiting the importation of alum from abroad.

Sir John Bourchier, as we have seen, made strenuous endeavours to regain his position as lessee of the works (3). His scheme was to obtain the patent for soap (which then produced but ten pounds a year) and to work the two patents together. He boasted that if his application for a lease was successful he would be able to bring in as a fine Sir Paul Pindar's great diamond, a jewel which, as he had reason to know, the King greatly coveted.

He learnt that William Turner was his rival, and he offered to give £1,000 a year more than Turner. But his financial position was too well-known, his constant lawsuits

(1) In the action against Tappsfield, see post p. 156, this was stated at £20,000.
(2) S.P. 15 (Chas. I.), 38/13.
(3) D.S.P., Jas. I., 155/25, and see S.P., Chas. I., 126/58. This letter was obviously written in 1625. In the Calendar of State Papers it is attributed to 1628, when the writer was dead.

must have cost him a pretty penny, and the only effect of his offer was to increase Turner's proposed rent by another £1,000. Bourchier died in 1626, and therefore his tenancy would have been short. Eventually, on the 20th July, 1625 (1), directions were given for the payment to Sir Paul Pindar and William Turner, as farmers of the alum works of two sums, one of £2,185, described as due under an agreement, and the other of £18,000 for a jewel, showing that without the help of Bourchier the great jewel had found its way into the King's coffers. Here it remained until financial stringency during the Civil War caused it to be pawned in Holland for £5,000, redeemable on payment of £5,300 (2).

The negotiations were finally completed by a lease dated 13th August, 1625, and enrolled on the Patent Rolls (3). The term ran from Michaelmas and was co-extensive with the duration of the original patent, i.e., until the 3rd January, 1637-38, and the rent was £11,000.

James Lord Ley (afterwards Earl of Marlborough) was then Lord Treasurer, and Sir Richard Weston (afterwards his successor and Earl of Portland) was Chancellor of the Exchequer; they were mentioned in the lease as advising the King. The lessees had to rely upon Arthur Ingram repairing the works before the 31st October and supplying the deficiencies. Thereafter they had to maintain boiling pans, seventy in number, or more if necessary, up to eighty, sufficient to make 1,800 tons of alum. Three hundred chaldrons of coal of the measure (4) of Whitby and Guisborough were to be left at the conclusion of the lease at the workhouses, and two thousand more at the waterside calculated at the rate of five hundred chaldrons to every fifteen pans. No sums were to be left unpaid to workmen, carriers and other creditors. Precautions were to be taken to provide that the home market should not be left surcharged or over-glutted. The yearly pensions of one hundred marks to William Ward, preacher of God's word and lecturer at Guisborough, of forty pounds to Richard Leake, the same at Lythe, and of £26 13s. 4d. to Thomas Chaloner, and of all other sums payable (no doubt including the salary of Robert Wemyss, the schoolmaster at Kirkleatham) were to be defrayed by the lessees, but the King covenanted to indemnify them against the annuities

(1) D.S.P., Chas. I., 38/13.
(2) D.S.P., Commonweatlh, 1655, 94/113.
(3) Pat. Rolls., Chas. I., pt. 13.
(4) i.e., not keel measure, which was half as much again.

payable to the original patentees. The manufacture of the alum must be improved in order to remove the disgrace and discredit into which it had fallen abroad, and to re-establish the foreign sale.

In case of war defalcations from the rent were to be allowed.

As soon as the arrangements were completed, in order to rehabilitate his reputation, Ingram, on 5th November, 1625, filed a bill in Chancery (1) against his kinsman and associate, William Tappsfield, and against John Turner and Richard Wynne—Richard Haslam having died.

He alleged that he had leased the works to Tappsfield, Haslam, Turner and Wynne for seven years at a rent of £2,700 (2), on condition that 1,800 tons a year were made, but that in fact never more than 1,300 tons were made; that two thousand men were employed and never paid in money, but forced to take corn and victuals for wages.

He then tells the story to which reference has previously been made (3), how in a time of scarcity—on 1st February, 1621-2, he provided a ship's lading of Danske (Dantzig) rye to be sold to the poor workmen at 5s. a bushel, water measure (which was one-eighth better than the ordinary market measure), but the defendants sold it in the country at 6s. the land bushel, gaining thereby £150, and suffered not the poor workmen to have any part of the same. In consequence of these unlawful acts Ingram had had to compound with King Charles for £20,000, although he had supplied the defendants with over £60,000.

Only the bill of complaint is to be found, and it is not improbable that there was never any serious intention of proceeding with the suit, which may be regarded as a tactical but unsuccessful method of restoring Ingram's reputation.

Soon after he secured the lease William Turner, with whom George Lowe and Thomas Jones were associated, conceived the idea of removing the works to Wapping (4). In 1626 he built a wooden house at the west end near the Tower of London, and occupied some rooms in the Parish of St. Mary Matfelon Whitechapel, a district abounding in brewhouses, whence the wants of the Navy were supplied. Here urine was boiled, alum made, and the alum scum conveyed in lighters and cast overboard into the Thames.

(1) C.5, 614/13.
(2) Obviously this represented his profit of 30s. on every ton.
(3) ante p. 149.
(4) Stow's Survey, Book iv., Ch. 2.

In July, 1627, there were complaints by the inhabitants that the detestable stench was intolerable and dangerous to health. Sickness and disease resulted, many fish were found dead, cattle refused to feed on the adjoining pastures. A bill of indictment was preferred, and the Grand Jury found it to be true.

The Privy Council directed the President of the College of Physicians with six other doctors of physic to report upon the matter. They certified that after viewing the alum works in St. Catherine's they found that they must of necessity breed annoyance and endanger health. Upon the petition of London dyers the works were allowed to continue till Ladyday, 1628, but it was forbidden to cast any refuse into the Thames; all such was directed to be buried in quick-lime. Needless to say, this injunction was consistently disregarded.

Meantime the works were also carried on in Yorkshire with practically the same working staff as before. John Turner, not because of any relationship with his namesake, for, as has been said, none such can be found, gradually acquired a more leading position, but we also find the names of William Tappsfield, Richard Haslam (until his death) and Richard Wynne.

William Turner, whose sister Anne will be remembered as having married Thomas Lane (1), took the opportunity to find employment for his nephew, George Lane, at Whitby.

The unnecessary and unpopular war with France was now being waged, and the French Navy made the North Sea most dangerous for merchant vessels. In January, 1626-7, an order in Council (2) permitted the farmers of alum to have an armed vessel at their own charges for four months to guard their ships and goods between London and the Tees, but no advantage appears to have been taken of this permission. Next month (3) they were allowed a rebate of one quarter's rent in respect of their losses through the plague and the capture of two ships. On 8th May following (4), seven weeks before the Duke of Buchingham sailed with a large expedition to relieve La Rochelle, George Lane despatched to his uncle a budget of

(1) The connection of Thomas Lane with the Lanes of Walgrave is not absolutely proved.
(2) D.S.P., Chas. I., 49/1.
(3) id., 54/29.
(4) id., 62/87.

misfortune. A ship employed to bring coals to Whitby had been sunk by the Dunkirkers the previous Sunday. " God for his mercy comfort them, for there was like to be nothing but sorrow." He begged for two ships of war, otherwise one of the Company's ships laden with alum could not put to sea.

An undated petition by Sir Paul Pindar and William Turner, attributed in the Calendar of State Papers to 1630 (1), but more probably written in 1627, is to the same effect. The petitioners complained that they had undertaken the farm of the alum works for divers years to come at a rent of £11,000, and yet could not enjoy the benefit. They could get no coals or other materials, and were forced to discontinue the manufacture of alum. They had lost one ship, taken by the Dunkirkers, and another lay at Scarborough laden with alum for London, not daring to put to sea for fear of the enemy, nor could they effect any insurance upon it. Manufacturers engaged in dyeing and dressing cloth and leather, especially in London, were much hindered, the workpeople impoverished and the alum works like to be ruined with consequent loss to the Revenue. They also prayed for a sufficiency of shipping to conduct their wares in safety.

The war terminated on the 29th October, 1628, and therefore it is difficult to see how the letter could have been written in 1630.

Petty pilferings at the works must always have been a source of annoyance and loss. We find constant references to these in the Quarter Sessional records. Nor did the prosecutions produce much consolation. Usually they resulted in a verdict of acquittal, and when a plea of guilty was recorded the punishment awarded was an insufficient deterrent.

On 8th July, 1613, Peter Walker of Borrowby (2) was indicted for stealing a stone of iron from the Mulgrave works, described as belonging to the King. He threw himself on the mercy of the Court, the fine was *nil* on account of his poverty, but he was ordered to sit in the stocks during the remainder of the sessions. On 2nd May, 1622 (3), three Guisborough labourers were indicted for

(1) id., 530/120.
(2) Sessions Book A2, 98b. In N.R.R.S., Vol. 2, p. 22, Canon Atkinson unfortunately omits the sentence of the Court.
(3) N.R.R.S., Vol. 3, pp. 137, 141.

having on the previous 13th January stolen 35 lbs. of alum (value 8s. 9d.) belonging to the King. They did not appear and were outlawed. On 9th July following, Ellen Gickill, who was charged with the theft of five *pondera* of alum (translated stones in the record, but valued at 5d. and, therefore, pounds), was acquitted.

Another case was subsequent in date to this period (1). Roger Tadcastle, son of the tenant of Margrave Park of the same name, was indicted in April, 1637, on three separate charges of stealing 21½ cwts. (£27 19s.), 4 cwts. (£5 4s.), and 3 cwts. (£3 18s.) of alum at Slape Wath, the property of a person unknown. He was acquitted; the circumstances rather point to a dispute as to ownership, but young Roger was not an estimable character. He finished his days on the gallows near Thirsk (2), probably at Busby Stoop.

It would rather appear that this state of things was in the minds of certain persons describing themselves as inhabitants of Whitby, but in fact all (with one possible exception) interested in the alum trade, who on 30th January, 1629-30, presented a petition to the King.

The names of these persons were: T. Brooke, William Turner, Edw. Smythe, George Lowe, Thos. Jones, John Coventry and Thos. Russell. The documents are very fully set out in the Port and Haven of Whitby, by R. T. Gaskin (3), and need only to be summarised here, but the author misses the connection between the petition and the farm of the alum works. The petition called attention to the antiquity of Whitby as an ancient borough and haven town, commodious for navigation and fishing, and to its more recent trade in alum and victuals with London.

By reason that the inhabitants of the town had not a settled and constant government with powers to make ordinances and wholesome laws for the town and river the same were much decayed and like to come to ruin. They therefore asked to be incorporated under the name of one Alderman, eight burgesses and sixteen assistants, with certain privileges set out in a schedule containing, amongst other things, a gaol or prison within the town, and the exclusion of the jurisdiction of the Justices of the Peace for the County.

(1) id., Vol. 4, p. 71.
(2) Book of Session, 1651, Fol. 41.
(3) pp. 311-315, and see S.P. 15, 159/43, 160/9, 162/84.

The matter was referred to the Attorney General (Sir Robert Heath), and while his report was on the whole favourable to the petition, he did not approve the ousting of the jurisdiction of the County Justices and the establishment of a separate Court of Quarter Sessions.

The matter was not dropped at once, but eventually it passed out of mind. It is most probable that the cause of this indifference was the refusal of the only privilege which was of any value to the petitioners. In any case, Whitby is still waiting for its Charter of Incorporation.

Coals for the works still came from Harraton, but the farmers now purchased at a fixed price and no longer took a lease of the mines in order to work them themselves. A dispute which arose in 1634 about the quantity delivered throws some light upon the methods of business (1).

One Richard Quintin had made a bargain on behalf of the farmers with Sir John Hedworth for the purchase of coals at 6s. 8d. the chalder for five years, from 1st January, 1629-30. Thomas Jackson contracted with Hedworth to get the coal and deliver it at Harraton Staith at 4s. 6d. the chalder. The dispute turned upon the question whether during a certain period 3,110 or 2,419 chalders had been delivered. Evidence in favour of the larger amount was directed to show that the keels in which the coal was carried from Harraton Staith down the Wear, though marked to carry thirty-five chalders only (probably to reduce payment of the impost of 1s. per chalder), really carried forty-five chalders. It was common ground that the chalders were to be sea-chalders, i.e., half as much again as land chalders, but both Sir William Lambton of Lambton, then aged 44, and Sir John Hedworth of Harraton, then 55, deposed that the Harraton chalders were the same size as at Newcastle, and that the keels employed were similar to those used in the time of William Wilson.

The original grant of privileges to the four patentees and, what was of more importance, the transfer of their rights to the Crown were due to expire on the 3rd January, 1637-8, the date fixed for the determination of the lease to William Turner and Sir Paul Pindar. While the Crown claimed the right to make a fresh lease of the privilege of manufacturing alum, permission to work on the lands of third parties had to be acquired by direct negotiation.

(1) Exch. Depns. 9, Car. I. Michaelmas. Durham No. 11.

In the Ingram papers (1) we find much information about these negotiations. Although Sir Arthur Ingram made no further attempt to acquire possession himself he took a very active interest in the matter.

A new aspirant now entered the lists in the person of the Earl of Strafford, then Viscount Wentworth, who had succeeded Emanuel Scrope, Earl of Sunderland, as Lord President of the Council in the North Parts in 1630, and was appointed Lord Deputy of Ireland in 1632. In his first position he was obviously brought into close working connection with Ingram, and as the latter had been for many years interested in the Irish farm of customs, Wentworth's appointment to Ireland was another link in the chain.

It may be that Ingram claimed a greater share in Wentworth's honours than he should have done. A mutual friend, Sir George Ratcliffe, also interested in the same Irish customs, wrote to him from Dublin on 28th October, 1634 (2), that he was accused of taking to himself as though by his means he had procured Wentworth to be President of York, Viscount, farmer of the alums, Lord of Tankersley, farmer of the customs and Deputy of Ireland. Ratcliffe then declared that such a boast was absolutely unfounded in the cases of the Presidentship, Viscountship and Deputyship. He admitted that Ingram had given information with respect to the alum and the values or expected profit thereof, but reminded him with what difficulty and by what means the lease was obtained.

So far as the grant of exclusive privileges by the Crown was concerned the negotiations resulted in a reversionary lease, duly enrolled upon the Patent Rolls (3), dated the 14th May, 1630, and made between the King of the one part and Sir John Gibson, of Welburn Hall, of the other part, by which the alum works were leased at a rent of £12,500 to Sir John Gibson for thirty-one years to commence on 4th January, 1637/8, i.e., after the expiration of the lease to Turner and Pinder. In accordance with a practice well-known at the present time Sir John Gibson had no apparent beneficial interest in the lease but was merely a trustee for Lord Wentworth, to whose party he was strongly attached.

(1) Hist. MSS., Com., Various, Vol. 8.
(2) Ingram Papers ut supra, p. 49.
(3) C.66, 2456, No. 8.

For the most part the covenants were similar to those in earlier leases. The lessee could pull down, rebuild and alter the existing alum houses so long as he maintained a sufficient number to produce the yearly quantity of 1,800 tons. No one except himself, his deputies and agents could dig for or manufacture alum. He had general powers of search in case he had any suspicions that alum was being imported contrary to the prohibition. On the expiration of the lease he had to surrender the works in the same condition, furnished with the same utensils, and supplied with the same quantity of coal as was provided in the lease to Turner and Pinder (1). In addition there were to be left 20 tons of urine for every fifteen pans and enough calcined mine to make 450 tons during the succeeding three months. There was the same injunction to pay wages and other debts, and the same direction to pay the three several pensions to William Ward, Richard Leake and Thomas Chaloner. The indemnity against payment of the annuities to the four original patentees and their assignees is drawn in a more detailed form than in the lease to Pinder and Turner, probably in consequence of claims by the unsatisfied beneficiaries which were then being asserted (2).

There was a covenant that if the King should do or cause to be done any matter or thing whereby the patentee should be hindered from enjoying any benefit or privilege granted to him, that then recompense or satisfaction should be made by defalcations out of the rents payable to the King.

Having succeeded in obtaining this lease from the Crown, the next difficulty to be surmounted was the consent of the Landowners. Sir William Chaloner was now in possession of Belman Bank and Newgate Bank; Sir William Pennyman in right of his wife Ann, granddaughter of John Atherton and Katherine Conyers, in possession of Slape Wath and Selby Hagg, and Lord Mulgrave of Sandsend and Asholme.

It has already been remarked that although so far no evidence has been discovered of early alum workings at Mulgrave, the probabilities lead to the inference that they were contemporaneous with, if not earlier than, those at Slape Wath. Lord Sheffeild, as he then was, had retained on his own estate one of the Liège workmen, Lambert Russell, the only one who is mentioned as having remained in Yorkshire after the termination of the first year, and his

(1) p. 155 ante.
(2) Conway letter book, p. 307.

stewards (not independent contractors) took the principal part in the conduct of the operations. He was continually after the transfer to the Crown, making proposals for a lease to himself.

So far as his share as one of the original patentees in the stipulated payments under the deed of transfer to the Crown was concerned he had assigned part, mortgaged part, compounded for part to such an extent and by such a series of complicated transactions that while he claimed £10,000 the advisers of the Crown maintained that he had been more than paid all that was due to him.

He had been created Earl of Mulgrave shortly after the accession of King Charles. In 1630, if the conjectured date is correct, he was putting forward a wonderful scheme, under which he was to be granted the privilege of coining copper to the value of £100,000 (1). Out of the profits he was to work copper mines, provide brass ordnance, stock the soap works and release his claim to the alum monies. His scheme did not mature, but it may well have been the cause of the delays to which we find reference in the Ingram Papers (2). There are four letters dealing with the subject (3). The first in order of arrangement is incorrectly attributed to 1623, and assumed to have been written by an unknown correspondent to Sir Arthur Ingram, although it is evidently written in 1633 by Ingram to Lord Mulgrave, and must be subsequent in date to the three others.

These show very clearly the transaction. Lord Mulgrave's eldest son had long been dead; he had been accidentally drowned. On his death the Wardship of his son, another Edmund Sheffeild, and now Lord Sheffeild, had been granted to Arthur Ingram (4), but Lord Sheffeild was now of age and married to Elizabeth Cranfield, daughter of Lionel, Earl of Middlesex. Whether the concurrence of the grandson in the lease was or was not necessary was a doubtful question, but at least it was considered advisable. Lord Wentworth, who was anxious for the conclusion of the arrangement without delay, writing from Dublin in November, 1633 (5), offered that so long as he continued receiver of the revenue from recusants he would pay £1,000 a year to Arthur Ingram as assignee of Lord Mulgrave. The actual transaction is disclosed in the pleadings of some

(1) S.P., Chas. I., 531/100-103.
(2) Ingram Papers ut supra, p. 24.
(3) id. pp. 38, 40, 41.
(4) Patent Rolls, 16, Jas. I., pt. 13, m.3.
(5) Ingram Papers ut supra, p. 41.

litigation, which took place after the death of Lord Mulgrave between various members of his family (1). The offer of Lord Wentworth was accepted, and on 1st March, 1633-4, a deed was executed by which the alum works in the Lordship of Mulgrave were demised to Sir John Gibson for a term co-terminous with that of the Crown lease of 14th July, 1630, and at the same rent of £12,500, but payable as to £10,860 to the King and as to the balance of £1,640 to Sir Ferdinand Fairfax, Sir John Wray, Sir William Ermine (2), Sir John Monson, Sir William Pelham and William Anderson as trustees for Lord Mulgrave. On the 10th of the same month, Thomas Viscount Wentworth, described as Lord Deputy of Ireland and President of the Council in the North Parts, and Sir John Gibson conveyed the annuity of £1,640 to the trustees, and finally, on 1st May following, a settlement was made under which the same annuity was to be held by the trustees upon trust to pay £600 to Maryon Countess of Mulgrave (the second wife), £200 to each of the sons, James, Thomas and Robert, of the second marriage, and the balance of £440 was left at the disposal of Lord Mulgrave. Although the lease was in reversion, as soon as the arrangements with Lord Mulgrave were completed, Lord Wentworth prevailed upon the Earl of Portland, then Lord High Treasurer (3), to issue a commission dated 17th July, 1634, addressed to Sir William Pennyman and Richard Wynne, to survey the works. Apparently the survey has not survived, but on 17th June, 1637, in some later proceedings, Sir William Pennyman deposed that it had been duly made (4).

Meantime death had been busy. Robert Wemyss, the Scotch Schoolmaster, later Vicar of Kirkleatham, died in 1624 (5). On the 17th June, 1631, a warrant (6) directed the payment of the pension of £12 to James Wemyss, who was described as causing a school to be taught at Kirkleatham for the children of the poor who worked in the alum mines. Possibly it was this institution which later gave the idea to Sir William Turner, son of John Turner, of founding the school there which still survives. The receipts for the payments of the several so-called pensions for the quarter ended Lady Day, 1634, are preserved in

(1) C.5, 15/73.
(2) Irwin.
(3) Ingram Papers, p. 40.
(4) E.178, 5789.
(5) Yorks. Arch. Soc. Records, Vol. 73, p. 28.
(6) Docquet of that date.

the Public Record Office (1).   Thomas Chaloner was still alive; he must have been 85 or 86, and yet his signature is nearly as firm as when he signed his petitions to the Queen after the death of his father some fifty years earlier (2). George Thorpe had now succeeded William Ward as preacher at Guisborough (3).

The preceding year, 1633, had witnessed the trial of of one of the surviving patentees, Sir David Foulis, in the Star Chamber, ostensibly on the charge of compounding with persons who refused the honour of knighthood, and the payment of the necessary fees, but, as malicious gossip maintained, rather to satisfy the private spite of Lord Wentworth.   Certainly Wentworth left no stone unturned to secure a conviction.   He reminded Ingram (4) of the date fixed for hearing the cause, 20th November, and added that should Ingram meet any of his noble friends he might do Wentworth a favour by mentioning it and desiring their presence.   The sentence given on 30th November condemned Foulis to pay £5,000 to the King, and £3,000 to Wentworth; Archbishop Laud, in delivering judgment, making the undignified pun: " To all fowls a moulting time, especially of sick feathers."   On 16th July, 1636 (5), Sir David was still in the Fleet Prison, and thence appealed to the Secretary of State for leave to go into the country for fear of sickness, offering to enter into a bond for his appearance.

Wentworth, who was not created Earl of Strafford until January, 1639-40, was actively engaged in Ireland up to the time of his trial and execution on 12th May, 1641.   Lady Burghclere, in her recent interesting life, although she appears to have had access to the unpublished Fitzwilliam manuscripts at Wentworth Woodhouse, makes no mention of the alum trade.   It is improbable that he found time to direct operations or to take any active part in the organisation of the work.

But another name now appears.   Philip Burlamachi was one of the many foreign financiers whose services were in much request during the early part of the seventeenth century.   He was first brought to the notice of the public in 1612 as one of eighteen merchant-strangers, who were

(1) S.P., Chas. I., 260/26.
(2) Ante p. 16.
(3) S.P., Chas. I., 265/37.
(4) Ingram Papers, p. 47.
(5) S.P., Chas. I., 328/75.

fined by the Star Chamber for exporting gold in breach of proclamations. Amongst his associates were Sir Wm. Courteen, Peter Vanlore and other members of the Alum Company (1). The amount exported was put at seven millions pounds, but the offences went back some sixteen years, and the witnesses upon whose depositions the case rested were so exceptionable that, in the general opinion, the proceedings would have fallen through had not the attorney of Courteen and Burlamachi tampered with the principal witness by attempting to induce him to recant. The attempt was discovered and both the culprit and his clients were fined in the Star Chamber. Burlamachi, who for some reason found sympathy on the ground that he had only erred through indiscretion, made his peace in January following for £10,000 ready money, and later was fined £4,000 in the Star Chamber for the offence of exporting coin. He got his discharge in August.

During the next few years his activities increased. He advanced £6,000 at 10 per cent. in 1622 to pay the forces of the Palatinate, and was repaid out of the farm of the customs (2). His brother, James, took back three geldings from England to Italy under special licence (3). When Lady Carlton wanted to raise £2,000 for her husband, Sir Dudley (later Lord Dorchester), she had no one to whom to apply other than Burlamachi though, as she complained, he required £40 or £50 for exchange and paid with much light gold (4).

From 1620 to Easter, 1628, £713,364 15s. 10d. passed through his hands or represented sums due to him. In particular, he expended £46,000 in victualling ships and paying their crew in preparation for the expedition to Rochelle, of which £600 was the cost of victualling 1,200 men for 20 days at 6d. a day. He provided, in September, 1628, £4,200 being one month's pay of officers who served the King of Denmark, for the repayment of which he received a Treasury Warrant.

In 1631 he was transmitting news from Germany to Lord Dorchester, then Secretary of State, purchasing for over £15,000 pictures and statues at Venice for the King, and negotiating the receipt of the dowry of Queen Henrietta Maria (5).

(1) S.P., Jas. I., Vols. 109, 110, 111.
(2) id, Vol. 133.
(3) id, Vol. 150.
(4) id, Vol. 148.
(5) S.P., Chas. I., 323/212, 374/33, 376/170.

What exactly were the relations between him on the one hand and the farmers on the other are somewhat doubtful, but he was the contractor for whom John Turner, in 1635, made 1,960 tons of alum at £8 a ton, principally at Asholm and Sandsend.

As the date for the expiration of the lease to Turner and Pinder drew near rumours gained ground that John Turner was working for the present only, irrespective of the future (1).

Another commission was therefore issued in June, 1637, directed on this occasion to James Pennyman, William Bulmer, Robert Stoope and Thomas Lyle, to inquire as to the state of the works and as to their capability to make the requisite yearly quantity of 1,800 tons (2).

The lease to Sir Paul Pinder and William Turner contained a covenant to surrender the works at the end of the term in good condition, and the suggestion was made that in breach of this covenant John Turner of Kirkleatham, who was now managing all the alum works, was so treating them that they might serve his time and, after the expiration of the lease be treated as valueless. In particular, he was charged with having neglected to bare sufficient of the rock to enable the alum shale to be worked continuously, and with allowing the face to be blocked with rubbish that had fallen from above. Several witnesses were examined; amongst them Lambert Russell, who by that time had completed thirty years at Sandsend. He drew a very gloomy picture. For lack of sufficient baring in due season there was the fear that the calcining place at the Holmes would in time of wet and unseasonable weather be completely overwhelmed with rubbish. At Sandsend £400 would be required to put the rock in order. In his opinion, 70 pans were necessary in order to make 1,800 tons annually.

But notwithstanding this evidence, it cannot be said that the whole of the charges were established. Most of the witnesses, Lambert Russell amongst them, considered that it would be quite safe for the new patentee, Sir John Gibson, to work the mines. William Belwood, then steward to Lord Mulgrave, who for the last nine years had carefully observed the state of Asholme and Sandsend that he might give an account to his master, took the opposite view.

(1) Ingram Papers, p. 40.
(2) E., 178, 5789.

167

But the essential point was that the stipulated quantity of 1,800 tons yearly was for the first time being made by John Turner as from August, 1635. Of this quantity, 1,300 tons or thereabouts was being made at Asholm and Sandsend, which appear to have had their proper complement of pans. It was not, therefore, necessary to make many tons at the Guisborough group, where most of the deficiencies in baring and equipment occurred.

Richard Wynne was one of the witnesses, and while he admitted the success of his brother-in-law, John Turner, he claimed that in 1620 he contracted with Sir Arthur Ingram to make 1,800 tons yearly for seven years, and actually made 150 tons the first month, but had then to decrease the quantity manufactured as Sir Arthur could not sell so much.

As far as one can judge, Sir John Gibson, in his capacity as trustee, duly entered upon the lease. As was the invariable custom, he merely drew a profit rental. A copy of the lease to him in the form of a book is to be found at Kirkleatham Hospital, which supports the view that John Turner was still the alum-maker.

Philip Burlamachi was anxious to continue his interest in the works. In an undated petition, attributed to 1633 (1), he proposed to take the alum works as sub-lessee to Lord Wentworth, paying him £1,000 and increasing the King's rent from £12,500 to £14,000 (2). He was then heavily in debt, enjoying a temporary protection from his creditors, but earnest though his supplications were, by the 16th March, 1637-8, he was still waiting for an answer from Wentworth to his petition (3).

He took upon himself the credit of having during the four years during which he was connected with the works paid £15,000 to the then patentees and advanced the manufacture from 900 tons a year to 2,000 tons (4). But, as we have seen, John Turner claimed that the credit was due to himself. His name does not appear again as principal, and, like so many other persons interested in the alum farm, he died in great poverty. After the Restoration in 1660, his daughters, Magdalen and Susannah, petitioned for relief on the ground that their late father had been ruined by advances

(1) S.P., Chas. I., 257/36.
(2) id, 537/87.
(3) id 323/212.
(4) id 274/33, id 376/170.

of money to Charles I.   They alleged that the Post Office had been given to him, but as a loyal subject to the Crown he had been deprived of his office during the Commonwealth in favour of the Attorney-General Prideaux (1).

It may not be out of place here to refer to a statement in Young's History of Whitby, Vol. 2, p. 759.   The author describes some works, the ruins of which existed in his day, situated in the angle which the left bank of the Murk Esk makes with the River Esk.   The name of the field where they were to be found was the Alum Garth, and the sketch of the works makes the author's conjecture extremely probable, namely, that they were the ruins of some former alum works.   He attempts to place their origin at the date with which we are now dealing, on the ground that the name " Alum Garth " occurs on a map dated 1636 in the possession of Mr. R. C. Elwes, the owner of the Egton Estate.   This map is still in existence and in the possession of the present owner of Egton, Mr. Lionel Foster, and though the name of the close cannot be clearly deciphered as Alumgarth, it certainly looks as if " allome " is its first member.   The plot of ground where the works stood is now occupied by the Church of St. Matthew, its churchyard and some gardens, and all trace of the pitholes shown by Young has disappeared, though observant men think that they can distinguish in the adjoining alum shale the workings whence the mineral was derived.   As far as one can make out the Salvins were still in possession of Egton at the date in question.   Later the Estate passed into the hands of the Elwes family, who had previously (but subsequent to 1636) lent money on the Slape Wath Works, and who were therefore quite likely to be interested in the trade.   But if alum was being manufactured in Grosmont in 1636 contrary to the proclamation it seems strange that the lessees made no complaint upon that ground, and the probabilities are that the manufacture took place some years later.

(1) S.P. 29, 17/104.

CHAPTER XIII.

THE COMMONWEALTH.

It may be no more than a coincidence, but it is at least worthy of note, that not one of the original patentees or of their descendants fought on the King's side during the Civil War.

Lord Mulgrave, notwithstanding that he had been promoted to his Earldom shortly after the accession of Charles I., was up to his death in 1646 one of the strongest supporters of Parliament, and his grandson, the second Earl, followed his lead. Sir Thomas Chaloner had died in 1615 before any sums became payable under the arrangement of 1609, but amongst his sons were to be found the two previously described as regicides.

Sir David Foulis had other grievances against the King's Party, besides the non-payment of stipulated annuities. His animosity against Strafford, his prosecution in the Star Chamber, the hope that his fine might be reduced, all have their share in determining his action, even though it entailed disloyalty to his former pupil. He died in 1642 in the early stages of the struggle.

Like Sir Thomas Chaloner, Sir John Bourchier died before he was called upon to choose his party; it was his nephew and namesake who took the lead on Heworth Moor, 3rd June, 1642, when the free-holders of Yorkshire made their protest to the King (1). He, too, had his own grievances against the high-handed proceedings of Wentworth when President of the North.

The troubles with Scotland over the Prayer Book, which were pregnant with such mighty consequences, had hardly begun when the new lease came into operation. It would seem as if they had no effect upon the alum working for the first few years. Sir John Gibson, whether he was beneficially entitled or merely a trustee, whether his was the directing mind or whether Philip Burlamachi succeeded in retaining the control, was treated by the Exchequer as the accounting party, and seems to have found no difficulty in making sufficient alum to satisfy the rent. When, many years later, on the 14th March, 1647-8, the accounts were produced to the committee of His Majesty's Revenues (2), which took the place of the Exchequer, the Committee found that Gibson duly paid up to Christmas, 1641, inclusive, the

(1) Yorks. Arch. Journal VII., 63.
(2) E. 407, Box 8, Roll 165.

rents already stated, namely, £10,860, every Christmas at the Receipt of the Exchequer, and £1,640 to Sir Ferdinand Fairfax and other feoffees in trust for the Earl of Mulgrave.

Sir Paul Pinder, as assignee of Sir John Gibson, accounted for subsequent years. He produced tallies of sums paid into the Exchequer, some going back before the commencement of the lease. At first the payments to preachers at Guisborough and Lythe, and to the schoolmaster at Kirkleatham, were continued. There was no payment to preachers or schoolmaster in 1644, but the former was subsequently revived by dormant order (1) of the Committee for the King's Revenue in favour first of Alan Smallwood and later of Thomas Smallwood at Guisborough, and of Richard Conyers at Lythe. Payment to the schoolmaster was not revived, and the omission of any mention of Thomas Chaloner leads to the inference that he was then dead. Indeed, had he been alive he would have been well over ninety years old. The net result of payments and allowances was to leave a debit balance of £24,884 claimed as due from Sir Paul Pinder.

As against these arrears, Sir Paul Pinder, relying upon the covenant before stated (2) claimed £55,301 18s. 6d. by way of defalcations, made up as follows:—He claimed £22,366 8s. (3), representing 3,195 tons 8 cwts. at £7 a ton, on the ground that in five years ending, respectively, at Christmas 1640, 1641, 1643, 1645 and 1647, he could only make 5,804 tons 12 cwts. in place of 9,000 tons at the rate of 1,800 tons a year. Divers men, so he maintained, who had been employed in the alum works testified that in those five years the Northern parts were troubled with such a large number of soldiers that the usual quantity of alum could not be made. For the year ending Christmas, 1644, no alum at all could be made, for which he claimed £12,500. Between 30th March, 1643, and 30th November, 1645, 262 tons 11 cwts. were imported into the Port of London from parts beyond the seas, as certified by the principal officers of the customs. As alum then sold for £26 a ton, £18 a ton (after deducting £8 for the cost of manufacture) was claimed, or, in other words, £6,526 11s. 6d.

In the years ended 25th December, 1646 and 1647, 260 tons 8 cwts. were similarly imported, but as the price of alum had then been reduced to £20, only £12 a ton, or

(1) A dormant order was one that was not satisfied by a single payment, but continued until revoked.

(2) p. 162 ante.

£3,124 16s., was claimed. But, in consequence of this reduction, he had in 1646 sold in England 572 tons 16 cwts. 24 lbs., and in 1647, 896 tons 16 cwts. 7 lbs. at £20 by order of the Committee of His Majesty's revenue in lieu of £25 as stipulated by the lease, and for this he claimed £6 a ton—in all £8,817 13s.

In addition, two cargoes had been lost at sea, for which claims were made. Eighty-two tons of alum laden in a ship of Whitby, the True Love, whereof Thomas Bower was Master, had been taken by a Man-of-War of Jersey. For this he claimed £656 at the rate of £8 a ton. One hundred tons eleven cwts. of kelp carried in a ship whereof Ralph Lascelles was master had been seized by a man-of-war belonging to the rebels of Ireland. At 26s. the ton the claim for this came to £130 14s.

Then again a new imposition or excise of 4s. a chalder had been charged by an ordinance of Parliament on Durham coals exported to the alum works, besides the old excise of 1s. 5,899 chalders of coal had been shipped between August, 1644, and December, 1645, and refund of the excess excise, namely, £1,179 16s., was demanded.

The total of the sums so claimed amounted to the above sum of £55,301 18s. 6d. (1).

It is to be noted that no claim for deficiencies was made in respect of the years 1642 and 1646, and therefore it is to be presumed that comparative tranquility reigned in Cleveland during these years.

The total defalcations therefore were more than double the arrears, and the balance of over £30,000 formed the subject of a claim submitted to the consideration of the Committee of the Revenue, but so far as it is possible to form an opinion, no ruling was ever given upon the several questions involved, nor did the estate of Sir Paul Pinder benefit to the extent of one penny in respect of the above claim.

It was not until 1648 that steps were taken to call in the Letters Patent granted to Sir John Gibson for the sole making and sale of alum. The first Earl of Mulgrave, as we have seen, died on the 6th October, 1646, and was succeeded by his grandson, a very constant attendant in the House of Lords, where the business was seldom conducted by more than eighteen peers.

(1) The calculation is not exact.

On Friday, 17th March, 1647-8, in his presence a message was brought from the House of Commons requesting the concurrence of the Lords in an order for recalling these Letters Patent.

A delay of a few days took place occasioned, as one must assume, through uncertainty as to the person having their custody. Then, after directing Sir Paul Pinder to surrender them, the order for cancelling them was read a third time on 31st March, 1648. This order was duly served upon Sir Paul, but he failed to comply with it. An ordinance was therefore passed, directing that the patent should be brought in and cancelled and also vacated on the Rolls or wherever else it was on record, as being illegal and void under the Statute of Monopolies. On the 4th May the peers present (twelve in number, of whom Mulgrave was again one) made a further order that Edmund Earl of Mulgrave might forthwith enter upon the alum works, houses and mines in his Manor of Mulgrave, and receive the profits for his own use.

It was now necessary for Sir Paul Pinder to make some move, and he applied to be heard by Counsel on the ground that his interest in the alum farm included other matters besides the alum mines monopoly. In other words, he and his predecessors in title had built up a successful business, kept the works in repair and fully equipped and duly paid rent for them. The widow of the first Earl and her children were also affected by the order. Her husband had concurred in the grant and had bargained that a large part of the rent reserved on his part should be for the benefit of his second marriage.

On Monday, 29th May, again in the presence of Lord Mulgrave, the House of Lords decided to have a conference with the House of Commons upon the subject. The House of Lords declared that by concurring with the Commons in the votes for damning the patent granted to Sir John Gibson of sole making of alum as a monopoly it was never in their intentions to take away any legal right or title which Sir Paul Pinder or any other person had in these alum mines.

The litigation dragged on for a few more weeks, and then on Tuesday, 27th June, 1648, Lord Mulgrave was in a position to acquaint the House that he and Sir Paul Pinder had come to an amicable agreement. This agreement was embodied in an indenture dated 14th July, 1648, and made between Sir Paul Pinder and the Earl, and was expressed to be for the composition of the dispute which had arisen

(1) Lords Journals X., 117a.

about the alum works and the lease to Sir John Gibson (deceased), which Sir Paul Pinder then held as assignee for the residue of the original term. The latter agreed to pay an additional sum of £500 a year over and above the original rent of £1,640 payable to the trustees of the late Earl (1).

As the cancelling of the letters patent and lease had also extinguished the rent of £10,860 to the State, Pinder had no doubt as to the possibility of paying this extra sum of £500 a year, but he failed to appreciate the effect of the competition which ensued when the alum trade was thrown open to all who desired to engage in it. Hardly had eighteen months expired before (on 9th November, 1649) the Earl sued Pinder in Chancery (1) on the ground that the latter refused to pay the rent, and that the Earl sustained much loss and prejudice inasmuch as a great part of his lands had been digged up to burn for extracting alum, and a very great number of poor and beggarly people had been brought thither, who proved themselves chargeable and burthensome to the Earl and his tenants. He alleged (whether truthfully or not it is impossible to say in the absence of more direct evidence) that certain substantial merchants of London had offered to pay £4,000 a year for what Pinder refused to pay the £500.

Apparently before the case was heard Sir Paul Pinder died in 1650, and appointed as his executors William Toomes, of Hackney, and his nephew, Matthew Pinder. William Toomes must have been a person of considerable wealth before he intermeddled with alum. On the 8th May, 1654 (2), Evelyn mentions that he visited his garden at Hackney and admired his banqueting house of cedar and his pictures, amongst them Vandyke's " Man in his Shirt." As his brother, Richard Toomes, who was his heir at his death, resided at Pottersbury in Northamptonshire (3), he also might have been connected with that County. Soon after his arrival in Yorkshire he bought lands in Normanby from James Morley and James Pennyman to the value of £300 a year. He then managed all the alum works up to May, 1652, when he handed over the Mulgrave works to Thomas Shipton, the steward to Lord Mulgrave, and Thomas Coventry, but continued to carry on those at Guisborough and Skelton, of which Slape Wath alone was in working order.

(1) C.2 (Chas. I.), M. 59/51.
(2- Evelyn's Memoirs, Vol. 1, 273.
(3) E. 178, 6329.

His occupation was not free from trouble. Constant indictments at Quarter Sessions (1) for various offences, mostly trivial, such as carrying away oak trees, probably for his calcining heaps, digging up the highway at Combe Bank, casting alum slam into the beck at Slape Wath, even though the majority were unsustained, could not have made his life too pleasant.

Disputes over the title to the land whereon the alum works stood caused further complications. Katherine Atherton was left a widow in 1617 or thereabouts (2). She had had an only son called John of Skelton to distinguish him from his half-brother, who was also called John. John of Skelton married a lady of whom all that we know is that her name was Anne, though the fact that he held by Knight service nine acres of land in Redcar of William Bellasis as of the Manor of Kirkleatham suggests a possible connection. John himself died on the 12th November, 1613, under the age of twenty-one, but leaving an only daughter, also called Anne (3), who was four years old at her father's death, therefore he could have been barely 16 years old at the date of his marriage. Katherine Atherton survived her husband by some eight years and died on 13th March, 1625-6. Her granddaughter Anne, who was sixteen years and four months at the date of her death (4), and who at the date of her grandmother's inquisition post mortem (21st January, 1633-4) was the wife of Sir William Pennyman, Baronet, was described as her next heir (5). She outlived her husband by a few months, and died about June 1644. Conyers Lord Darcy and Conyers of Hornby Castle, who was said to have been 45 years old at her death was found to be her next heir by an inquisition which was not taken until 13th December, 1657 (6), and the jurymen were unable to state who, after her death, had received the issues of her lands (which included an undivided third part of the Manor of Skelton and other Bruce lands). The explanation of the vagueness in the verdict was due to a claim by Sir Gervase Elwes and his sons, Gervase and Jeremy, that having advanced sums of money to pay Sir William's fine for delinquency they had a charge on the lands (7). Lord

(1) North Riding Records, Vol. V., pp. 68, 84, 104, 154, 169, 173. In one case Hackney is mis-copied as Hackness.
(2) St. Ch. 8, 24/13.
(3) C. 142, 347/25.
(4) C. 142, 495/90.
(5) Consanguinea et proprior heres.
(6) C. 142, 766/69.
(7) Yorks. Arch. Records (Royalist Composition Papers), Vol. 3, p. 140.

Darcy and Conyers later claimed that the debt had been satisfied, and on the 15th February, 1653-4, William Toomes as assignee of Lord Darcy put in an information of discovery of the estate, and an order was made by the Committee for Compounding that the representatives of Sir Gervase Elwes should shew cause why the premises (including the alum mines in Skelton) should not be re-sequestered.

The situation was perplexing enough to drive a man mad. It is therefore not very surprising that on 4th June, 1655, William Toomes hanged himself. Indeed, it came out in evidence that only a few months previously he had made an earlier attempt to commit suicide, when a surgeon named Brown had attended to him, but had received no fee for his skill in saving his life.

There were no merciful verdicts of insanity in those days. On 26th October, 1655, the Sheriff (sic) summoned a Jury to inquire of what goods he died possessed in order that they might be forfeited to the State.

The inquisition does not appear to have been preserved, but the foreman, Robert Stoope, of Tolesby, kept a copy of the finding on the Jury, and gave it in evidence at a subsequent inquiry held in March, 1664 (1).

Slapewath was then furnished with 20 boiling pans of iron valued at £30 or £40 each, 28 settlers, 2 roaching pans, 125 chalders of coal, 64 tons 9 cwts. of kelp, 12 pits furnished with pumps and troughs, 82 coolers, 4 mother cisterns and pumps, one washing cistern with troughs to convey the washings to the pans, and various other things. Gerard Fox, whose name appears later, collected and sold a very large quantity of the above, but it does not appear that he handed over the proceeds.

In any case it is quite clear that a second inquisition, which is still in existence was taken, as one of the witnesses expressed it, after His Majesty's happy restoration.

The inquiry related to goods both in Middlesex and Yorkshire, and two separate inquisitions were taken. At the latter, not only Robert Stoope but several other witnesses were examined. They detailed the furniture at Slape Wath in much the same language as in the earlier inquisition. They include a lead pipe, 100 yards long and $1\frac{1}{2}$in. bore for conveying water out of " Maister Challenger's " grounds to the pits, a spelling of the name Chaloner for another instance of which we to go back to Machin's diary.

(1) E.178, 6329.
(2) Camden Society O.S., Vol. 42.

After the death of Toomes the works at Slape Wath lay idle while the Mulgrave Mines alone continued to make alum. It will be remembered that under the settlement made by the first Earl in May, 1634, the greater portion of the annuity of £1,640 was settled upon his second wife, Marian, and the sons of the second marriage (1). In case the alum mines ceased to be worked like annuities were charged upon the Mulgrave estates. Up to the end of the year 1651 William Toomes continued to pay the annuities, but his surrender to the second Earl precluded any hope of their future payment.

That the works were in fairly serviceable state is shown by the evidence taken in 1662 of John Barwick, an alum boiler, then 68 years old (2), who had been employed at Guisborough as far back as the days when Arthur Ingram was lessee, and subsequently had been employed for seven years at Asholme. The valuation at Asholme, Ducking Grave and the Holmes amounted to £4,135; that at Sandsend to £3,732.

Most of the items are those to which we are well accustomed, but it is noteworthy that three alum houses at Asholme had only 20 lead boiling pans between them, and one alum house at Sandsend 11 pans.

The evidence was directed to the period between 1st April, 1652, when the works were said to have been taken out of the hands of William Toomes, described as executor of Sir Paul Pinder, one of the Farmers of the alum works, and 21st October, 1662, the date of the Inquisition. A certain Thomas Coventry, then deceased, and Thomas Shipton, the steward at Mulgrave Castle, had carried on the works by virtue of a commission from the then Earl of Mulgrave. For the first three years up to 1655, when Thomas Coventry died, the yearly output was from 400 to 500 tons or thereabouts; for the next three years it was increased to 700 tons; in 1659, to 900 tons; in 1660, 1,000 tons; in 1661, 1,100 tons; and a contract with Sir John Monson had been negotiated to make 1,200 tons in 1662.

The second Earl was now in possession of the family estates in Yorkshire and Lincolnshire, but there had been considerable delay in the payment of annuities to his step-grandmother and half-uncles. On 30th June, 1652, Marian, then Dowager Countess of Mulgrave, filed her bill (3) against the 2nd Earl, his wife and the then surviving trustees, Sir

(1) C.5, M. 15/73.
(2) E. 178, 6548.
(3) C.5, M. 15/73.

John Monson and Sir John Wray. She stated that not only were the pretended privileges for making alum not continued, but by several votes and declarations of the two Houses of Parliament they were declared illegal and a monopoly. The letters patent with the lease to Sir John Gibson were ordered to be vacated and declared void. She therefore asked that the trustees might be directed to execute the trusts of the settlement, and raise the annuity out of the alum mines, or otherwise out of the Mulgrave Estates. In their answers, the trustees expressed their desire to discharge their duties, but appear to suggest, rather than to allege, that the costs and charges of repair and manufacture exceeded the profits arising from the sale. It may be that the increased output in subsequent years redressed the balance, for so far as the records go, there seems to have been no subsequent default in the payment of the annuitants, none of whom enjoyed a long life.

Edmund, second Earl of Mulgrave, made his will on 5th August, 1656, and died in October, 1658. In his lifetime he had spent about £3,000 in fitting up the works with suitable implements and other utensils, and the question arose whether these were to be treated as passing with the alum mines, of which there was a special bequest to his wife of one half of the surplus after payment of the annuities charged by his grandfather, or as passing as personal estate to his wife as executrix. Elizabeth, Lady Mulgrave, naturally asserted her rights as executrix, but expressed her willingness to waive her rights and to be content with an additional jointure that had been devised to her and her moiety of the overplus of the profits. It is more than probable that these proceedings were merely instituted to put on record a family arrangement. Those who are interested will find the details in the bill filed by Lady Mulgrave on the 18th May, 1659, to which Sir John Monson, K.B., put in his defence on the 21st May and in the cross bill filed on the 3rd June by John, the third Earl, then an infant, by his next friend, Sir John Monson, to which his mother put in her defence on 10th June following (1).

(1) C.5, 402/103, 402/104, 94/2.

CHAPTER XIV.

THE TERMINATNON OF THE ALUM FARM.

The joint declaration of the two Houses of Parliament that the letters patent to Sir John Gibson were invalid had at once given the signal for a rush of speculators allured by the enticing prospect of making alum at £7 a ton and selling it at £26 a ton. Had the sale price been maintained the result would have been only realisable on paper by treating the overhead charges as non-existent, but in fact during the Commonwealth the price of alum was soon reduced to £10 or thereabouts.

Amongst these speculators one of the most prominent was Zacharie Stewart of Loftus-in-Cleveland. He was a man of some importance. In his pedigree, recorded by Dugdale, he claimed descent from the Stewards of Cambridgeshire, but, as Mr. Clay says (1), there is no confirmation of his claim to be found in the Visitation of Cambridgeshire of 1619 (2). His father, also Zacharie Steward, clerke, S.T.P. Rector of Easington from 1559, died in 1618 (3) whilst his son was still a child, having married Elizabeth Watson of Hutton Bushell, a lady apparently connected with the Conyers family of Sockburn. He himself in 1634, at the age of 21 or thereabouts, married Anne, daughter of Sir Thomas Norcliffe of Nunnington, a marriage which connected him with the family of Conyers of Boulby (4). His mother, shortly after the death of her first husband, married Philip Wheath, Clerk in Holy Orders, who would appear to have been curate to the succeeding Rector.

He described himself in 1661 as having been clerk in some alum works for forty years, which, if his other dates are correct, would imply that he first acted as such clerk at the age of seven; but like those of many other actors in the alum trade drama his statements are not distinguished for their pedantic accuracy. It will be sufficient for our purpose if we consider him as the son of a Rector, who had partly inherited and partly purchased small parcels of land in an adjoining parish; connected by marriage with several county familes and yet employed from an early age in the trade in which he was later to take a prominent part. His step-father, Philip Wheath (5), had induced the son of a

(1) Dugdale by J. W. Clay, Vol. 2, p. 484.
(2) Harl. Soc. Pubns.
(3) Yorks. Arch. Soc. (Records), Vol. 73, p. 25.
(4) Yorks. Arch. Soc. (Records), Vol. 49, p. 52.
(5) E.112 (Com.), Yorks. 80.

deceased neighbour to reside with him during his minority, and it was alleged, though strenuously denied by Zacharie, that the object was to gain possession of the infant's land. Certain it was that this land adjoined his own, and together they offered an ideal site for alum works (1).

In 1655 he succeeded in persuading three citizens of London, Thomas Goodyer, Thomas Lechmere and Humphrey Aldersey, Salters and Dyers, that this parcel of ground, one-hundred-and-thirty-three acres in extent, near Lingberry Hill, contained the richest and most suitable alum ore, plenty of kelp and sufficient water to keep thirty or forty pans in working order, whilst its proximity to the sea rendered it more commodious than any of its rivals for importing coal and exporting alum. He maintained that alum could be worked here at less expense and more profit than elsewhere.

The negotiations lasted some time, and it was not until February, 1656-7 that a lease was executed by Zacharie Stewart to his three co-partners of the land and alum mines at a yearly rent of £30 for forty-one years from Michaelmas, 1657. At the same time a deed of partnership was sealed under which the three London citizens bound themselves to spend up to £3,000 in making a channel of sufficient width and depth for vessels requisite for the works before Lady-day, 1658, within seven years to erect a dock or harbour sheltered by a pier, to bare the rock and provide a workhouse at Lingberry Hill for seven pans with calcined mine, kelp, coals, brushwood and all necessary requisites. If £3,000 should prove insufficient the balance was to be supplied by all four partners in equal shares, Zacharie Stewart thus being only bound to bear one-fourth part of the excess. The produce of the mines was to be divided equally between the four partners.

The sum of £3,000 was soon expended and an additional £4,000 had to be provided. It was alleged that Stewart claimed his fourth share of all the alum that was made and yet refused to contribute towards the additional expenditure.

A works manager, Daniel Butler, was appointed, whether by all four partners or by the three Londoners only, was a matter of controversy. Stewart alleged that Butler was extravagant, paying 12d. a yard in lieu of 6d. for cleansing the channel, and 2½d. in lieu of 2d. for baring the rock. The latter measurements were probably cubic yards. What the former were it is impossible to say.

(1) E. 112 (Chas. II.), Yorks. 67.

That the channel was cleansed was admitted on all sides; the pier was finished to the length of forty-eight yards within eighteen months; it was six yards in height, six yards broad at the bottom and three yards at the top, and cost 2d. a cubic yard to make; two staiths were added each three yards high, one fourteen and the other twenty-three yards in length.

Not much alum was made. A witness speaking some thirteen years after the event deposed (1) that he kept five pans going at one time for three weeks and made nine tons in a fortnight, a rate which he could have maintained indefinitely, the cost of one ton being twenty nobles, or seven pounds at the most. He only made alum for seven months, and the inference must be drawn that the production for the whole period was proportionately less than for the three weeks.

There is no record of any division of profits; under a verbal promise Stewart was entitled to receive six chalders of coal at his manor house at Loftus every year, and for the first three or four years these were duly delivered. The proximity to a harbour reduced the cost of carrying coals from the ships to the works to 7d. or 8d. a chalder, and alum to the ships from the works to 4d. a ton, in place of 2s. 6d. or 2s. 8d. for either service elsewhere. But notwithstanding this advantage, there was not sufficient encouragement to carry on the works, and they had ceased operations in 1664.

The other mines which had been started during the Commonwealth had an equally short life. It is more probable that the Grosmont works mentioned by Dr. Young (2) belonged to this period than to the date to which he attributed them, but here, too, we are without any record of sales. It would therefore appear that at the Restoration of Charles II., while several of the smaller works were in a moribund condition not capable of being revived, the Mulgrave works alone showed signs of vitality.

Notwithstanding these adverse conditions, attention was at once directed to the Alum Farm. One of the first to move was a certain Lieutenant Thomas Wade, who had recently been appointed Postmaster at Whitby (3). His information was limited to Mulgrave; to the effect, namely, that stock and furniture which had been provided by Sir Paul Pinder and William Toomes, to the value of £11,000,

(1) Exch. Depns. 23, Chas. II., Easter 41, Mich: 32. 25 Chas. II., Easter 23.
(2) Ante p. 169.
(3) S.P., Chas. II., 22/46.

had been seized by the Earl of Mulgrave, who confessed that in the first three years that he held the works he had gained £11,000 (1). Wade then petitioned for the usual allowance to persons who made discovery of concealed goods. Whether he received the reward for his tale-bearing does not appear. It is incredible that those who advised the King were ignorant of these notorious facts. The statement contained in some pleadings (2) of the Attorney General some years later correctly expressed the ministerial view. The King being minded to be re-invested in his right of making alum according to the example of his Royal father and grandfather of famous memory (the work of alum-making having been brought into this realm and set up at the great expense and charge of the Crown) had been pleased to re-assume the same rather by contract than by Royal Prerogative. In other words, while the Crown claimed the exclusive right of working the alum mines, it was quite prepared to buy out the interests of competing concerns.

The Earl of Southampton was then Lord High Treasurer, and Lord Ashley (afterwards Earl of Shaftesbury) Chancellor and Under-Treasurer of the Exchequer. For this purpose they appointed Sergeant Charnock (afterwards Sir George Charnock) and the same Gerard Fox, whose name has appeared before (3), to treat with all or most of the owners of alum mines in order to amalgamate all in one over-riding concern.

As we have seen, the works at Asholme and Sandsend were being carried on by Sir John Monson in accordance with the trusts contained in the settlement of the first Earl and the will of the second. At some time in the year 1661 Sir John Monson entered into an agreement with Sir Nicholas Crispe, Bart., John Twisden, Dr.Ph., Francis Pargiter and John Sammes, who eventually became, and no doubt were then intended to become, farmers of the alum works, to supply them with 1,200 tons a year, and this contract was substantially carried out under the supervision of Thomas Shipton, then steward at Mulgrave Castle. The result would therefore appear to be that the alum continued to be manufactured by those interested in the Mulgrave estates while the farmers were merely the factors who placed it upon the market.

(1) There is no record of this confession.
(2) E.112, Car. II., Yorks. 264.
(3) Ante p. 176.

On September 13th, 1662 (1), Sergeant Charnock received £100 for an intended journey to Yorkshire about the alum mines. At this time, besides Asholme and Sandsend, managed by Sir John Monson, and Lingberry Hill, there were the following works, potentially capable of producing alum, although not all in active operation:—

(1) Alum Mines at Whitby opened by Sir Hugh Cholmley, to which was attached a new wharf at Spittle Bridge.

(2) Like mines at Dunsley on grounds belonging to Thomas Fairfax or Isaac Fairfax.

(3) Slape Wath, described as lately in the possession of Sir William Darcy of Witton Castle, Co. Durham (the next brother to Conyers Lord Darcy) and George Darcy his son.

(4) Samlesbury, near Preston, in Lancashire, in the possession of Sir Richard Hoghton (2) of Hoghton Towers, Baronet, Dame Sarah his wife, and James Ramsay.

The scheme of the Treasury was to obtain a lease to the King of all these concerns, which were afterwards to be assigned to the farmers already named. A proclamation was then to be issued in the stereotyped form forbidding the importation of foreign alum, and the price of English alum was to be raised to the old figure of £26 a ton.

The farmers were Sir Nicholas Crispe, a nephew of his namesake in the early days of the farm; Dr. John Twisden (as trustee, though not so expressed, for his brother-in-law, Sir Hugh Cholmley, then about to sail for Tangiers where he was to engineer the mole), and two London merchants called Francis Pargiter and John Sammes. The proprietors of the majority of the concerns were quite ready to accept the scheme propounded by the Treasury. To manufacture alum at £7 the ton and sell at £26 sounds alluring enough, but, as we have seen, the mathematical result was only attained by neglecting items of repair and renewal that recurred at far too frequent intervals. Besides, the negotiators had no difficulty in proving that unless the scheme matured the price would be nearer £9 than £26, and there had been many instances in the past ten years to support their argument.

(1) Early Entry Book III., 438.
(2) Grandson of Sir Richard, p. 80 ante.

A provisional agreement must have been made with the eventual farmers, of whom Sir Nicholas Crispe was the moving spirit. Sir Hugh Cholmley, whose interests were secured by his trustee, Dr. Twisden, was quite obviously ready to bring his works into the pool. The Dunsley and Salmesbury works came in with equal facility.

In the case of Slape Wath the only difficulty arose with regard to its title. On the death of Dame Anne Pennyman, who survived her husband, the interest of the Elwes family in the rents and property was treated as at an end, and the property was taken to have descended upon her heir at law, Lord Conyers, from whom by some family arrangement it appears to have fallen to the share of his next brother, Sir William Darcy. He tells his own story (1), namely, that in the late rebellious times, about 1653, being much pressed for money, owing to his loyalty, he contracted debts by means of bonds and recognisances, for which he and his brother Henry were bound to an attorney of Gray's Inn, by name Robert Wolrich. Robert Wolrich was then dead, leaving a child, Sarah, married to Sir John Hewley of York. The mortgagees had entered into the lands so charged, which included the alum mines at Slape Wath, and many others, and proceedings were instituted in the Court of Exchequer (2) to determine the rights of the various parties, which were not settled for several years. So as not to delay the scheme an arrangement was made under which the alum mines were leased to the Crown at a yearly rent of £400, of which Sir John and Lady Hewley received one-third, namely, £133 6s. 8d., in payment of interest and part payment of principal (3), while the balance went to the Darcy's.

But the real delay was caused by the Lingberry works. The London merchants were only too glad to get out. Goodyer had, in 1660, assigned his interest to Lechmere, who was then dead, leaving his widow, Anne, his executrix. She and Humphrey Aldersey agreed to lease the mines to the King. But Zacharie Stewart utterly refused to join with them. At first the rent offered was £300 a year, and in October, 1664, he based his refusal on the ground of the inadequacy of the rent.

The negotiations were at first conducted by Sir George Charnock and Gerard Fox in the country. Insinuations were made that if Stewart would offer Charnock and Fox £160

(1) E.112, Car. II., Yorks. 352.
(2) E.154, 27 Car. II., Easter, York, No. 17.
(3) Lady Hewley's trust, which is still in existence, holds some of the lands so charged.

they would be prepared to recommend the increase of rent from £300 to £400; indeed, Charnock was quoted as having said that it had cost Isaac Fairfax £200 to get a rent of £300 for the Dunsley works.

Stewart next, at Charnock's request, went up to London, and had a long interview with the Commissioners (Charnock and Fox) in the Strand. There was here a conflict of evidence; the Commissioners maintained that Zacharie Stewart definitely offered to accept a rent of £400. Stewart's story was that Charnock claimed that the alum mines belonged to the Crown, to which claim Stewart replied that even if this were so the expenditure on the works entitled him and his partners to a rent of £400, and that if the decision of Chief Baron Sir Matthew Hale (later Chief Justice of England) was adverse to him, he would accept that sum.

Lord Ashley, as Chancellor of the Exchequer (one of the witnesses calls him Lord Anthony Ashley Cooper) then took a more prominent part in arranging the scheme. He sent for Stewart to attend him at Exeter House in the Strand, and the latter, acting on Counsel's advice, took with him two of his workmen as witnesses and his first cousin, once removed, Marmaduke Norcliffe of Furnival's Inn (1). Dryden's description of Shaftesbury under the name of Achitophel comes to mind as one reads the account of the interview.

> For close designs and crooked counsels fit
> Sagacious, bold and turbulent of wit (2).

Ashley met them at the stairs' head, and asked Stewart sharply: " Are you he that opposes the King's revenue in this matter?" " No," replied Stewart, " I would rather advance the King's revenue by supplying alum at £16 a ton without any rent in place of that which Lord Mulgrave with his rent of £1,800 supplies."

Ashley then bade him take notice that he should land no more coals at his works. He answered that he trusted that his lordship would not take the liberty of a subject from him, and that he intended to continue to land coals. Then Ashley threatened to cause an information to be exhibited against him in the Exchequer, and Stewart desired him to do so whilst he was in London, so that he might put in his answer before he returned home (3).

(1) See Dugdale, by J. W. Clay, Vol. 2, p. 428.
(2) Absalom and Achitophel 1, 152.
(3) E.112, Car. II., Yorks. 264.

The interview then terminated, but no information was filed till seven years had elapsed. The grounds upon which the Treasury denied the right of Zacharie Stewart to mine for alum was that the mines had not passed by the original grant from the Crown. The Manor of Loftus had been granted to Ralph Wise and Henry Harryman, together with numerous other lands and possessions in Yorkshire, Durham and elsewhere as trustees for Christopher, Earl of Anglesey, from whom Stewart derived title. That there might be no doubt as to what passed with the manor the grant specified all and singular the mines and quarries. The enrolment on the Patent Rolls (1) shows signs of having been examined in this connection and supports Stewart's contention. In any case it was quite clear that Sir Matthew Hale, after consulting the Attorney General, Sir Jeffrey Palmer, on 13th December, 1664, reported that the mines duly passed under the grant. Notwithstanding the obstructive attitude adopted by Stewart, the scheme proceeded as if his consent had been obtained.

It was first thought advisable to draw up the agreement under which for some four years Monson had been supplying alum from the Mulgrave works to the farmers designate. This draft agreement was dated 19th June, 1665 (2), but by reason of the great Plague and of the Dutch War, was never perfected, in so much that a fresh agreement embodying most of its terms had to be executed in 1667. The earlier document had been intended to be made between Sir John Monson of the one part, and Sir Nicholas Crispe, Dr. John Twisden, Francis Pargiter and John Sammes of the other part. Monson agreed to deliver to Crispe, Twisden, Pargiter and Sammes in every year for four years, from the 24th June, 1665, out of ships and store-houses, 1,200 tons of good alum (every ton to contain 20 cwts. and every cwt. 112 lbs.) (3). Six hundred tons of these were to be delivered in bags at the Port of London, between London Bridge and the Tower, or at some other usual place for unloading alum, at the price of £11 15s. a ton, and the remainder, after due notice, at Whitby, without bags, at the price of £11 5s. for the first three hundred, and £10 15s. for the remaining portion.

(1) C. 66/2474 (30th July, 4 Ch. I.).
(2) S.P. 29, 330/64 (Chas. II.).
(3) This was by no means a matter of course. See later p. 193.

To prevent glutting the market, no more than 150 tons were to be shipped to London at one time, and within less than twenty days interval, except in the cases of cargoes delayed through stress of weather. The alum delivered in London was to be paid for at the house of Andrew Halliburton, St. Olave's Hart Street, and that delivered in Whitby at the house of Charles Fairfax in that town. So long as this arrangement lasted Monson was to acquit Crispe, Twisden, Pargiter and Sammes of the rent of £1,800 payable to the Earl of Mulgrave. Since the latter attained his majority in 1669 there was good reason for fixing four years as the duration of the arrangement; if it continued beyond the period, one year's notice to determine was necessary.

Monson was to have all the rights and privileges granted to the farmers by the King.

The actual lease of these rights and privileges as enrolled on the Patent Rolls (1) only bears date the year 1665 with the day and month in blank, but was later described as having been executed on 8th November, 1665. The King granted to the four farmers the six sets of alum mines above mentioned at the following rents, namely:— £1,800 to John, Earl of Mulgrave and Sir John Monson, £1,500 to Sir Henry Yelverton, William Twisden, John Saville and Richard Stephens, trustees for Sir Wm. Cholmley (son of one Sir Hugh and father of another); £300 to Isaac Fairfax; £400 (2) to Sir William and George Darcy; £400 for the Lingberry Mines, in the proportion of £100 to Zacharie Stewart (3), £200 to Thomas Lechmere and £100 to Humphrey Aldersey; and £340 to John Ramsay as trustee for Sir Richard Hoghton and his wife in respect of the mines at Samlesbury. The rent to the King was £5,260, of which £1,000 for each of the first four years was assigned to Sir Edmund Turner by appointment of Sir John Harrison, and appears to represent compensation for the surrender of the old lease to Sir John Gibson, which was not due to expire until 1668.

The total of these yearly payments amounted to £10,000, which spread over an output of 1,200 tons, increased the ton price by £8 6s. 8d. No doubt part of the rents represented interest upon capital invested in the plant,

(1) Pat. Rolls 17, Car. 2, pt. 8, C.66/3079, m. 19.
(2) Of which the third part was to go to Sir John and Lady Hewley. See p. 184 ante.
(3) Who, as we have seen, repudiated the supposed agreement.

but the remainder was the measure of the cost of restricting competition by limiting the output with a view to keeping up the price.

Several of the leases to the King of these competing alum works are enrolled on the same Patent Roll (1) as that on which the Crown lease to the farmers was enrolled. They all contained a clause that if three months after the commencement of the lease alum was not being made, the lessors (i.e., the original proprietors) might take down and remove all pans, houses, sheds, buildings, utensils and implements, and dispose of them as they should think fit without any abatement in the rent. An ingenious provision to encourage sterilisation of the works. The general terms of the Crown lease to the farmers were very similar to those which had been inserted in all leases ever since the Crown had acquired the mines. To the end that the lessees might enjoy the profit and benefit of making alum, and that the dominions might be supplied therewith without any foreign importation, the King commanded that no one other than the lessees should, during the term of the lease boil or work liquors of alum or any juices, minerals or excrescencies thereof brought in and imported from any country, or bring in any alum made in parts beyond the seas, or bring back any alum which should have been exported out of the realm into foreign countries upon pain of forfeiture of the alum and materials, and of such further penalties as could be inflicted under the laws and statutes of the realm or the royal prerogative.

The lessees could export alum or materials used in its manufacture free of all customs, imposts, subsidies and other dues.

There were the customary rights of search at all ports of discharge to discover foreign alum, and powers of attorney to prosecute delinquents in the name of the King. As the use of kelp was coming more into fashion there were very large powers of gathering it in all places within the King's dominions. No servants employed in making alum, or mariners or seamen on any of the alum ships were to be pressed to serve by land or sea. The lessees were to provide sufficient alum for the use of the King's subjects at no higher rate than 26s. per cwt.

Power was reserved for the Crown to enter and view the state of repair of the houses, and to ascertain whether the mines were digged in an orderly manner, and whether

(1) C.66, 3079, Nos. 17, 19.

the workmen, carriers and other creditors were duly paid, a provision rendered necessary by the troubles when Sir Arthur Ingram was lessee.

Finally, there was a provision that in case of war, plague or general interruption of trade, allowance was to be made by the Lord Treasurer and Chancellor of the Exchequer, and the rents reduced. By letters of Privy Seal, contemporaneous with this lease (18th November, 1665), the King had also agreed to make abatement in case any other person should erect alum works, and make alum, whereby the price should be reduced below £26 a ton.

On the 27th April, 1667, the proclamation (1) was issued forbidding the import or sale of foreign alum in England on the ground that the manufacture thereof set up by King James I. produced a sufficient quantity to supply the Kingdom.

The arrangement under which Sir John Monson so to speak bartered the fixed rent of £1,800 for the right of supplying alum by no means satisfied everyone. Elizabeth, Countess of Mulgrave, had married Sir John Bennet (later Viscount Ossulton) shortly after the death of her first husband, under whose will she was, amongst other things, to enjoy a moiety of the profits arising from the alum mines. Her step-grandmother-in-law, Countess Marian, was now dead, as were the three sons of the second marriage of the first Earl, and there were therefore no deductions to be made under the settlement executed by the last mentioned.

This being so, in 1667, Countess Elizabeth and Sir John Bennet instituted proceedings (2) against the trustee, alleging that the bargain was most improvident, inasmuch as by reason of the deadness in trade, the war with Holland and the great cost of manufacture, the alum could yield little profit. Monson put in his answer, in which he mainly relied upon his obligation under the will of the second Earl to carry on the alum works. He admitted the losses sustained during the late war, the increase in freight and in the price of materials, and the loss of several ships laden with coal.

He estimated the cost of manufacture at £9 12s. 6d. a ton, which, at the prices per ton contained in the agreement, should yield a yearly profit of £2,175.

(1) Proclamations Collections, p. 243.
(2) S.P.29 (Chas. II.), 240/132, 224/141.

Apparently the suit was eventually compromised. Sir John Bennet, under a privy seal dated 22nd May, 1666, received the yearly sum of £400 charged on the alum rent payable to the King.

Confirmation of the damage caused to the works during the Dutch War is found in a letter dated 2nd May, 1667 (1), from the same Thomas Wade, previously described as Postmaster at Whitby, to Secretary Williamson. A Dutch dogger had forced into Runswick three Whitby vessels laden with coals for the alum works and had taken two others. One of the refugee vessels had three guns with which she protected the other two until the Whitby trained bands (2) and some volunteers got aboard and brought them safe into harbour.

Another Whitby ketch, worth £500 or £600, laden with alum, would have been taken, but Captain Wickham's trained bands came on the scene and saved her. Two days later another correspondent sent Williamson a similar account of the two transactions. Fortunately, the Dutch War, never very popular, was at its close, and no further casualties of a like nature were recorded.

Lord Mulgrave came of age in 1669, and at once took advantage of the clause entitling him to determine the arrangement with the farmers, but at almost the same time, on 29th June, 1669, he entered into a new agreement under which he continued to supply the 1,200 tons. We may therefore safely assume that the modifications introduced upon the attainment of his majority were not of much importance.

The King's rents were not paid into the Exchequer with any regularity, and it is only when the accounts came to be audited that we can learn what allowances the farmers claimed. In respect of the Plague and the Great Fire in London in the years 1635 and 1666 they claimed £1,735. There are two separate sets of accounts (3), both vouched the same year (1686) seven years after the close of the period to which they relate, the first for eight-years-and-a-half from Christmas, 1665, to Midsummer '74, the second for four-years-and-a-half to Christmas, 1678.

(1) S.P.29, 199/22.
(2) The name "trained bands" was still constantly used for the militia.
(3) E. 351/3382, 3383.

The rents to the lessors of abandoned mines were duly met, and Lord Mulgrave was satisfied. For the first period, in place of £44,710, only £24,610 10s. 6d. was paid into the Exchequer; for the second period, which should have produced £23,670, only £4,560 was so paid. The explanation was that new alum works were springing up all over the country and had to be leased by the Crown in order to prevent their competition.

Two alum mines had been opened, one on either side of Saltburn mouth; that on the West side by Sir John Lowther and Edward Trotter, which was then leased to the King at a rent of £500 from Midsummer, 1670, and that on the East side, Saltburn, in the Parish of Brotton, by John Turner, Sergeant-at-law, eldest son of John Turner, whose name occurs so often above, likewise leased at a rent of £400 from Christmas, 1670. Another alum mine was opened in Marske by Anthony Lowther and demised to Sir Hugh Cholmley, Sir Nicholas Crispe and others, likewise at a rent of £400 from Christmas, 1672.

Other mines had been opened in the neighbourhood which were not leased to the King, and made alum in competition. Sir David Foulis (1) had, during the years 1673 and 1674 made alum to the amount of 28 tons 3 cwts. in Staintondale, near the Peak. The farmers claimed and were allowed £464 9s. 6d. at the rate of £16 10s. a ton, being £26 less £9 10s. for the cost of manufacture.

For the next following four years no details are given, but it is clear that while the Peak works were still in existence, Nicholas Conyers had also opened out mines at Easington and Boulby. In addition, 143 tons had been made at some new or more probably re-opened mines at Guisborough, whose exact locality was not further specified. The total claims under these headings amounted to £11,672 12s·, and would have almost entirely exhausted the payments into the Exchequer.

The Crown lease to the farmers was not due to expire until 20th June, 1586, but it was now becoming evident that the payments to proprietors of newly-opened mines and compensation for alum manufactured by strangers would soon exceed the rents payable to the King, and negotiations were on foot to induce the Crown to accept a surrender of what was after all a liability rather than an asset. The surrender became an accomplished fact on 3rd May, 1679 (2).

(1) Grandson of the original patentee.
(2) Cal, Treasury Books, Vol. 6, p. 37; Vol. 5, p. 12.

A few days before, on 28th April, Henry Guy wrote to each of Sergeant Turner, Sir William Darcy, Mr. Trotter, Mr. Anthony Lowther, Humphrey Aldersey, Isaac Fairfax, Sir David Foulis, the executors of Thomas Lechmere, John Ramsay, Zacharie Stewart (1) and Sir John Lowther, that the King, having accepted a surrender of the alum farm, had no further use of their alum works and would pay them no further rent beyond arrears.

It may be that some of the lessors had no relish for this summary method of determining their leases. Certain it is that Sir William Darcy, George Darcy and Sir John Hewley, on the ground that they had leased Slape Wath to the Crown for 21 years from 24th June, 1665, were, on the 7th August, 1679 (2), granted an annuity to be divided between them of £400 for seven-and-a-half years from the preceding Lady Day, payable quarterly out of the customs of alum, imported or exported.

On 9th August, 1679, Sir John Bennet had petitioned the Lords of the Treasury that his annuity of £400 might be secured on some other branch of the revenue now that the alum farm had been determined.

Gerard Fox, finding his occupation gone, on 12th March, 1679-80, complained that since the alum contract had been destroyed, numerous alum works had been set up all along the coast, which would necessitate a riding surveyor to prevent the fraudulent shipping of alum into foreign parts, as had lately been done. He then (apparently without success) prayed that he might be appointed to that post.

As has been mentioned above, it was not until 1686 that the accounts were finally audited and were balanced by reducing the claim of the farmers from £11,672 12s. to £7,520.

Soon after he had attained his majority, Lord Mulgrave took that place at Court to which his position as a large landed proprietor entitled him, notwithstanding the ingratitude that his great-grandfather had displayed towards the King's father. His town house was then at Charing Cross, near the new great ordinary, where Pepys relates that in 1669 he enjoyed his two grilled pigeons.

(1) But he had died in 1676.   See his will.   Yorks. Arch. Soc. Records, Vol. 68, p. 112.
(2) Cal. Treasury Books, Vol. 6, p. 173.

In January, 1673, he succeeded the Duke of Richmond as Gentleman of the Bedchamber, and was granted a pension of £1,000 a year, to be paid out of the alum farm, or if that ceased, out of such part of the revenue as should be thought fit. When the alum farm was surrendered, he continued to manufacture alum for his own benefit, using the services of Matthew Shipton, son of the Thomas Shipton whose name has occurred above, and who died shortly before the surrender. The Chancery records (1) show that the agency of father and son was not free from scandal. What were the rights and wrongs of the case is immaterial to the present purpose. One fact only which has previously been mentioned is of interest, namely, that the alum contracted to be manufactured consisted of tons, every ton being 20 cwts., but every cwt. of 92½ lbs. only.

Lord Mulgrave, who was created in 1694 Marquess of Normanby, and 1703 Duke of Buckinghamshire, died on 24th February, 1720. As the builder of Buckingham Palace, his name is not likely to be forgotten, even though the man-in-the-street usually confuses him with another holder of the title. He had married for his third wife Katherine, illegitimate daughter of James II. (2) by Catherine Sedley, and by her alone had male issue, of whom only one son, Edmund survived him, and died an infant and unmarried in 1735. On his death there was no heir made of the body of the first Earl of Mulgrave, and the Mulgrave estates reverted to the Crown, but his mother, the Duchess of Buckinghamshire, purchased the reversion and continued the alum works (3).

At her death she left the estates and alum works to her grandchild by her first husband, Charles Phipps, from whom the present Marquess of Normanby is descended.

It is beyond the scope of this work to trace the development of the alum trade under private enterprise. All that has been attempted is to record its varying fortunes so long as it was buttressed by the protective hand of the Crown. Without such aid it must have failed at the outset, but whether all the measures adopted for its protection were necessary is quite a different question.

That the price of the manufactured article was at the outset enhanced instead of reduced is obvious, but it may

(1) C.5, 527/82, 94/2.
(2) But see Walpole as to her paternity.
(3) Mr. J. W. Clay is not quite correct at p. 208 of his Extinct Peerages of the Northern Counties.

well be argued that the low price at which it was subsequently produced was the direct result of experiences gained during the period of protection.

Again, while the labourers were scandalously exploited during the earlier years of the alum farm, both by irregular payment of wages and by unfair pressure to accept in part payment of arrears corn and meat of inferior quality at exorbitant prices, yet, on the other hand, a steady rise in the rate of wages is noticeable, and measures were taken, after the disclosures in the proceedings against Arthur Ingram, to prevent any similar breaches of faith.

It is uncertain whether the Exchequer gained or lost by acquiring the alum rights from the first patentees. Enough has perhaps been said to prove that the estimates of loss after the event were quite as unreliable as the estimates of profit before the acquisition. That it did not turn out a gold mine, or perhaps more correctly that it suffered the same fate as many investments in gold mines, goes without saying. For many years the Crown was decidedly out of pocket, but from 1617 onward a steady flow into the Exchequer resulted, which must have almost, if not quite wiped out the debit balance. The fact that persons entitled to pensions preferred to have them charged upon the alum farm rather than on any other part of revenue shows the opinion of those best qualified to judge.

For many years after the termination of the alum farm the works at Mulgrave and Sandsend attained a reputation which outstripped that of any of its rivals, and it must be a source of regret that the industry should now revert to Lancashire and to a region where it had formerly struggled so ineffectively with its Yorkshire competitors.

INDEX

Bower, Thos., 172.
Bowyer, Agnes, 26; Sir Wm., 26; Wm., 141.
Bowdler, Rich., 91, 92, 111, 118.
Branksea, 41, 46, 53.
Bransby, John, 109.
Branthwaite, R., 49.
Brockett, Edw., 27; Sir John, 27, 29; John, 27.
Brook House, 39.
Brooke, Sir John, 124, 131; T., 159; Lord (see Greville).
Brotton, 191.
Browne, Geo., 10; John, 36; Wm., 35, 36.
Brough, Thos., 152.
Buck, Hy., 148.
Buckingham, Duke of, 154, 157.
Buckinghamshire, Duke of, 193; Duchess, 193.
Bulmer, Wm., 167.
Burghley, Lord (see Cecil).
Burlamachi, Jas., 166; Magdalen, 168; Ph., 165-168, 170; Susannah, 168.
Burton, John, 2.
Butler, Dan., 180.

Caesar, Sir Julius, 46, 123, 129.
Calais, 10, 36.
Canford, 35, 36, 38, 40, 41, 48-58, 74.
Canning, Wm., 95, 99.
Canterbury, Archbishop of, 123, 128.
Cargo Fleet, 62, 79, 143, 148.
Carlton, 129; Geo., 19, 40, 49, 55.
Carpenter, Thos., 99-114, 124.
Catesby, John, 55.
Cabe, Sir Ambrose, 25.
Cecil, Wm. (Lord Burghley), 12, 18, 20-28, 41-46, 56, 72.
Robert (Earl of Salisbury), 30, 83-86, 111, 129 ; Thos. (Lord
    Burghley), 30.
Chamberlain, Abr., 73, 86, 94, 97.
Chapman, Wm., 152; Fras., 13, 18, 23-26.
Chaloner, Edw., 32; Jas., 33, 122; Roger, 10; John, 9, 10, 12, 16;
    Judith, 32; Sir Thos., senr., 10, 12, 18, 31, 130; Marriage of, 25;
    Death of, 122; Sir Thos., junr., 1, 59, 71, 74, 85, 122, 170;
    Thomas (of Lambay), 9, 16, 17, 23, 26, 33, 60, 63-77, 87, 122,
    128, 130, 142, 155, 162 165, 171 Wm., 32.; Sir Wm., 128, 162.
Charlton, L., 2.
Charnock, Sir Geo., 182, 185.
Cholmley, Fras., 101; Sir Hugh, 183, 184, 187, 191; Sir Wm., 187.
Church, Ralph, 148.
Clarke, Ralph, 146.
Clavell, Sir Wm., 94.
Cleveland, description of, 59.
Clonmines, 6, 11, 13.
Cobham, Lord Geo., 23; Henry, 23.
Clough, R., 25.
Coatham, 101.
Cochineal, 143.
Cockeram, Thos., 140.
Cole, Rich., 11.
Coulthirst, Rob., 145.
Compton, Wm., 4.
Constantine, Wm., 49, 50.
Conyers (Boulby), 179; Kath., 162; Lord, 64, 184; Nich., 191; Rich.,
    171.
Cotton, Anne, 19; Joan, 19; Sir Robt., 59; Thos., 40, 49; Sir Wm., 19.
Courteen, Sir Wm., 166.
Courtenay, Hy., 35.
Cope, Sir Walt., 29, 85, 95, 96.
Corney, Cuthbert, 149.
Coste, A. de la, 4.
Cowell, Hy., 66.

197

ERRATA

P.   3, L. 3, Footnote 3, for plusseurs read plusiers.
P.   7, L. 10, for Treaties read Treatise.
P. 11, L. 29, for superseded read succeeded.
P. 19, L. 33, for Heath read Hoath.
P. 31, L. 29, for Edmund read Edward.
P. 45, L. 34, for Hutingdon read Huntingdon.
P. 53, L. 38, for Gryfin read Gryffin.
P. 56, L. 9, for Burleigh read Burghley.
P. 56, L. 24, for deterent read deterrent.
P. 60. L. 26, for James read John.
P. 61, L. 31, for James read John.
P. 67, L. 31, for James read John.
P. 68, L. 14, for Startcliffe read Stantcliffe.
P. 75, L. 13, for H. W. read Hist.
P. 106, Ls. 5 and 12, for Folder read Fodder.
P. 119, L. 33, for Reeve read Reade.
P. 130, ADD: The transcript of the Guisborough Register in the
        York Diocesan Registry shows that Thomas Chaloner
        generosus sepultus est 4 May, 1634.
P.133, last line, for released read received.
P. 147, L. 10, for the read one.
P. 147, L. 32, for Guisboorough read Guisborough.